Get the eBooks FREE!

(PDF, ePub, and Kindle all included)

We believe that once you buy a book from us, you should be able to read it in any format we have available. To get electronic versions of this book at no additional cost to you, purchase and then register this book at the Manning website following the instructions inside this insert.

That's it!

Thanks from Manning!

Making Sense of NoSQL

A GUIDE FOR MANAGERS
AND THE REST OF US

DAN McCREARY
ANN KELLY

MANNING
SHELTER ISLAND

For online information and ordering of this and other Manning books, please visit www.manning.com. The publisher offers discounts on this book when ordered in quantity. For more information, please contact

 Special Sales Department
 Manning Publications Co.
 20 Baldwin Road
 PO Box 261
 Shelter Island, NY 11964
 Email: orders@manning.com

Manning Publications Co.
20 Baldwin Road
PO Box 261
Shelter Island, NY 11964

Development editor: Elizabeth Lexleigh
Copyeditor: Benjamin Berg
Proofreader: Katie Tennant
Typesetter: Dottie Marsico
Cover designer: Leslie Haimes

ISBN 9781617291074
Printed in the United States of America
1 2 3 4 5 6 7 8 9 10 – MAL – 18 17 16 15 14 13

To technology innovators and early adopters...
those who shake up the status quo

We dedicate this book to people who understand the limitations of our current way of solving technology problems. They understand that by removing limitations, we can solve problems faster and at a lower cost and, at the same time, become more agile. Without these people, the NoSQL movement wouldn't have gained the critical mass it needed to get off the ground.

Innovators and early adopters are the people within organizations who shake up the status quo by testing and evaluating new architectures. They initiate pilot projects and share their successes and failures with their peers. They use early versions of software and help shake out the bugs. They build new versions of NoSQL distributions from source and explore areas where new NoSQL solutions can be applied. They're the people who give solution architects more options for solving business problems. We hope this book will help you to make the right choices.

brief contents

contents

foreword

Where does one start to explain a topic that's defined by what it isn't, rather than what it is? Believe me, as someone who's been trying to educate people in this field for the past three years, it's a frustrating dilemma, and one shared by lots of technical experts, consultants, and vendors. Even though few think the name *NoSQL* is optimal, almost everyone seems to agree that it defines a category of products and technologies better than any other term. My best advice is to let go of whatever hang-ups you might have about the semantics, and just choose to learn about something new. And trust me please…the stuff you're about to learn is worth your time.

Some brief personal context up front: as a publisher in the world of information management, I had heard the term *NoSQL*, but had little idea of its significance until three years ago, when I ran into Dan McCreary in the corridor of a conference in Toronto. He told me a bit about his current project and was obviously excited about the people and technologies he was working with. He convinced me in no time that this NoSQL thing was going to be huge, and that someone in my position should learn as much as I could about it. It was excellent advice, and we've had a wonderful partnership since then, running a conference together, doing webinars, and writing white papers. Dan was spot on…this NoSQL stuff *is* exciting, and the people in the community are quite brilliant.

Like most people who work in arcane fields, I often find myself trying to explain complex things in simple terms for the benefit of those who don't share the same passion or context that I have. And even when you understand the value of the perfect elevator pitch, or desperately want to explain what you do to your mother, the right explanation can be elusive. Sometimes it's even more difficult to explain new things to people who have *more* knowledge, rather than less. Specifically in terms of NoSQL, that's the huge community of relational DBMS devotees who've existed happily and efficiently for the past 30 years, needing nothing but one toolkit.

That's where *Making Sense of NoSQL* comes in. If you're in an enterprise computing role and trying to understand the value of NoSQL, then you're going to appreciate this book, because it speaks directly to you. Sure, you startup guys will get something out of it, but for enterprise IT folks, the barriers are pretty daunting—not the least of which will be the many years of technical bias accumulated against you from the people in your immediate vicinity, wondering why the heck you'd want to put your data into anything but a nice, orderly table.

The authors understand this, and have focused a lot of their analysis on the technical and architectural trade-offs that you'll be facing. I also love that they've undertaken so much effort to offer case studies throughout the book. Stories are key to persuasion, and these examples drawn from real applications provide a storyline to the subject that will be invaluable as you try to introduce these new technologies into your organization.

Dan McCreary and Ann Kelly have provided the first comprehensive explanation of what NoSQL technologies are, and why you might want to use them in a corporate context. While this is not meant to be a technical book, I can tell you that behind the scenes they've been diligent about consulting with the product architects and developers to ensure that the nuances and features of different products are represented accurately.

Making Sense of NoSQL is a handbook of easily digestible, practical advice for technical managers, architects, and developers. It's a guide for anyone who needs to understand the full range of their data management options in the increasingly complex and demanding world of big, fast data. The title of chapter 1 is "NoSQL: It's about making intelligent choices," and based on your selection of this book, I can confirm that you've made one already.

TONY SHAW
FOUNDER AND CEO
DATAVERSITY

preface

Sometimes we're presented with facts that force us to reassess what we think we know. After spending most of our working life performing data modeling tasks with a focus on storing data in rows, we learned that the modeling process might not be necessary. While this information didn't mean our current knowledge was invalid, it forced us to take a hard look at how we solved business technology problems. Armed with new knowledge, techniques, and problem-solving styles, we broadened the repertoire of our solution space.

In 2006, while working on a project that involved the exchange of real estate transactions, we spent many months designing XML schemas and forms to store the complex hierarchies of data. On the advice of a friend (Kurt Cagle), we found that storing the data into a native XML database saved our project months of object modeling, relational database design, and object-relational mapping. The result was a radically simple architecture that could be maintained by nonprogammers.

The realization that enterprise data can be stored in structures other than RDBMSs is a major turning point for people who enter the NoSQL space. Initially, this information may be viewed with skepticism, fear, and even self-doubt. We may question our own skills as well as the educational institutions that trained us and the organizations that reinforce the notion that RDBMS and objects are the only way to solve problems. Yet if we're going to be fair to our clients, customers, and users, we must take a holistic approach to find the best fit for each business problem and evaluate other database architectures.

In 2010, frustrated with the lack of exposure NoSQL databases were getting at large enterprise data conferences, we approached Tony Shaw from DATAVERSITY about starting a new conference. The conference would be a venue for anyone interested in learning about NoSQL technologies and exposing individuals and organizations to the NoSQL databases available to them. The first NoSQL Now! conference was successfully held in San Jose, California, in August of 2011, with approximately 500 interested and curious attendees.

One finding of the conference was that there was no single source of material that covered NoSQL architectures or introduced a process to objectively match a business problem with the right database. People wanted more than a collection of "Hello World!" examples from open source projects. They were looking for a guide that helped them match a business problem to an architecture first, and then a process that allowed them to consider open source as well as commercial database systems.

Finding a publisher that would use our existing DocBook content was the first step. Luckily, we found that Manning Publications understands the value of standards.

acknowledgments

We'd like to thank everyone at Manning Publications who helped us take our raw ideas and transform them into a book: Michael Stephens, who brought us on board; Elizabeth Lexleigh, our development editor, who patiently read version after version of each chapter; Nick Chase, who made all the technology work like it's supposed to; the marketing and production teams, and everyone who worked behind the scenes— we acknowledge your efforts, guidance, and words of encouragement.

To the many people who reviewed case studies and provided us with examples of real-world NoSQL usage—we appreciate your time and expertise: George Bina, Ben Brumfield, Dipti Borkar, Kurt Cagle, Richard Carlsson, Amy Friedman, Randolph Kahle, Shannon Kempe, Amir Halfon, John Hudzina, Martin Logan, Michaline Todd, Eric Merritt, Pete Palmer, Amar Shan, Christine Schwartz, Tony Shaw, Joe Wicentowski, Melinda Wilken, and Frank Weige.

To the reviewers who contributed valuable insights and feedback during the development of our manuscript—our book is better for your input: Aldrich Wright, Brandon Wilhite, Craig Smith, Gabriela Jack, Ian Stirk, Ignacio Lopez Vellon, Jason Kolter, Jeff Lehn, John Guthrie, Kamesh Sampah, Michael Piscatello, Mikkel Eide Eriksen, Philipp K. Janert, Ray Lugo, Jr., Rodrigo Abreu, and Roland Civet.

We'd like to say a special thanks to our friend Alex Bleasdale for providing us with working code to support the role-based, access-control case study in our chapter on NoSQL security and secure document publishing. Special thanks also to Tony Shaw for contributing the foreword, and to Leo Polovets for his technical proofread of the final manuscript shortly before it went to production.

about this book

In writing this book, we had two goals: first, to describe NoSQL databases, and second, to show how NoSQL systems can be used as standalone solutions or to augment current SQL systems to solve business problems. We invite anyone who has an interest in learning about NoSQL to use this book as a guide. You'll find that the information, examples, and case studies are targeted toward technical managers, solution architects, and data architects who have an interest in learning about NoSQL.

This material will help you objectively evaluate SQL and NoSQL database systems to see which business problems they solve. If you're looking for a programming guide for a particular product, you've come to wrong place. In this book you'll find information about the motivations behind NoSQL, as well as related terminology and concepts. There might be sections and chapters of this book that cover topics you already understand; feel free to skim or skip over them and focus on the unknown.

Finally, we feel strongly about and focus on standards. The standards associated with SQL systems allow applications to be ported between databases using a common language. Unfortunately, NoSQL systems can't yet make this claim. In time, NoSQL application vendors will pressure NoSQL database vendors to adopt a set of standards to make them as portable as SQL.

Roadmap

This book is divided into four parts. Part 1 sets the stage by defining NoSQL and reviewing the basic concepts behind the NoSQL movement.

In chapter 1, "NoSQL: It's about making intelligent choices," we define the term *NoSQL*, talk about the key events that triggered the NoSQL movement, and present a high-level view of the business benefits of NoSQL systems. Readers already familiar with the NoSQL movement and the business benefits might choose to skim this chapter.

In chapter 2, "NoSQL concepts," we introduce the core concepts associated with the NoSQL movement. Although you can skim this chapter on a first read-through, it's important for understanding material in later chapters. We encourage you to use this chapter as a reference guide as you encounter these concepts throughout the book.

In part 2, "Database patterns," we do an in-depth review of SQL and NoSQL database architecture patterns. We look at the different database structures and how we access them, and present use cases to show the types of situations where each architectural pattern is best used.

Chapter 3 covers "Foundational data architecture patterns." It begins with a review of the drivers behind RDBMSs and how the requirements of ERP systems shaped the features we have in current RDBMS and BI/DW systems. We briefly discuss other database systems such as object databases and revision control systems. You can skim this chapter if you're already familiar with these systems.

In chapter 4, "NoSQL data architecture patterns," we introduce the database patterns associated with NoSQL. We look at key-value stores, graph stores, column family (Bigtable) systems, and document databases. The chapter provides definitions, examples, and case studies to facilitate understanding.

Chapter 5 covers "Native XML databases," which are most often found in government and publishing applications, as they are known to lower costs and support the use of standards. We present two case studies from the financial and government publishing areas.

In part 3, we look at how NoSQL systems can be applied to the problems of big data, search, high availability, and agile web development.

In chapter 6, "Using NoSQL to manage big data," you'll see how NoSQL systems can be configured to efficiently process large volumes of data running on commodity hardware. We include a discussion on distributed computing and horizontal scalability, and present a case study where commodity hardware fails to scale for analyzing large graphs.

In chapter 7, "Finding information with NoSQL search," you'll learn how to improve search quality by implementing a document model and preserving the document's content. We discuss how MapReduce transforms are used to create scalable reverse indexes, which result in fast search. We review the search systems used on documents and databases and show how structured search solutions are used to create accurate search result rankings.

Chapter 8 covers "Building high-availability solutions with NoSQL." We show how the replicated and distributed nature of NoSQL systems can be used to result in systems that have increased availability. You'll see how many low-cost CPUs can provide higher uptime once data synchronization technologies are used. Our case study shows how full peer-to-peer architectures can provide higher availability than other distribution models.

In chapter 9, we talk about "Increasing agility with NoSQL." By eliminating the object-relational mapping layer, NoSQL software development is simpler and can quickly adapt to changing business requirements. You'll see how these NoSQL systems allow the experienced developer, as well as nonprogramming staff, to become part of the software development lifecycle process.

In part 4, we cover the "Advanced topics" of functional programming and security, and then review a formalized process for selecting the right NoSQL system.

In chapter 10, we cover the topic of "NoSQL and functional programming" and the need for distributed transformation architectures such as MapReduce. We look at how functional programming has influenced the ability of NoSQL solutions to use large numbers of low-cost processors and why several NoSQL databases use actor-based systems such as Erlang. We also show how functional programming and resource-oriented programming can be combined to create scalable performance on distributed systems with a case study of the NetKernel system.

Chapter 11 covers the topic of "Security: protecting data in your NoSQL systems." We review the history and key security considerations that are common to NoSQL solutions. We provide examples of how a key-value store, a column family store, and a document store can implement a robust security model.

In chapter 12, "Selecting the right NoSQL solution," we walk through a formal process that organizations can use to select the right database for their business problem. We close with some final thoughts and information about how these technologies will impact business system selection.

Code conventions and downloads

Source code in listings or in text is in a `fixed-width font like` this to separate it from ordinary text. You can download the source code for the listings from the Manning website, www.manning.com/MakingSenseofNoSQL.

Author Online

The purchase of *Making Sense of NoSQL* includes free access to a private web forum run by Manning Publications, where you can make comments about the book, ask technical questions, and receive help from the authors and from other users. To access the forum and subscribe to it, point your web browser to www.manning.com/Making-SenseofNoSQL. This page provides information on how to get on the forum once you are registered, what kind of help is available, and the rules of conduct on the forum.

Manning's commitment to our readers is to provide a venue where a meaningful dialogue between individual readers and between readers and the authors can take place. It is not a commitment to any specific amount of participation on the part of the authors, whose contribution to the forum remains voluntary (and unpaid). We suggest you try asking the authors some challenging questions lest their interest stray!

The Author Online forum and the archives of previous discussions will be accessible from the publisher's website as long as the book is in print.

About the authors

DAN MCCREARY is a data architecture consultant with a strong interest in standards. He has worked for organizations such as Bell Labs (integrated circuit design), the supercomputing industry (porting UNIX) and Steve Job's NeXT Computer (software evangelism), as well as founded his own consulting firm. Dan started working with US federal data standards in 2002 and was active in the adoption of the National Information Exchange Model (NIEM). Dan started doing NoSQL development in 2006 when he was exposed to native XML databases for storing form data. He has served as an invited expert on the World Wide Web XForms standard group and is a cofounder of the NoSQL Now! Conference.

ANN KELLY is a software consultant with Kelly McCreary & Associates. After spending much of her career working in the insurance industry developing software and managing projects, she became a NoSQL convert in 2011. Since then, she has worked with her customers to create NoSQL solutions that allow them to solve their business problems quickly and efficiently while providing them with the training to manage their own applications.

Part 1

Introduction

In part 1 we introduce you to the topic of NoSQL. We define the term *NoSQL*, talk about why the NoSQL movement got started, look at the core topics, and review the business benefits of including NoSQL solutions in your organization.

In chapter 1 we begin by defining NoSQL and talk about the business drivers and motivations behind the NoSQL movement. Chapter 2 expands on the foundation in chapter 1 and provides a review of the core concepts and important definitions associated with NoSQL.

If you're already familiar with the NoSQL movement, you may want to skim chapter 1. Chapter 2 contains core concepts and definitions associated with NoSQL. We encourage everyone to read chapter 2 to gain an understanding of these concepts, as they'll be referenced often and applied throughout the book.

NoSQL: It's about making intelligent choices

This chapter covers

- What's NoSQL?
- NoSQL business drivers
- NoSQL case studies

The complexity for minimum component costs has increased at a rate of roughly a factor of two per year…Certainly over the short term this rate can be expected to continue, if not to increase.
> —Gordon Moore, 1965

…Then you better start swimmin'…Or you'll sink like a stone…For the times they are a-changin'.
> —Bob Dylan

In writing this book we have two goals: first, to describe NoSQL databases, and second, to show how NoSQL systems can be used as standalone solutions or to augment current SQL systems to solve business problems. Though we invite anyone who has an interest in NoSQL to use this as a guide, the information, examples, and case studies are targeted toward technical managers, solution architects, and data architects who are interested in learning about NoSQL.

This material will help you objectively evaluate SQL and NoSQL database systems to see which business problems they solve. If you're looking for a programming guide for a particular product, you've come to the wrong place. Here you'll find information about the motivations behind NoSQL, as well as related terminology and concepts. There may be sections and chapters of this book that cover topics you already understand; feel free to skim or skip over them and focus on the unknown.

Finally, we feel strongly about and focus on *standards*. The standards associated with SQL systems allow applications to be ported between databases using a common language. Unfortunately, NoSQL systems can't yet make this claim. In time, NoSQL application vendors will pressure NoSQL database vendors to adopt a set of standards to make them as portable as SQL.

In this chapter, we'll begin by giving a definition of NoSQL. We'll talk about the business drivers and motivations that make NoSQL so intriguing to and popular with organizations today. Finally, we'll look at five case studies where organizations have successfully implemented NoSQL to solve a particular business problem.

1.1   What is NoSQL?

One of the challenges with NoSQL is defining it. The term *NoSQL* is problematic since it doesn't really describe the core themes in the NoSQL movement. The term originated from a group in the Bay Area who met regularly to talk about common concerns and issues surrounding scalable open source databases, and it stuck. Descriptive or not, it seems to be everywhere: in trade press, product descriptions, and conferences. We'll use the term NoSQL in this book as a way of differentiating a system from a traditional relational database management system (RDBMS).

For our purpose, we define NoSQL in the following way:

> *NoSQL is a set of concepts that allows the rapid and efficient processing of data sets with a focus on performance, reliability, and agility.*

Seems like a broad definition, right? It doesn't exclude SQL or RDBMS systems, right? That's not a mistake. What's important is that we identify the core themes behind NoSQL, what it is, and most importantly what it isn't.

So what is NoSQL?

- *It's more than rows in tables*—NoSQL systems store and retrieve data from many formats: key-value stores, graph databases, column-family (Bigtable) stores, document stores, and even rows in tables.
- *It's free of joins*—NoSQL systems allow you to extract your data using simple interfaces without joins.
- *It's schema-free*—NoSQL systems allow you to drag-and-drop your data into a folder and then query it without creating an entity-relational model.

- *It works on many processors*—NoSQL systems allow you to store your database on multiple processors and maintain high-speed performance.
- *It uses shared-nothing commodity computers*—Most (but not all) NoSQL systems leverage low-cost commodity processors that have separate RAM and disk.
- *It supports linear scalability*—When you add more processors, you get a consistent increase in performance.
- *It's innovative*—NoSQL offers options to a single way of storing, retrieving, and manipulating data. NoSQL supporters (also known as *NoSQLers*) have an inclusive attitude about NoSQL and recognize SQL solutions as viable options. To the NoSQL community, NoSQL means "Not only SQL."

Equally important is what NoSQL is not:

- *It's not about the SQL language*—The definition of NoSQL isn't an application that uses a language other than SQL. SQL as well as other query languages are used with NoSQL databases.
- *It's not only open source*—Although many NoSQL systems have an open source model, commercial products use NOSQL concepts as well as open source initiatives. You can still have an innovative approach to problem solving with a commercial product.
- *It's not only big data*—Many, but not all, NoSQL applications are driven by the inability of a current application to efficiently scale when big data is an issue. Though volume and velocity are important, NoSQL also focuses on variability and agility.
- *It's not about cloud computing*—Many NoSQL systems reside in the cloud to take advantage of its ability to rapidly scale when the situation dictates. NoSQL systems can run in the cloud as well as in your corporate data center.
- *It's not about a clever use of RAM and SSD*—Many NoSQL systems focus on the efficient use of RAM or solid state disks to increase performance. Though this is important, NoSQL systems can run on standard hardware.
- *It's not an elite group of products*—NoSQL isn't an exclusive club with a few products. There are no membership dues or tests required to join. To be considered a NoSQLer, you only need to convince others that you have innovative solutions to their business problems.

NoSQL applications use a variety of data store types (databases). From the simple key-value store that associates a unique key with a value, to graph stores used to associate relationships, to document stores used for variable data, each NoSQL type of data store has unique attributes and uses as identified in table 1.1.

Table 1.1 Types of NoSQL data stores—the four main categories of NoSQL systems, and sample products for each data store type

Type	Typical usage	Examples
Key-value store—A simple data storage system that uses a key to access a value	• Image stores • Key-based filesystems • Object cache • Systems designed to scale	• Berkeley DB • Memcache • Redis • Riak • DynamoDB
Column family store—A sparse matrix system that uses a row and a column as keys	• Web crawler results • Big data problems that can relax consistency rules	• Apache HBase • Apache Cassandra • Hypertable • Apache Accumulo
Graph store—For relationship-intensive problems	• Social networks • Fraud detection • Relationship-heavy data	• Neo4j • AllegroGraph • Bigdata (RDF data store) • InfiniteGraph (Objectivity)
Document store—Storing hierarchical data structures directly in the database	• High-variability data • Document search • Integration hubs • Web content management • Publishing	• MongoDB (10Gen) • CouchDB • Couchbase • MarkLogic • eXist-db • Berkeley DB XML

NoSQL systems have unique characteristics and capabilities that can be used alone or in conjunction with your existing systems. Many organizations considering NoSQL systems do so to overcome common issues such as volume, velocity, variability, and agility, the business drivers behind the NoSQL movement.

1.2 NoSQL business drivers

The scientist-philosopher Thomas Kuhn coined the term *paradigm shift* to identify a recurring process he observed in science, where innovative ideas came in bursts and impacted the world in nonlinear ways. We'll use Kuhn's concept of the paradigm shift as a way to think about and explain the NoSQL movement and the changes in thought patterns, architectures, and methods emerging today.

Many organizations supporting single-CPU relational systems have come to a crossroads: the needs of their organizations are changing. Businesses have found value in rapidly capturing and analyzing large amounts of variable data, and making immediate changes in their businesses based on the information they receive.

Figure 1.1 shows how the demands of volume, velocity, variability, and agility play a key role in the emergence of NoSQL solutions. As each of these drivers applies pressure to the single-processor relational model, its foundation becomes less stable and in time no longer meets the organization's needs.

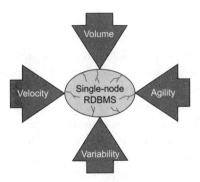

Figure 1.1 **In this figure, we see how the business drivers volume, velocity, variability, and agility apply pressure to the single CPU system, resulting in the cracks. Volume and velocity refer to the ability to handle large datasets that arrive quickly. Variability refers to how diverse data types don't fit into structured tables, and agility refers to how quickly an organization responds to business change.**

1.2.1 *Volume*

Without a doubt, the key factor pushing organizations to look at alternatives to their current RDBMSs is a need to query big data using clusters of commodity processors. Until around 2005, performance concerns were resolved by purchasing faster processors. In time, the ability to increase processing speed was no longer an option. As chip density increased, heat could no longer dissipate fast enough without chip overheating. This phenomenon, known as the power wall, forced systems designers to shift their focus from increasing speed on a single chip to using more processors working together. The need to scale out (also known as *horizontal scaling*), rather than scale up (faster processors), moved organizations from serial to parallel processing where data problems are split into separate paths and sent to separate processors to divide and conquer the work.

1.2.2 *Velocity*

Though big data problems are a consideration for many organizations moving away from RDBMSs, the ability of a single processor system to rapidly read and write data is also key. Many single-processor RDBMSs are unable to keep up with the demands of real-time inserts and online queries to the database made by public-facing websites. RDBMSs frequently index many columns of every new row, a process which decreases system performance. When single-processor RDBMSs are used as a back end to a web store front, the random bursts in web traffic slow down response for everyone, and tuning these systems can be costly when both high read and write throughput is desired.

1.2.3 *Variability*

Companies that want to capture and report on exception data struggle when attempting to use rigid database schema structures imposed by RDBMSs. For example, if a business unit wants to capture a few custom fields for a particular customer, all customer rows within the database need to store this information even though it doesn't apply. Adding new columns to an RDBMS requires the system be shut down and ALTER TABLE commands to be run. When a database is large, this process can impact system availability, costing time and money.

1.2.4   Agility

The most complex part of building applications using RDBMSs is the process of putting data into and getting data out of the database. If your data has nested and repeated subgroups of data structures, you need to include an object-relational mapping layer. The responsibility of this layer is to generate the correct combination of INSERT, UPDATE, DELETE, and SELECT SQL statements to move object data to and from the RDBMS persistence layer. This process isn't simple and is associated with the largest barrier to rapid change when developing new or modifying existing applications.

Generally, object-relational mapping requires experienced software developers who are familiar with object-relational frameworks such as Java Hibernate (or NHibernate for .Net systems). Even with experienced staff, small change requests can cause slowdowns in development and testing schedules.

You can see how velocity, volume, variability, and agility are the high-level drivers most frequently associated with the NoSQL movement. Now that you're familiar with these drivers, you can look at your organization to see how NoSQL solutions might impact these drivers in a positive way to help your business meet the changing demands of today's competitive marketplace.

1.3   NoSQL case studies

Our economy is changing. Companies that want to remain competitive need to find new ways to attract and retain their customers. To do this, the technology and people who create it must support these efforts quickly and in a cost-effective way. New thoughts about how to implement solutions are moving away from traditional methods toward processes, procedures, and technologies that at times seem bleeding-edge.

The following case studies demonstrate how business problems have successfully been solved faster, cheaper, and more effectively by thinking outside the box. Table 1.2 summarizes five case studies where NoSQL solutions were used to solve particular business problems. It presents the problems, the business drivers, and the ultimate findings. As you view subsequent sections, you'll begin to see a common theme emerge: some business problems require new thinking and technology to provide the best solution.

Table 1.2   The key case studies associated with the NoSQL movement—the name of the case study/standard, the business drivers, and the results (findings) of the selected solutions

Case study/standard	Driver	Finding
LiveJournal's Memcache	Need to increase performance of database queries.	By using hashing and caching, data in RAM can be shared. This cuts down the number of read requests sent to the database, increasing performance.
Google's MapReduce	Need to index billions of web pages for search using low-cost hardware.	By using parallel processing, indexing billions of web pages can be done quickly with a large number of commodity processors.

Table 1.2 The key case studies associated with the NoSQL movement—the name of the case study/ standard, the business drivers, and the results (findings) of the selected solutions *(continued)*

Case study/standard	Driver	Finding
Google's Bigtable	Need to flexibly store tabular data in a distributed system.	By using a sparse matrix approach, users can think of all data as being stored in a single table with billions of rows and millions of columns without the need for up-front data modeling.
Amazon's Dynamo	Need to accept a web order 24 hours a day, 7 days a week.	A key-value store with a simple interface can be replicated even when there are large volumes of data to be processed.
MarkLogic	Need to query large collections of XML documents stored on commodity hardware using standard query languages.	By distributing queries to commodity servers that contain indexes of XML documents, each server can be responsible for processing data in its own local disk and returning the results to a query server.

1.3.1 Case study: LiveJournal's Memcache

Engineers working on the blogging system LiveJournal started to look at how their systems were using their most precious resource: the RAM in each web server. LiveJournal had a problem. Their website was so popular that the number of visitors using the site continued to increase on a daily basis. The only way they could keep up with demand was to continue to add more web servers, each with its own separate RAM.

To improve performance, the LiveJournal engineers found ways to keep the results of the most frequently used database queries in RAM, avoiding the expensive cost of rerunning the same SQL queries on their database. But each web server had its own copy of the query in RAM; there was no way for any web server to know that the server next to it in the rack already had a copy of the query sitting in RAM.

So the engineers at LiveJournal created a simple way to create a distinct "signature" of every SQL query. This signature or *hash* was a short string that represented a SQL SELECT statement. By sending a small message between web servers, any web server could ask the other servers if they had a copy of the SQL result already executed. If one did, it would return the results of the query and avoid an expensive round trip to the already overwhelmed SQL database. They called their new system Memcache because it managed RAM memory cache.

Many other software engineers had come across this problem in the past. The concept of large pools of shared-memory servers wasn't new. What was different this time was that the engineers for LiveJournal went one step further. They not only made this system work (and work well), they shared their software using an open source license, and they also standardized the communications protocol between the web front ends (called the *memcached protocol*). Now anyone who wanted to keep their database from getting overwhelmed with repetitive queries could use their front end tools.

1.3.2   *Case study: Google's MapReduce—use commodity hardware to create search indexes*

One of the most influential case studies in the NoSQL movement is the Google MapReduce system. In this paper, Google shared their process for transforming large volumes of web data content into search indexes using low-cost commodity CPUs.

Though sharing of this information was significant, the concepts of *map* and *reduce* weren't new. Map and reduce functions are simply names for two stages of a data transformation, as described in figure 1.2.

The initial stages of the transformation are called the *map operation*. They're responsible for data extraction, transformation, and filtering of data. The results of the map operation are then sent to a second layer: the reduce function. The reduce function is where the results are sorted, combined, and summarized to produce the final result.

The core concepts behind the map and reduce functions are based on solid computer science work that dates back to the 1950s when programmers at MIT implemented these functions in the influential LISP system. LISP was different than other programming languages because it emphasized functions that transformed isolated lists of data. This focus is now the basis for many modern functional programming languages that have desirable properties on distributed systems.

Google extended the map and reduce functions to reliably execute on billions of web pages on hundreds or thousands of low-cost commodity CPUs. Google made map and reduce work reliably on large volumes of data and did it at a low cost. It was Google's use of MapReduce that encouraged others to take another look at the power of functional programming and the ability of functional programming systems to scale over thousands of low-cost CPUs. Software packages such as Hadoop have closely modeled these functions.

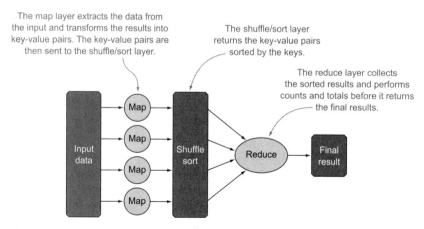

Figure 1.2   The map and reduce functions are ways of partitioning large datasets into smaller chunks that can be transformed on isolated and independent transformation systems. The key is isolating each function so that it can be scaled onto many servers.

The use of MapReduce inspired engineers from Yahoo! and other organizations to create open source versions of Google's MapReduce. It fostered a growing awareness of the limitations of traditional procedural programming and encouraged others to use functional programming systems.

1.3.3 Case study: Google's Bigtable—a table with a billion rows and a million columns

Google also influenced many software developers when they announced their Bigtable system white paper titled *A Distributed Storage System for Structured Data*. The motivation behind Bigtable was the need to store results from the web crawlers that extract HTML pages, images, sounds, videos, and other media from the internet. The resulting dataset was so large that it couldn't fit into a single relational database, so Google built their own storage system. Their fundamental goal was to build a system that would easily scale as their data increased without forcing them to purchase expensive hardware. The solution was neither a full relational database nor a filesystem, but what they called a "distributed storage system" that worked with structured data.

By all accounts, the Bigtable project was extremely successful. It gave Google developers a single tabular view of the data by creating one large table that stored all the data they needed. In addition, they created a system that allowed the hardware to be located in any data center, anywhere in the world, and created an environment where developers didn't need to worry about the physical location of the data they manipulated.

1.3.4 Case study: Amazon's Dynamo—accept an order 24 hours a day, 7 days a week

Google's work focused on ways to make distributed batch processing and reporting easier, but wasn't intended to support the need for highly scalable web storefronts that ran 24/7. This development came from Amazon. Amazon published another significant NoSQL paper: *Amazon's 2007 Dynamo: A Highly Available Key-Value Store*. The business motivation behind Dynamo was Amazon's need to create a highly reliable web storefront that supported transactions from around the world 24 hours a day, 7 days a week, without interruption.

Traditional brick-and-mortar retailers that operate in a few locations have the luxury of having their cash registers and point-of-sale equipment operating only during business hours. When not open for business, they run daily reports, and perform backups and software upgrades. The Amazon model is different. Not only are their customers from all corners of the world, but they shop at all hours of the day, every day. Any downtime in the purchasing cycle could result in the loss of millions of dollars. Amazon's systems need to be iron-clad reliable and scalable without a loss in service.

In its initial offerings, Amazon used a relational database to support its shopping cart and checkout system. They had unlimited licenses for RDBMS software and a consulting budget that allowed them to attract the best and brightest consultants for their projects. In spite of all that power and money, they eventually realized that a relational model wouldn't meet their future business needs.

Many in the NoSQL community cite Amazon's Dynamo paper as a significant turning point in the movement. At a time when relational models were still used, it challenged the status quo and current best practices. Amazon found that because key-value stores had a simple interface, it was easier to replicate the data and more reliable. In the end, Amazon used a key-value store to build a turnkey system that was reliable, extensible, and able to support their 24/7 business model, making them one of the most successful online retailers in the world.

1.3.5   *Case study: MarkLogic*

In 2001 a group of engineers in the San Francisco Bay Area with experience in document search formed a company that focused on managing large collections of XML documents. Because XML documents contained *markup*, they named the company *MarkLogic*.

MarkLogic defined two types of nodes in a cluster: query and document nodes. *Query nodes* receive query requests and coordinate all activities associated with executing a query. *Document nodes* contain XML documents and are responsible for executing queries on the documents in the local filesystem.

Query requests are sent to a query node, which distributes queries to each remote server that contains indexed XML documents. All document matches are returned to the query node. When all document nodes have responded, the query result is then returned.

The MarkLogic architecture, moving queries to documents rather than moving documents to the query server, allowed them to achieve linear scalability with petabytes of documents.

MarkLogic found a demand for their products in US federal government systems that stored terabytes of intelligence information and large publishing entities that wanted to store and search their XML documents. Since 2001, MarkLogic has matured into a general-purpose highly scalable document store with support for ACID transactions and fine-grained, role-based access control. Initially, the primary language of MarkLogic developers was XQuery paired with REST; newer versions support Java as well as other language interfaces.

MarkLogic is a commercial product that requires a software license for any datasets over 40 GB. NoSQL is associated with commercial as well as open source products that provide innovative solutions to business problems.

1.3.6   *Applying your knowledge*

To demonstrate how the concepts in this book can be applied, we introduce you to Sally Solutions. Sally is a solution architect at a large organization that has many business units. Business units that have information management issues are assigned a solution architect to help them select the best solution to their information challenge.

Sally works on projects that need custom applications developed and she's knowledgeable about SQL and NoSQL technologies. Her job is to find the best fit for the business problem.

Now let's see how Sally applies her knowledge in two examples. In the first example, a group that needed to track equipment warranties of hardware purchases came to Sally for advice. Since the hardware information was already in an RDBMS and the team had experience with SQL, Sally recommended they extend the RDBMS to include warranty information and create reports using joins. In this case, it was clear that SQL was appropriate.

In the second example, a group that was in charge of storing digital image information within a relational database approached Sally because the performance of the database was negatively impacting their web application's page rendering. In this case, Sally recommended moving all images to a key-value store, which referenced each image with a URL. A key-value store is optimized for read-intensive applications and works with content distribution networks. After removing the image management load from the RDBMS, the web application as well as other applications saw an improvement in performance.

Note that Sally doesn't see her job as a black-and-white, RDBMS versus NoSQL selection process. Sometimes the best solution involves using hybrid approaches.

1.4   Summary

This chapter began with an introduction to the concept of NoSQL and reviewed the core business drivers behind the NoSQL movement. We then showed how the power wall forced systems designers to use highly parallel processing designs and required a new type of thinking for managing data. You also saw that traditional systems that use object-middle tiers and RDBMS databases require the use of complex object-relational mapping systems to manipulate the data. These layers often get in the way of an organization's ability to react quickly to changes (agility).

When we venture into any new technology, it's critical to understand that each area has its own patterns of problem solving. These patterns vary dramatically from technology to technology. Making the transition from SQL to NoSQL is no different. NoSQL is a new paradigm and requires a new set of pattern recognition skills, new ways of thinking, and new ways of solving problems. It requires a new cognitive style.

Opting to use NoSQL technologies can help organizations gain a competitive edge in their market, making them more agile and better equipped to adapt to changing business conditions. NoSQL approaches that leverage large numbers of commodity processors save companies time and money and increase service reliability.

As you've seen in the case studies, these changes impacted more than early technology adopters: engineers around the world realize there are alternatives to the RDBMS-as-our-only-option mantra. New companies focused on new thinking, technologies, and architectures have emerged not as a lark, but as a necessity to solving real business problems that don't fit into a relational mold. As organizations continue to change and move into global economies, this trend will continue to expand.

As we move into our next chapter, we'll begin looking at the core concepts and technologies associated with NoSQL. We'll talk about simplicity of design and see how it's fundamental to creating NoSQL systems that are modular, scalable, and ultimately lower-cost to you and your organization.

NoSQL concepts

2

This chapter covers

- NoSQL concepts
- ACID and BASE for reliable database transactions
- How to minimize downtime with database sharding
- Brewer's CAP theorem

Less is more.
　　　　　　　—Ludwig Mies van der Rohe

In this chapter, we'll cover the core concepts associated with NoSQL systems. After reading this chapter, you'll be able to recognize and define NoSQL concepts and terms, you'll understand NoSQL vendor products and features, and you'll be able to decide if these features are appropriate for your NoSQL system. We'll start with a discussion about how using simple components in the application development process removes complexity and promotes reuse, saving you time and money in your system's design and maintenance.

2.1 Keeping components simple to promote reuse

If you've worked with relational databases, you know how complex they can be. Generally, they begin as simple systems that, when requested, return a selected row from a single flat file. Over time, they need to do more and evolve into systems that manage multiple tables, perform join operations, do query optimization, replicate transactions, run stored procedures, set triggers, enforce security, and perform indexing. NoSQL systems use a different approach to solving these complex problems by creating simple applications that distribute the required features across the network. Keeping your architectural components simple allows you to reuse them between applications, aids developers in understanding and testing, and makes it easier to port your application to new architectures.

From the NoSQL perspective, simple is good. When you create an application, it's not necessary to include all functions in a single software application. Application functions can be distributed to many NoSQL (and SQL) databases that consist of simple tools that have simple interfaces and well-defined roles. NoSQL products that follow this rule do a few things and they do them well. To illustrate, we'll look at how systems can be built using well-defined functions and focus on how easy it is to build these new functions.

If you're familiar with UNIX operating systems, you might be familiar with the concept of UNIX pipes. UNIX pipes are a set of processes that are chained together so that the output of one process becomes the input to the next process. Like UNIX pipes, NoSQL systems are often created by integrating a large number of modular functions that work together. An example of creating small functions with UNIX pipes to count the total number of figures in a book is illustrated in figure 2.1.

What's striking about this example is that by typing about 40 characters you've created a useful function. This task would be much more difficult to do on systems that don't support UNIX-style functions. In reality, only a query on a native XML database might be shorter than this command, but it wouldn't also be general-purpose.

Many NoSQL systems are created using a similar philosophy of modular components that can work together. Instead of having a single large database layer, they often

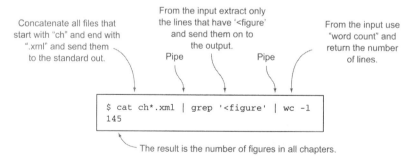

Figure 2.1   UNIX pipes as an example of reusing simple tools to create new functions. This figure concatenates (puts together) all chapter files in a book into a single file and counts the number of figures in all chapters. With UNIX pipes, we do this by stringing together three simple commands: concatenate (`cat`), a search function called `grep`, and word count (`wc`). No additional code is needed; each function takes the output from the previous function and processes it.

have a number of simpler components that can be reassembled to meet the needs of different applications. For example, one function allows sharing of objects in RAM (memcache), another function runs batch jobs (MapReduce,) and yet another function stores binary documents (key-value stores). Note that most UNIX pipes were designed to transform linear pipelines of line-oriented data streams on a single processor. NoSQL components, though modular, are more than a series of linear pipeline components. Their focus is on efficient data services that are frequently used to power distributed web services. NoSQL systems can be documents, messages, message stores, file stores, REST, JSON, or XML web services with generic application program interfaces (APIs). There are tools to load, validate, transform, and output large amounts of data, whereas UNIX pipes were really designed to work on a single processor.

STANDARDS WATCH: UNIVERSAL PIPES FOR STRUCTURED DATA   At this point you might be asking if you can still use the concepts behind UNIX pipes to process your structured data. The answer is yes, if you use JSON or XML standards! The World Wide Web Consortium has recognized the universal need for standard pipe concepts that work with any unstructured data. They have provided a standard for processing pipelined data called *XProc*. Several NoSQL databases have XProc built in as part of their architecture. XProc standards allow data transformation pipelines built with one NoSQL database to be ported to other XProc systems without modification. You can read more about XProc at http://www.w3.org/TR/xproc/. There's also a version of the UNIX shell that's specifically used for XML called XMLSH. You can read more about XMLSH at http://www.xmlsh.org.

The concept of simple functions in NoSQL systems will be a recurring theme. Don't be afraid to suggest or use a NoSQL system even if it doesn't meet all your needs in a single system. As you come to learn more about NoSQL systems, you'll think of them as collections of tools that become more useful the more you know about how they fit together. Next, we'll see how the concept of simplicity is important in the development of the application layer with respect to NoSQL applications.

2.2   *Using application tiers to simplify design*

Understanding the role of tiered applications is important to objectively evaluate one or more application architectures. Since functions move between tiers, the comparison at times might not be as clear as when you look at a single tier. The best way to fairly and objectively compare systems is to take a holistic approach, looking at the overall application and how well it meets system requirements.

Using application tiers in your architecture allows you to create flexible and reusable applications. By segregating an application into tiers, you have the option of modifying or adding a specific layer instead of reworking an entire application when modifications are required. As you'll see in the following example, which compares RDBMSs and NoSQL systems, functions in NoSQL applications are distributed differently.

When application designers begin to think about software systems that store persistent data, they have many options. One choice is to determine whether they need to use application tiers to divide the overall functionality of their application. Identifying each layer breaks the application into separate architectural components, which allows the software designer to determine the responsibility of each component. This *separation of concerns* allows designers to make the complicated seem simple when explaining the system to others.

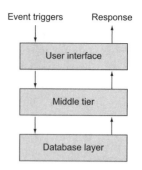

Figure 2.2   Application tiers are used to simplify system design. The NoSQL movement is concerned with minimizing bottlenecks in overall system performance, and this sometimes means moving key components out of one tier and putting them into another tier.

Application tiers are typically viewed in a layer-cake-like drawing, as shown in figure 2.2. In this figure, user events (like a user clicking a button on a web page) trigger code in the user interface. The output or response from the user interface is sent to the middle tier. This middle tier may respond by sending something back to the user interface, or it could access the database layer. The database layer may in turn run a query and send a response back to the middle tier. The middle tier then uses the data to create a report and sends it to the user. This process is the same whether you're using Microsoft Windows, Apple's OS X, or a web browser with HTML links.

When designing applications it's important to consider the trade-offs when putting functionality in each tier. Because relational databases have been around for a long time and are mature, it's common for database vendors to add functionality at the database tier and release it with their software rather than reusing components already delivered or developed. NoSQL system designers know that their software must work in complex environments with other applications where reuse and seamless interfaces are required, so they build small independent functions. Figure 2.3 shows the differences between RDBMS and NoSQL applications.

In figure 2.3 we compare the relational versus NoSQL methods of distributing application functions between the middle and database tiers. As you can see, both models have a user interface tier at the top. In the relational database, most of the application functionality is found in the database layer. In the NoSQL application, most of the application functionality is found in the middle tier. In addition, NoSQL systems leverage more services for managing BLOBs of data (the key-value store), for storing full-text indexes (the Lucene indexes), and for executing batch jobs (MapReduce).

A good NoSQL application design comes from carefully considering the pros and cons of putting functions in the middle versus the database tier. NoSQL solutions allow you to carefully consider all the options, and if the requirements include a high-scalability component, you can choose to keep the database tier simple. In traditional relational database systems, the complexity found in the database tier impacts the overall scalability of the application.

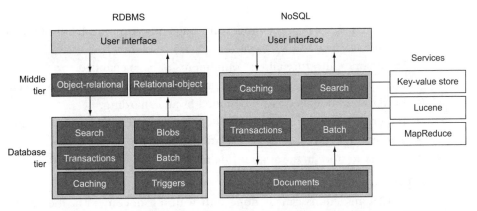

Figure 2.3 This figure compares application layers in RDBMSs and NoSQL systems. RDBMSs, on the left, have focused on putting many functions into the database tier where you can guarantee security and transactional integrity. The middle tier is used to convert objects to and from tables. NoSQL systems, on the right, don't use object-relational mapping concepts; they move database functions into the middle tier and leverage external services.

Remember, if you focus on a single tier you'll never get a fair comparison. When performing a trade-off analysis, you should compare RDBMSs with NoSQL systems as well as think about how repartitioning will impact functionality at each tier. This process is complex and requires an understanding of *both* RDBMS and NoSQL architectures. The following is a list of sample pros and cons you'll want to consider when performing a trade-off analysis.

RDBMS pros:

- ACID transactions at the database level makes development easier.
- Fine-grained security on columns and rows using views prevents views and changes by unauthorized users.
- Most SQL code is portable to other SQL databases, including open source options.
- Typed columns and constraints will validate data before it's added to the database and increase data quality.
- Existing staff members are already familiar with entity-relational design and SQL.

RDBMS cons:

- The object-relational mapping layer can be complex.
- Entity-relationship modeling must be completed before testing begins, which slows development.
- RDBMSs don't scale out when joins are required.
- Sharding over many servers can be done but requires application code and will be operationally inefficient.
- Full-text search requires third-party tools.
- It can be difficult to store high-variability data in tables.

NoSQL pros:

- Loading test data can be done with drag-and-drop tools before ER modeling is complete.
- Modular architecture allows components to be exchanged.
- Linear scaling takes place as new processing nodes are added to the cluster.
- Lower operational costs are obtained by autosharding.
- Integrated search functions provide high-quality ranked search results.
- There's no need for an object-relational mapping layer.
- It's easy to store high-variability data.

NoSQL cons:

- ACID transactions can be done only within a document at the database level. Other transactions must be done at the application level.
- Document stores don't provide fine-grained security at the element level.
- NoSQL systems are new to many staff members and additional training may be required.
- The document store has its own proprietary nonstandard query language, which prohibits portability.
- The document store won't work with existing reporting and OLAP tools.

Understanding the role of placing functions within an application tier is important to understanding how an application will perform. Another important factor to consider is how memory such as RAM, SSD, and disk will impact your system.

Terminology of database clusters

The NoSQL industry frequently refers to the concept of *processing nodes in a database cluster*. In general, each cluster consists of racks filled with commodity computer hardware, as shown in figure 2.4.

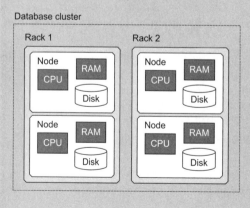

Figure 2.4   Some of the terminology used in distributed database clusters. A cluster is composed of a set of processors, called nodes, grouped together in racks. Nodes are commodity processors, each of which has its own local CPU, RAM, and disk.

(continued)
Each independent computer is called a *node*.

For the purposes of this book, unless we're discussing custom hardware, we'll define nodes as containing a single logical processor called a *CPU*. Each node has its own local RAM and disk. The CPU may in fact be implemented using multiple chips, each with multiple core processors. The disk system may also be composed of several independent drives.

Nodes are grouped together in racks that have high-bandwidth connections between all the nodes within a rack. Racks are grouped together to form a database cluster within a data center. A single data center location may contain many database clusters. Note that some NoSQL transactions must store their data on two nodes in different geographic locations to be considered successful transactions.

2.3 Speeding performance by strategic use of RAM, SSD, and disk

How do NoSQL systems use different types of memory to increase system performance? Generally, traditional database management systems weren't concerned with memory management optimization. In contrast, NoSQL systems are designed to be cost effective when creating fast user response times by minimizing the amount of expensive resources you need.

If you're new to database architectures, it's good to start with a clear understanding about the difference in performance between queries that retrieve their data from RAM (volatile random access memory) and queries that retrieve their data from hard drives. Most people know that when they turn off their computer after a long work day, the data in RAM is erased and must be reloaded. Data on *solid state drives (SSDs)* and *hard disk drives (HDDs)* persists. We also know that RAM access is fast and, in comparison, disk access is much slower. Let's assume 1 nanosecond is equal to approximately a foot, which is in fact roughly the time it takes for light to travel one foot. That means your RAM is 10 feet away from you, but your hard drive is over 10 million feet away, or about 2,000 miles. If you use a solid state disk, the result is slower than RAM, but not nearly as slow as a spinning disk drive (see figure 2.5).

Let's start by putting you in the city of Chicago, Illinois. If you want to get something from your RAM, you can usually find it in your back yard. If you're lucky enough to have data stored in a solid state disk, you can find it by making a quick trip somewhere in your neighborhood. But if you want to get something from your hard drive, you'll need to go to the city of Los Angeles, California, which is about 2,000 miles away. Not a round trip you want to make often if you can avoid it.

Rather than drive all the way to Los Angeles and back, what if you could check around your neighborhood to see if you already have the data? The time it takes to do a calculation in a chip today is roughly the time it takes light to travel across the chip.

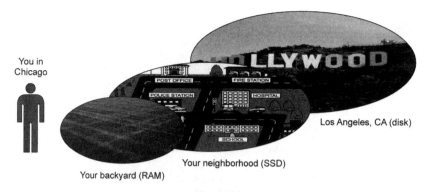

You in
Chicago

Los Angeles, CA (disk)

Your neighborhood (SSD)

Your backyard (RAM)

Figure 2.5   To get a feel for how expensive it is to access your hard drive compared to finding an item in RAM cache, think of how long it might take you to pick up an item in your back yard (RAM). Then think of how long it would take to drive to a location in your neighborhood (SSD), and finally think of how long it would take to pick up an item in Los Angeles if you lived in Chicago (HDD). This shows that finding a query result in a local cache is more efficient than an expensive query that needs HDD access.

You can do a few trillion calculations while you're waiting for your data to get back from LA. That's why calculating a hash is much faster than going to disk, and the more RAM you have, the lower the probability you need to make that long round trip.

The solution to faster systems is to keep as much of the right information in RAM as you can, and check your local servers to see if they might also have a copy. This local fast data store is often called a *RAM cache* or *memory cache*. Yet, accomplishing this and determining when the data is no longer current turn out to be difficult questions.

Many memory caches use a simple timestamp for each block of memory in the cache as a way of keeping the most recently used objects in memory. When memory fills up, the timestamp is used to determine which items in memory are the oldest and should be overwritten. A more refined view can take into account how much time or resources it'll take to re-create the dataset and store it in memory. This "cost model" allows more expensive queries to be kept in RAM longer than similar items that could be regenerated much faster.

The effective use of RAM cache is predicated on the efficient answer to the question, "Have we run this query before?" or equivalently, "Have we seen this document before?" These questions can be answered by using *consistent hashing*, which lets you know if an item is already in the cache or if you need to retrieve it from SSD or HDD.

2.4   *Using consistent hashing to keep your cache current*

You've learned how important it is to keep frequently used data in your RAM cache, and how by avoiding unnecessary disk access you can improve your database performance. NoSQL systems expand on this concept and use a technique called *consistent hashing* to keep the most frequently used data in your cache.

Consistent hashing is a general-purpose process that's useful when evaluating how NoSQL systems work. Consistent hashing quickly tells you if a new query or

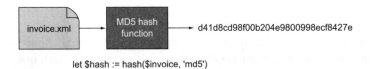

let $hash := hash($invoice, 'md5')

Figure 2.6 Sample hashing process. An input document such as a business invoice is sent through a hashing function. The result of the hashing function is a string that's unique to the original document. A change of a single byte in the input will return a different hash string. A hash can be used to see if a document has changed or if it's already located in a RAM cache.

document is the same as one already in your cache. Knowing this information prevents you from making unnecessary calls to disk for information and keeps your databases running fast.

A hash string (also known as a *checksum* or *hash*) is a process that calculates a sequence of letters by looking at each byte of a document. The hash string uniquely identifies each document and can be used to determine whether the document you're presented with is the same document you already have on hand. If there's any difference between two documents (even a single byte), the resulting hash will be different. Since the 1990s, hash strings have been created using standardized algorithms such as MD5, SHA-1, SHA-256, and RIPEMD-160. Figure 2.6 illustrates a typical hashing process.

Hash values can be created for simple queries or complex JSON or XML documents. Once you have your hash value, you can use it to make sure that the information you're sending is the same information others are receiving. Consistent hashing occurs when two different processes running on different nodes in your network create the same hash for the same object. Consistent hashing confirms that the information in the document hasn't been altered and allows you to

Hash collisions

There's an infinitesimally small chance that two different documents could generate the same hash value, resulting in a *hash collision*. The likelihood of this occurring is related to the length of the hash value and how many documents you're storing. The longer the hash, the lower the odds of a collision. As you add more documents, the chance of a collision increases. Many systems use the MD5 hash algorithm that generates a 128-bit hash string. A 128-bit hash can generate approximately 10^{38} possible outputs. That means that if you want to keep the odds of a collision low, for example odds of under one in 10^{18}, you want to limit the number of documents you keep to under 10^{13}, or about 10 trillion documents.

For most applications that use hashing, accidental hash collisions aren't a concern. But there are situations where avoiding hash collisions is important. Systems that use hashes for security verification, like government or high-security systems, require hash values to be greater than 128 bits. In these situations, algorithms that generate a hash value greater than 128 bits like SHA-1, SHA-256, SHA-384, or SHA-512 are preferred.

determine whether the object exists in your cache or message store, saving precious resources by only rerunning processes when necessary.

Consistent hashing is also critical for synchronizing distributed databases. For example, version control systems such as Git or Subversion can run a hash not only on a single document but also on hashes of hashes for all files within a directory. By doing this consistently, you can see if your directory is in sync with a remote directory and, if not, you can run update operations on only the items that have changed.

Consistent hashing is an important tool to keep your cache current and your system running fast, even when caches are spread over many distributed systems. Consistent hashing can also be used to assign documents to specific database nodes on distributed systems and to quickly compare remote databases when they need to be synchronized. Distributed NoSQL systems rely on hashing for rapidly enhancing database read times without getting in the way of write transactions.

2.5   *Comparing ACID and BASE—two methods of reliable database transactions*

Transaction control is important in distributed computing environments with respect to performance and consistency. Typically one of two types of transaction control models are used: ACID, used in RDBMS, and BASE, found in many NoSQL systems. Even if only a small percentage of your database transactions requires transactional integrity, it's important to know that both RDBMSs and NoSQL systems are able to create these controls. The difference between these models is in the amount of effort required by application developers and the location (tier) of the transactional controls.

Let's start with a simple banking example to represent a reliable transaction. These days, many people have two bank accounts: savings and checking. If you want to move funds from one account to the other, it's likely your bank has a transfer form on their website. This is illustrated in figure 2.7.

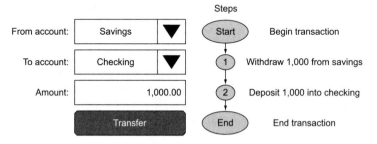

Figure 2.7   The atomic set of steps needed to transfer funds from one bank account to another. The first step subtracts the transfer amount from the source savings account. The second step adds the same transfer amount to the destination checking account. For the transaction to be considered reliable, both steps must work or both need to be undone. Between steps, no reports should be allowed to run that show the total amount as dropping by the transaction amount.

When you click the Transfer button on the web page, two discrete operations must happen in unison. The funds are subtracted from your savings account and then added to your checking account. Transaction management is the process of making sure that these two operations happen together as a single unit of work or not at all. If the computer crashes after the first part of the transaction is complete and before the second part of the transaction occurs, you'd be out $1,000 and very unhappy with your bank.

Traditional commercial RDBMSs are noted for their reliability in performing financial transactions. This reputation has been earned not only because they've been around for a long time and diligently debugged their software, but also because they've made it easy for programmers to make transactions reliable by wrapping critical transactions in statements that indicate where transactions begin and end. These are often called BEGIN TRANSACTION and END TRANSACTION statements. By adding them, developers can get high-reliability transaction support. If either one of the two atomic units doesn't complete, both of the operations will be rolled back to their initial settings.

The software also ensures that no reports can be run on the accounts halfway through the operations. If you run a "combined balance" report during the transaction, it'd never show a total that drops by 1,000 and then increases again. If a report starts while the first part of the transaction is in process, it'll be blocked until all parts of the transaction are complete.

In traditional RDBMSs the transaction management complexity is the responsibility of the database layer. Application developers only need to be able to deal with what to do if an entire transaction fails and how to notify the right party or how to keep retrying until the transaction is complete. Application developers don't need to know how to undo various parts of a transaction, as that's built into the database.

Given that reliable transactions are important in most application systems, the next two sections will take an in-depth look at RDBMS transaction control using ACID, and NoSQL transaction control using BASE.

2.5.1   *RDBMS transaction control using ACID*

RDBMSs maintain transaction control by using atomic, consistent, independent, and durable (ACID) properties to insure transactions are reliable. The following defines each of the associated properties:

- *Atomicity*—In the banking transaction example, we said that the exchange of funds from savings to checking must happen as an all-or-nothing transaction. The technical term for this is *atomicity*, which comes from the Greek term for "dividable." Systems that claim they have atomic transactions must consider all failure modes: disk crashes, network failures, hardware failures, or simple software errors. Testing atomic transactions even on a single CPU is difficult.
- *Consistency*—In the banking transaction example, we talked about the fact that when moving funds between two related accounts, the total account balance

must never change. This is the principle of consistency. It means that your database must never have a report that shows the withdrawal from savings has occurred but the addition to checking hasn't. It's the responsibility of the database to block all reports during atomic operations. This has an impact on the speed of a system when many atomic transactions and reports are all being run on the same records in your database.

- *Isolation*—Isolation refers to the concept that each part of a transaction occurs without knowledge of any other transaction. For example, the transaction that adds funds doesn't know about the transaction that subtracts funds from an account.
- *Durability*—Durability refers to the fact that once all aspects of a transaction are complete, it's permanent. Once the transfer button is selected, you have the right to spend the money in your checking account. If the banking system crashes that night and they have to restore the database from a backup tape, there must be some way to make sure the record of this transfer is also restored. This usually means that the bank must create a transaction log on a separate computer system and then play back the transactions from the log after the backup is complete.

If you think that the software to handle these rules must be complex, you're right; it's very complex and one of the reasons that relational databases can be expensive. If you're writing a database on your own, it could easily double or triple the amount of software that has to be written. This is why new databases frequently don't support database-level transaction management in their first release. That's added only after the product matures.

Many RDBMSs restrict transaction location to a single CPU. If you think about the situation where your savings account information is stored in a computer in New York and your checking account information is stored in a computer in San Francisco, the complexity increases, since you have a greater number of failure points and the number of reporting systems that must be blocked on both systems increases.

Although supporting ACID transactions is complex, there are well-known and well-publicized strategies to do this. All of them depend on *locking* resources, putting extra copies of the resources aside, performing the transaction and then, if all is well, unlocking the resources. If any part of a transaction fails, the original resource in question must be returned to its original state. The design challenge is to create systems that support these transactions, make it easy for the application to use transactions, and maintain database speed and responsiveness.

ACID systems focus on the consistency and integrity of data above all other considerations. Temporarily blocking reporting mechanisms is a reasonable compromise to ensure your systems return reliable and accurate information. ACID systems are said to be pessimistic in that they must consider all possible failure modes in a computing environment. At times ACID systems seem to be guided by Murphy's Law—if anything *can* go wrong it *will* go wrong—and must be carefully tested in order to guarantee the integrity of transactions.

While ACID systems focus on high data integrity, NoSQL systems that use BASE take into consideration a slightly different set of constraints. What if blocking one transaction while you wait for another to finish is an unacceptable compromise? If you have a website that's taking orders from customers, sometimes ACID systems are *not* what you want.

2.5.2 *Non-RDBMS transaction control using BASE*

What if you have a website that relies on computers all over the world? A computer in Chicago manages your inventory, product photos are on an image database in Virgina, tax calculations are performed in Seattle, and your accounting system is in Atlanta. What if one site goes down? Should you tell your customers to check back in 20 minutes while you solve the problem? Only if your goal is to drive them to your competitors. Is it realistic to use ACID software for every order that comes in? Let's look at another option.

Websites that use the "shopping cart" and "checkout" constructs have a different primary consideration when it comes to transaction processing. The issue of reports that are inconsistent for a few minutes is less important than something that prevents you from taking an order, because if you block an order, you've lost a customer. The alternative to ACID is BASE, which stands for these concepts:

- *Basic availability* allows systems to be temporarily inconsistent so that transactions are manageable. In BASE systems, the information and service capability are "basically available."
- *Soft-state* recognizes that some inaccuracy is temporarily allowed and data may change while being used to reduce the amount of consumed resources.
- *Eventual consistency* means eventually, when all service logic is executed, the system is left in a consistent state.

Unlike RDBMSs that focus on consistency, BASE systems focus on availability. BASE systems are noteworthy because their number-one objective is to allow new data to be stored, even at the risk of being out of sync for a short period of time. They relax the rules and allow reports to run even if not all portions of the database are synchronized. BASE systems aren't considered *pessimistic* in that they don't fret about the details if one process is behind. They're *optimistic* in that they assume that eventually all systems will catch up and become consistent.

BASE systems tend to be simpler and faster because they don't have to write code that deals with locking and unlocking resources. Their mission is to keep the process moving and deal with broken parts at a later time. BASE systems are ideal for web storefronts, where filling a shopping cart and placing an order is the main priority.

Prior to the NoSQL movement, most database experts considered ACID systems to be the only type of transactions that could be used in business. NoSQL systems are

Vs.

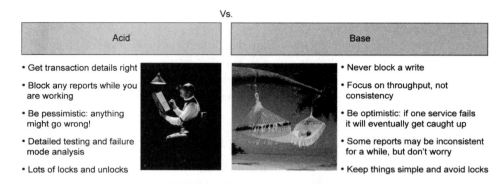

Acid	Base
• Get transaction details right	• Never block a write
• Block any reports while you are working	• Focus on throughput, not consistency
• Be pessimistic: anything might go wrong!	• Be optimistic: if one service fails it will eventually get caught up
• Detailed testing and failure mode analysis	• Some reports may be inconsistent for a while, but don't worry
• Lots of locks and unlocks	• Keep things simple and avoid locks

Figure 2.8   ACID versus BASE—understanding the trade-offs. This figure compares the rigid financial accounting rules of traditional RDBMS ACID transactions with the more laid-back BASE approach used in NoSQL systems. RDBMS ACID systems are ideal when all reports must always be consistent and reliable. NoSQL BASE systems are preferred when priority is given to never blocking a write transaction. Your business requirements will determine whether traditional RDBMS or NoSQL systems are right for your application.

highly decentralized and ACID guarantees may not be necessary, so they use BASE and take a more relaxed approach. Figure 2.8 shows an accurate and somewhat humorous representation of ACID versus BASE philosophies.

A final note: ACID and BASE aren't rigid points on a line; they lie on a continuum where organizations and systems can decide where and how to architect systems. They may allow ACID transactions on some key areas but relax them in others. Some database systems offer both options by changing a configuration file or using a different API. The systems administrator and application developer work together to implement the right choice after considering the needs of the business.

Transactions are important when you move from centralized to distributed systems that need to scale in order to handle large volumes of data. But there are times when the amount of data you manage exceeds the size of your current system and you need to use database sharding to keep systems running and minimize downtime.

2.6   *Achieving horizontal scalability with database sharding*

As the amount of data an organization stores increases, there may come a point when the amount of data needed to run the business exceeds the current environment and some mechanism for breaking the information into reasonable chunks is required. Organizations and systems that reach this capacity can use automatic database *sharding* (breaking a database into chunks called *shards* and spreading the chunks across a number of distributed servers) as a means to continuing to store data while minimizing system downtime. On older systems this might mean taking the system down for a few hours while you manually reconfigure the database and copy data from the old system to a new system, yet NoSQL systems do this automatically. How a database grows and its tolerance for automatic partitioning of data is important to NoSQL systems. Sharding has become a highly automated process in both big data and fault-tolerant systems. Let's look at how sharding works and explore its challenges.

Let's say you've created a website that allows users to log in and create their own personal space to share with friends. They have profiles, text, and product information on things they like (or don't like). You set up your website, store the information in a MySQL database, and you run it on a single CPU. People love it, they log in, create pages, invite their friends, and before you realize it your disk space is 95% full. What do you do? If you're using a typical RDBMS system, the answer is buy a new system and transfer half the users to the new system. Oh, and your old system might have to be down for a while so you can rewrite your application to know which database to get information from. Figure 2.9 shows a typical example of database sharding.

The process of moving from a single to multiple databases can be done in a number of ways; for example:

1 You can keep the users with account names that start with the letters A-N on the first drive and put users from O-Z on the new system.
2 You can keep the people in the United States on the original system and put the people who live in Europe on the new system.
3 You can randomly move half the users to the new system.

Each of these alternatives has pros and cons. For example, in option 1, if a user changes their name, should they be automatically moved to the new drive? In option 2, if a user moves to a new country, should all their data be moved? If people tend to share links with people near them, would there be performance advantages to keeping these users together? What if people in the United States tend to be active at the same time in the evening? Would one database get overwhelmed and the other be

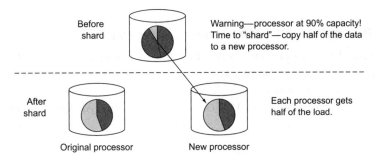

Figure 2.9 Sharding is performed when a single processor can't handle the throughput requirements of a system. When this happens you'll want to move the data onto two systems that each take half the work. Many NoSQL systems have automatic sharding built in so that you only need to add a new server to a pool of working nodes and the database management system automatically moves data to the new node. Most RDBMSs don't support automatic sharding.

idle? What happens if your site doubles in size again? Do you have to continue to rewrite your code each time this happens? Do you have to shut the system down for a weekend while you upgrade your software?

As the number of servers grows, you find that the chance of any one server being down remains the same, so for every server you add the chance of one part not working increases. So you think that perhaps the same process you used to split the database between two systems can also be used to duplicate data to a backup or mirrored system if the first one fails. But then you have another problem. When there are changes to a master copy, you must also keep the backup copies in sync. You must have a method of data replication. The time it takes to keep these databases in sync can decrease system performance. You now need more servers to keep up!

Welcome to the world of database sharding, replication, and distributed computing. You can see that there are many questions and trade-offs to consider as your database grows. NoSQL systems have been noted for having many ways to allow you to grow your database without ever having to shut down your servers. Keeping your database running when there are node or network failures is called *partition tolerance*—a new concept in the NoSQL community and one that traditional database managers struggle with.

Understanding transaction integrity and autosharding is important with respect to how you think about the trade-offs you're faced with when building distributed systems. Though database performance, transaction integrity, and how you use memory and autosharding are important, there are times when you must identify those system aspects that are most important and focus on them while leaving others flexible. Using a formal process to understand the trade-offs in your selection process will help drive your focus toward things most important to your organization, which we turn to next.

2.7 *Understanding trade-offs with Brewer's CAP theorem*

In order to make the best decision about what to do when systems fail, you need to consider the properties of consistency and availability when working with distributed systems over unreliable networks.

Eric Brewer first introduced the *CAP* theorem in 2000. The CAP theorem states that any distributed database system can have at most two of the following three desirable properties:

- *Consistency*—Having a single, up-to-date, readable version of your data available to all clients. This isn't the same as the consistency we talked about in ACID. Consistency here is concerned with multiple clients reading the same items from replicated partitions and getting consistent results.
- *High availability*—Knowing that the distributed database will always allow database clients to update items without delay. Internal communication failures between replicated data shouldn't prevent updates.

- *Partition tolerance*—The ability of the system to keep responding to client requests even if there's a communication failure between database partitions. This is analogous to a person still having an intelligent conversation even after a link between parts of their brain isn't working.

Remember that the CAP theorem only applies in cases when there's a broken connection between partitions in your cluster. The more reliable your network, the lower the probability you'll need to think about CAP.

The CAP theorem helps you understand that once you partition your data, you must consider the availability-consistency spectrum in a network failure situation. Then the CAP theorem allows you to determine which options best match your business requirements. Figure 2.10 provides an example of the CAP application.

The client writes to a primary master node, which replicates the data to another backup slave node. CAP forces you to think about whether you accept a write if the communication link between the nodes is down. If you accept it, you must take responsibility for making sure the remote node gets the update at a later time, and you risk a client reading inconsistent values until the link is restored. If you refuse the write, you sacrifice availability and the client must retry later.

Although the CAP theorem has been around since 2000, it's still a source of confusion. The CAP theorem limits your design options in a few rare end cases and usually only applies when there are network failures between data centers. In many cases, reliable message queues can quickly restore consistency after network failures.

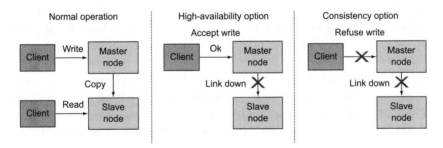

Figure 2.10   The partition decision. The CAP theorem helps you decide the relative merits of availability versus consistency when a network fails. In the left panel, under normal operation a client write will go to a master and then be replicated over the network to a slave. If the link is down, the client API can decide the relative merits of high availability or consistency. In the middle panel, you accept a write and risk inconsistent reads from the slave. In the right panel, you choose consistency and block the client write until the link between the data centers is restored.

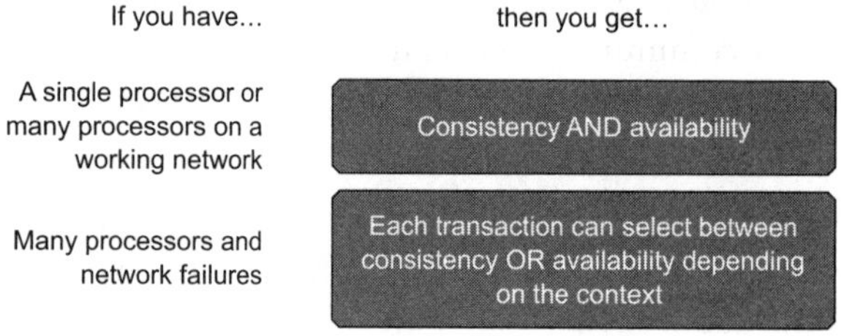

Figure 2.11 The CAP theorem shows that you can have both consistency and availability if you're only using a single processor. If you're using many processors, you can chose between consistency and availability depending on the transaction type, user, estimated downtime, or other factors.

The rules about when the CAP theorem applies are summarized in figure 2.11.

Tools like the CAP theorem can help guide database selection discussions within an organization and prioritize what properties (consistency, availability, and scalability) are most important. If high consistency and update availability are simultaneously required, then a faster single processor might be your best choice. If you need the scale-out benefits that distributed systems offer, then you can make decisions about your need for update availability versus read consistency for each transaction type.

Whichever option you choose, the CAP theorem provides you with a formal process that can help you weigh the pros and cons of each SQL or NoSQL system, and in the end you'll make an informed decision.

2.8   *Apply your knowledge*

Sally has been assigned to help a team design a system to manage loyalty gift cards, which are similar to bank accounts. Card holders can add value to a card (deposit), make a purchase (withdrawal), and verify the card's balance. Gift card data will be partitioned and replicated to two data centers, one in the U.S. and one in Europe. People who live in the U.S. will have their primary partition in the U.S. data center and people in Europe will have their primary partition in Europe.

The data line between the two data centers has been known to fail for short periods of time, typically around 10-20 minutes each year. Sally knows this is an example of a *split partition* and that it'll test the system's partition tolerance. The team needs to decide whether all three operations (deposit, withdraw, and balance) must continue when the data line is down.

The team decides that deposits should continue to work even if the data line is down, since a record of the deposit can update both sites later when the connection is restored. Sally mentions that split partitions may generate inconsistent read results if one site can't update the other site with new balance information. But the team decides that bank balance requests that occur when the link is down should still return the last balance known to the local partition.

For purchase transactions, the team decides that the transaction should go through during a link failure as long as the user is connecting to the primary partition. To limit risk, withdrawals to the replicated partition will only work if the transaction is under a specific amount, such as $100. Reports will be used to see how often multiple withdrawals on partitions generate a negative balance during network outages.

2.9 Summary

In this chapter, we covered some of the key concepts and insights of the NoSQL movement. Here's a list of the important concepts and architectural guidelines we've discussed so far; you'll see these concepts mentioned and discussed in future chapters:

- Use simple building blocks to build applications.
- Use a layered architecture to promote modularity.
- Use consistent hashing to distribute data over a cluster.
- Use distributed caching, RAM, and SSD to speed database reads.
- Relaxing ACID requirements often gives you more flexibility.
- Sharding allows your database cluster to grow gracefully.
- The CAP theorem allows you to make intelligent choices when there's a network failure.

Throughout this book we emphasize the importance of using a formal process in evaluating systems to help identify what aspects are most important to the organization and what compromises need to be made.

At this point you should understand the benefits of using NoSQL systems and how they'll assist you in meeting your business objectives. In the next chapter, we'll build on our pattern vocabulary and review the strengths and weaknesses of RDBMS architectures, and then move on to patterns that are associated with NoSQL data architectures.

2.10 Further reading

- Birthday problem. Wikipedia. http://mng.bz/54gQ.
- "Disk sector." Wikipedia. http://mng.bz/Wfm5.
- "Dynamic random-access memory." Wikipedia. http://mng.bz/Z09P.
- "MD5: Collision vulnerabilities." Wikipedia. http://mng.bz/157p.
- "Paxos (computer science)." Wikipedia. http://mng.bz/U5tm.
- Preshing, Jeff. "Hash Collision Probabilities." Preshing on Programming. May 4, 2011. http://mng.bz/PxDU.
- "Quorum (distributed computing)." Wikipedia. http://mng.bz/w2P8.
- "Solid-state drive." Wikipedia. http://mng.bz/sg4R.
- W3C. "XProc: An XML Pipeline Language." http://www.w3.org/TR/xproc/.
- XMLSH. http://www.xmlsh.org.

Part 2

Database patterns

Part 2 covers three main areas: legacy database patterns (which most solution architects are familiar with), NoSQL patterns, and native XML databases.

Chapter 3 reviews legacy SQL patterns associated with relational and data warehouse databases. If you're already familiar with online transactional processing (OLTP), online analytical processing (OLAP), and the concepts used in distributed revision control systems, you can skim this chapter.

Chapter 4 introduces and describes the new NoSQL patterns. You'll learn about key-value stores, graph stores, column family stores, and document stores. This chapter should be read carefully, as it'll be referenced throughout the text.

Chapter 5 looks at patterns that are unique to native XML databases and standards-driven systems. These databases are important in areas such as government, health care, finance, publishing, integration, and document search. If you're not concerned with portability, standards, and markup languages, you can skim this chapter.

Foundational data architecture patterns

This chapter covers

- Data architecture patterns
- RDBMSs and the row-store design pattern
- RDBMS implementation features
- Data analysis using online analytical processing
- High-availability, read-mostly systems
- Hash trees in revision control systems and databases

If I have seen further it is by standing on the shoulders of giants.

—Isaac Newton

You may be asking yourself, "Why study relational patterns? Isn't this book about NoSQL?" Remember, NoSQL means "Not only SQL." Relational databases will continue to be an appropriate solution to many business problems for the foreseeable future. But there are situations where relational databases aren't the best match for a business problem. This chapter will review how RDBMSs store data (in tabular and row-oriented structures) used by online transactional systems, and the performance challenges this creates in distributed environments.

We'll begin with a definition of data architecture patterns and look at how the needs of *enterprise resource planning (ERP)* systems drove RDBMS feature sets. We'll then look at the most common SQL patterns such as row stores (used in most RDBMSs) and star schemas (used in OLAP, data warehouse, and business intelligence systems). We'll become familiar with key SQL terms and discuss the main features of directory services, DNS services, and revision control systems.

After reading this chapter, you'll understand the strengths and weaknesses of RDBMS systems and know when a NoSQL solution is a better fit. You'll recognize key RDBMS terms and become familiar with some key features of directory services, DNS services, and document revision control systems. Before we dive into RDBMS's strengths and weaknesses, we'll start with a definition of a data architecture pattern and talk about its significance when selecting a database for your business application.

3.1   *What is a data architecture pattern?*

So what exactly is a data architecture pattern and why is it useful in selecting the right database? Architectural patterns allow you to give precise names to recurring high-level data storage patterns. When you suggest a specific data architecture pattern as a solution to a business problem, you should use a consistent process that allows you to name the pattern, describe how it applies to the current business problem, and articulate the pros and cons of the proposed solution. It's important that all team members have the same understanding about how a particular pattern solves your problem so that when implemented, business goals and objectives are met.

The word *pattern* has many meanings. In general, it implies that given a new problem, you have the ability to recognize structures that you've seen in the past. For our purposes, we define a *data architecture pattern* as a consistent way of representing data in a regular structure that will be stored in memory. Although the memory you store data in is usually long-term persistent memory, such as solid state disk or hard drives, these structures can also be stored in RAM and then transferred to persistent memory by another process.

It's also important to understand the difference between a broad high-level data architecture pattern that's used to identify how data is stored in a system versus a narrow low-level design pattern that identifies how you interact with the data. For example, figure 3.1 shows the high-level, row-store data architecture pattern used in RDBMSs at the top of the diagram, and the low-level design patterns like joins, transactions, and views in the bottom part of the diagram.

As we continue along the NoSQL journey, we'll talk about traditional RDBMS patterns as well as patterns specific to the NoSQL movement. You'll come to quickly recognize these patterns and how they're used to build solutions that apply to your organization's business requirements. We'll begin our pattern discussion by looking at the RDBMS row-store pattern and the design patterns associated with it.

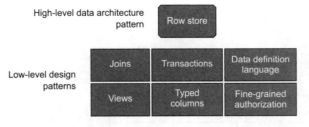

Figure 3.1   High-level data architecture patterns are used to discuss the fundamental ways data is stored in a system. Once you select a high-level data architecture pattern, there are many lower-level design patterns that a system may implement.

3.2   Understanding the row-store design pattern used in RDBMSs

Now that you have a basic understanding of an architectural pattern, let's look at the concepts and principles of the *row-store* pattern associated with relational database management systems. Understanding the row-store pattern and its use of joins is essential in helping you determine if a system can scale to a large number of processors. Unfortunately, the features that make row-store systems so flexible also limit their ability to scale.

Almost all RDBMSs store their data in a uniform object called a *row*. Rows consist of data fields that are associated with a column name and a single data type. Since rows are added and deleted as atomic units (a unit of work that's independent of any other transaction) using insert, update, or delete commands, the technical data architecture pattern name is called a *row store*, which is more commonly known as an *RDBMS* or *SQL database*.

We should note that not all SQL databases use the row-store pattern. Some databases use columns as an atomic unit of storage. As you might expect, these systems are called *column stores*. Column stores shouldn't be confused with the term *column family store*, which is used in Bigtable systems. Column-store systems are used when aggregate (counts, sums, and so on) reporting speed is a priority over insert performance.

3.2.1   How row stores work

Rows are an atomic unit of data storage in RDBMSs. The general concept of a row store is illustrated in figure 3.2.

The rows you insert comprise your tables in an RDBMS. Tables can be related to other tables and data relationships are also stored in tables. The following list shows how you might use an RDBMS to solve a business problem:

- A database modeling team meets with their business users. The business data is modeled in a logical way to understand data types, groupings, and repeating fields. When the modeling process is complete, the team has a physical table/column model. This process is used for new data created within the organization as well as for data that's transmitted to the organization from an external source.

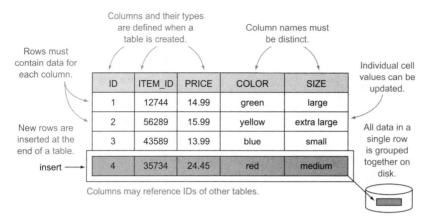

Figure 3.2   The basic rules of a row-store system. Row stores are created by first declaring a table with a fixed number of columns, each with a distinct name and a data type. Data is added row-by-row to the system, and each row must have data present for each column. All the data in a row is added as a unit and stored as a unit on disk.

- Tables are created using a specialized language called a *data definition language* or *DDL*. The entire table, with all column definitions and their data types, must be created before the first row is inserted into the table. Indexes are also created for columns on large tables that have many rows to increase access speed.
- Columns must have unique names within a table and a single data type (for example, string, date, or decimal) which is created when a table is first defined. The semantics or meaning of each column is stored in an organization's data dictionary.
- New data is added to a table by inserting new rows using INSERT statements or bulk loading functions. Repeating fields are associated with parent rows by referencing the parent's row identifier.
- The SQL INSERT statement can be used to insert a new row with any available data that's provided to the INSERT statement. SQL UPDATE operations can then be used to change specific values of a row, but row identifiers must be used to indicate what row to update.
- Reports are generated to create logical business documents from each table by selecting all related rows with JOIN statements.
- Database rules, called *triggers*, can be set up to automatically delete all rows associated with a business record.

Many commercial RDBMSs started with simple features. In time, new features were added to meet the needs of large *enterprise resource planning* (*ERP*) systems until they became robust and hardened for reliable commercial use. Initially, organizations needed a way to store financial information in order to produce accurate business statements. RDBMSs were created to store information about assets, sales, and purchases from which a SQL reporting system created queries (reports) to show the income, expenses, cash flow, and the organization's overall net worth. These financial statements were used to help decision makers think about whether to invest in new ventures or conserve their cash.

3.2.2 *Row stores evolve*

Beginning in the 1970s, many companies purchased separate siloed software applications for different aspects of their business, as seen in the left panel of figure 3.3.

In this stage, one database from a particular vendor might contain human resource (HR) information, another database from a different vendor might store sales information, and possibly a third vendor system would store customer relationship management (CRM) information. This structure mimicked the structure of the organization, where individual departments operated in their own world with limited communication between groups. Companies found these siloed systems to be appropriate and secure in situations where it was necessary to protect sensitive data (such as employee salary information or customer payment information). The isolated systems made it easy for each department to manage and protect their own resources, but it introduced challenges for the organization.

A key problem with siloed systems was the challenge of creating up-to-date reports that merged data from multiple systems. For example, a sales report in the sales tracking system might be used to generate commission information, but the list of sales staff and their commission rates might be stored in a separate HR database. As each change is made in the HR system, the new data must be moved to the sales tracking system. The costs of continually moving data between separate siloed systems became one of the largest budget items in many IT departments. To combat the problem of

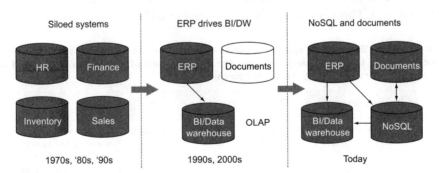

Figure 3.3 Understanding how NoSQL systems fit into the enterprise can be seen by looking at the three phases of enterprise databases. Initially organizations used standalone isolated systems (left panel). In time, the need arose to create integrated reports and the siloed systems were merged into ERP systems with fine-grained security controls, with separate systems for reporting on historical transactions (middle panel). These data warehouse and business intelligence systems use online analytical processing (OLAP) to create ad hoc reports without impacting ERP performance. The next stage (right panel) is when NoSQL systems are added for specialized tasks that RDBMSs aren't well suited for, and also serve as a bridge to document integration.

high integration costs, many organizations moved away from siloed systems and toward more integrated systems, as shown in the middle panel of figure 3.3.

As organizations evolved, the need for an integrated view of the enterprise became a requirement for assessing organization health and improving competitive position. Organizations could invest large sums to install and customize ERP packages, which incurred hefty vendor license fees and promises to add new features like fine-grained, role-based access to company data that would continue to support the customers' needs.

IT managers continued to face high customization costs and, in time, the lack of scalability began to cripple them. The license terms and associated technology didn't support migration to a large number of commodity processors, and most organizations lacked integrated document stores, making it difficult to retrieve information from disparate systems.

This was the technology landscape as we entered the twenty-first century. As we discussed in chapter 1, the power wall emerged, and with it the inability of CPUs to continue to get faster, which led to a new set of NoSQL technologies. In the right panel of figure 3.3, we see the emergence of NoSQL systems not as standalone systems, but in addition to the traditional RDBMSs. These systems are now key in solving problems that RDBMSs can't handle. The scalability of NoSQL solutions makes them ideal for transforming large amounts of data used in data warehouse applications. Additionally, their document nature and approach allows smooth integration of corporate documents directly into the analytical reporting and search services of an organization.

3.2.3   *Analyzing the strengths and weaknesses of the row-store pattern*

Let's take a look at some of the strengths and weaknesses of a typical enterprise RDBMS system. This information is summarized in table 3.1.

Table 3.1   **RDBMS strengths and weaknesses—you can see that RDBMSs were driven by early financial systems that stored data in tables. The pros and cons of RDBMSs drive the need to have consistent and secure reporting over a large number of tables.**

Feature	Strength	Weakness
Joins between tables	New views of data from different tables can easily be created.	All tables must be on the same server to make joins run efficiently. This makes it difficult to scale to more than one processor.
Transactions	Defining begin point, end point, and completion of critical transactions in an application is simple.	Read and write transactions may be slowed during critical times in a transaction unless the transaction isolation level is changed.

Table 3.1 (continued)

Feature	Strength	Weakness
Fixed data definitions and typed columns	Easy way to define structure and enforce business rules when tables are created. You can verify on insert that all data conforms to specific rules. Allows range indexes over columns.	Difficult to work with highly variable and exception data when adding to a column.
Fine-grained security	Data access control by row and column can be done with a series of view and grant statements.	Setup and testing security access for many roles can be a complex process.
Document integration	None. Few RDBMSs are designed to easily query document structures.	Difficult to create reports using both structured and unstructured data.

We should note that RDBMSs are continuing to evolve to add finer-grained control of ACID transactions. Some RDBMSs allow you to specify the isolation level of a transaction using a command such as SET TRANSACTION ISOLATION LEVEL READ UNCOMMIT-TED. Setting this option performs a *dirty read* or a read on data that hasn't yet been committed. If you add this option to a transaction, reports may have inconsistent results, but they can return faster, which can result in increased read performance.

When you look back at the information in this section, you can see that the needs of ERP systems were influential in the RDBMS feature sets of today. This means that if your business system has requirements that are similar to an ERP system, then an RDBMS might be the right choice for you. Now let's take a closer look at how these systems worked by using a sales order tracking example.

3.3 *Example: Using joins in a sales order*

Now that you know about row stores and how they work, we'll talk about how RDBMSs use joins to create reports using data from multiple tables. As you'll see, joins are flexible from a reporting perspective, but create challenges when trying to scale RDBMSs to multiple processors. Understanding joins is important since most NoSQL architecture patterns are free of joins (with the exception of graph patterns, discussed in chapter 4). The lack of joins allows NoSQL solutions to resolve the scalability problem associated with single-processor systems by scaling across multiple systems.

A *join* is a process of using a row identifier in a column of one table to reference a particular row in another table. Relational databases are designed to find ways to create relationships between tables of related data. The classic RDBMS example is a sales order tracking system similar to a virtual shopping cart you'll find on amazon.com. See figure 3.4 as an example of how the data associated with a sales order might be represented in an RDBMS.

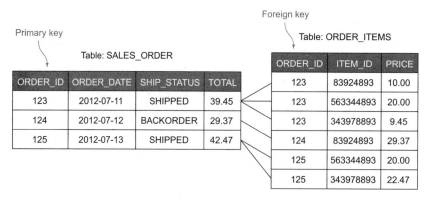

Figure 3.4   Join example using sales, orders, and line items—how relational databases use an identifier column to join records together. All rows in the SALES_ORDER table on the left contain a unique identifier under the column heading ORDER_ID. This number is created when the row is added to the table and no two rows may have the same ORDER_ID. When you add a new item to your order, you add a new row to the ORDER_ITEMS table and "relate" it back to the ORDER_ID that the table is associated with. This allows all the line items with an order to be joined with the main order when creating a report.

In this figure there are two distinct tables: the main SALES_ORDER table on the left and the individual ORDER_ITEMS table on the right. The SALES_ORDER table contains one row for each order and has a unique identifier associated with it called the *primary key*. The SALES_ORDER table summarizes all the items in the ORDER_ITEMS table but contains no detailed information about each item. The ORDER_ITEMS table contains one row for each item ordered and contains the order number, item ID, and price. When you add new items to an order, the systems application must add a new row in the ORDER_ITEMS table with the appropriate order ID and update the total in the SALES_ORDER table.

When you want to run a report that lists all the information associated with an order, including all the line items, you'd write a SQL report that joins the main SALES_ORDER table with the ORDER_ITEMS table. You can do this by adding a WHERE clause to the report that will select the items from the ORDER_ITEMS table that have the same ORDER_ID. Figure 3.5 provides the SQL code required to perform this join operation.

As you can see from this example, sales order and line-item information fit well into a tabular structure since there's not much variability in this type of sales data.

```
SELECT * FROM SALES_ORDER, ORDER_ITEMS
WHERE SALES_ORDER.ORDER_ID = ORDER_ITEMS.ORDER_ID
```

Figure 3.5   SQL JOIN example—the query will return a new table that has all of the information from both tables. The first line selects the data, and the second line restricts the results to include only those lines associated with the order.

There are challenges when retrieving the sales data information from all RDBMSs. Before you begin to write your query, you must know and understand the data structures and their dependencies. Tables themselves don't show you how to create joins. This information can be stored in other tools such as entity-relationship design tools—but this relationship metadata isn't part of the core structure of a table. The more complex your data is, the more complex your joins will be. Creating a report that has data from a dozen tables many require complex SQL statements with many WHERE statements to join tables together.

The use of row stores and the need for joins between tables can impact how data is partitioned over multiple processors. Complex joins between two tables stored on different nodes requires that a large amount of data be transferred between the two systems, making the process very slow. This slow-down can be circumvented by storing joined rows on the same node, but RDBMSs don't have automatic methods to keep all rows for objects together on the same system. To implement this strategy requires careful consideration, and the responsibility for this type of distributed storage may need to be moved from the database to the application tier.

Now that we've reviewed the general concepts of tables, row stores, and joins, and you understand the challenges of distributing this data over many systems, we'll look at other features of RDBMSs that make them ideal solutions for some business problems and awkward for others.

3.4   *Reviewing RDBMS implementation features*

Let's take a look at the key features found in most RDBMSs today:

- RDBMS transactions
- Fixed data definition language and typed columns
- Using RDBMS views for security and access control
- RDBMS replication and synchronization

Understanding that these features are generally built in to most RDBMS systems is critical when you're selecting a database for a new project. If your project needs some or all of these features, a RDBMS might be the right solution. Selecting the right data architecture can save your organization time and money by avoiding rework and costly mistakes before software implementation. It's our goal to provide you with a good understanding of the key features of RDBMS (transactions, indexes, and security) and how they are important in RDBMSs.

3.4.1   *RDBMS transactions*

Using our Sales_Order sample from section 3.3, let's look at how a typical RDBMS database controls transactions and the steps that an application performs to maintain consistency in the database, beginning with the following terms:

- *Transactions*—A single atomic unit of work within a database management system that's performed against a database

- *Begin/End transaction*—Commands to begin and end a batch of transactions (inserts, updates, or deletes) that either succeed or fail as a group
- *Rollback*—An operation that returns a database to some previous state

In our SALES_ORDER example, there are two tables that should be updated together. When new items are added to an order, a new record is inserted into the ORDER_ITEMS table (which contains the detail about each item) and the total in the SALES_ORDER table is updated to reflect the new amount owed.

In RDBMSs it's easy to make sure these two operations either both complete successfully or they don't occur at all by using the database transaction control statements shown in figure 3.6.

The first statement, BEGIN TRANSACTION, marks the beginning of the series of operations to perform. Following the BEGIN TRANSACTION, you'd then call the code that inserts the new order into the ORDER_ITEMS table followed by the code that updates the total in the SALES_ORDER table. The last statement, COMMIT TRANSACTION, signals to the system that your transaction is finished and no further processing is required. The database will prevent (block) any other operations from occurring on either table while this transaction is in process so that reports that access these tables will reflect the correct values.

If for some reason the database fails in the middle of a transaction, the system will automatically roll back all parts of the transaction and return the database to the status it was prior to the BEGIN_TRANSACTION. The transaction failure can be reported to the application, which can attempt a retry operation or request the user to try again later.

The functions that guarantee transaction reliability can be performed by any application. The key is that RDBMS implementations make some parts of this automatic and easy for the software developer. Without these functions, application developers must create an undo process for each part of the transactions, which may require a great deal of effort.

Some NoSQL systems don't support transactions across multiple records. Some support transaction control but only within atomic units of work such as within a

```
BEGIN TRANSACTION;
-- code to insert new item into the order here...
-- code to update the order total with new amount here...
COMMIT TRANSACTION;
GO
```

Figure 3.6   This code shows how the **BEGIN TRANSACTION** and **COMMIT TRANSACTION** lines are added to SQL to ensure that both the new items are added to a sales order *and* the total of the sales order is updated as an atomic transaction. The effect is that the transactions are done together or not at all. The benefit is that the SQL developer doesn't have to test to make sure that both changes occurred and then undo one of the transactions if the other one fails. The database will always be in a consistent state.

document. If your system has many places that require careful transaction control, RDBMSs may be the best solution.

3.4.2 *Fixed data definition language and typed columns*

RDBMSs require you to declare the structure of all tables prior to adding data to any table. These declarations are created using a SQL data definition language (DDL), which allows the database designer to specify all columns of a table, the column type, and any indexes associated with the table. A list of typical SQL data types from a MySQL system can be seen in table 3.2.

Table 3.2 Sample of RDBMS column types for MySQL. Each column in an RDBMS is assigned one type. Trying to add data that doesn't contain the correct data type will result in an error.

Category	Types
Integer	INTEGER, INT, SMALLINT, TINYINT, MEDIUMINT, BIGINT
Numeric	DECIMAL, NUMERIC, FLOAT, DOUBLE
Boolean	BIT
Date and time	DATE, DATETIME, TIMESTAMP
Text	CHAR, VARCHAR, BLOB, TEXT
Sets	ENUM, SET
Binary	TINYBLOB, BLOB, MEDIUMBLOB, LONGBLOB

The strength of this system is that it enforces the rules about your data up front and prevents you from adding any data that doesn't conform to the rules. The disadvantage is that in situations where the data may need to vary, you can't simply insert it into the database. These variations must be stored in other columns with other data types or the column type needs to be changed to be more flexible.

In organizations that have existing databases with millions of rows of data in tables, these tables must be removed and restored if there are changes to data types. This can result in downtime and loss of productivity to your staff, your customers, and ultimately the company bottom line. Application developers sometimes use the metadata associated with a column type to create rules to map the columns into object data types. This means that the object-relational mapping software must also be updated at the same time the database changes.

Though they may seem like minor annoyances to someone building a new system with a small test data set, the process of restructuring the database in a production environment may take weeks, months, or longer. There's anecdotal evidence of organizations that have spent millions of dollars to simply change the number of digits in a data field. The Year 2000 problem (Y2K) is one example of this type of challenge.

3.4.3 *Using RDBMS views for security and access control*

Now that you understand the concepts and structure of RDBMSs, let's think about how you might securely add sensitive information. Let's expand the SALES_ORDER example to allow customers to pay by credit card. Because this information is sensitive, you need a way to capture and protect this data. Your company security policy may allow some individuals with appropriate roles in the company to see sales data. Additionally, you may also have security rules which dictate that only a select few individuals in the organization are allowed to see a customer's credit card number. One solution would be to put the numbers in a separate hidden table and perform a join operation to retrieve the information when required, but RDBMS vendors provide an easier solution by creating a separate *view* of any table or query. An example of this is shown in figure 3.7.

In this example, users don't access the actual tables. Instead, they see only a report of information from the table, which excludes any sensitive information that they don't have access to based on your company security policy. The ability to use dynamic calculations to create table *views* and grant access to views using roles defined within an organization is one of the features that make RDBMSs flexible.

Many NoSQL systems don't allow you to create multiple views of physical data and then grant access to these views to users with specific roles. If your requirements

Figure 3.7 Data security and access control—how sensitive columns can be hidden from some users using views. In this example, the physical table that stores order information contains credit card information that should be restricted from general users. To protect this information without duplicating the table, RDBMSs provide a restricted view of the table that excludes this credit card information. Even if the user has a general reporting tool, they won't be able to view this data because they haven't been granted permission to view the underlying physical table, only a view of the table.

include these types of functions, then RDBMS solutions might be a better match to your needs.

3.4.4 *RDBMS replication and synchronization*

As we've mentioned, early RDBMSs were designed to run on single CPUs. When organizations have critical data, it's stored on a primary hard disk with a duplicate copy of each insert, update, and delete transaction replicated in a journal or log file on a separate drive. If the database becomes corrupt, a backup of the database is loaded and the journal "replayed" to get the database to the point it was when it was halted.

Journal files add overhead and slow the system down, but they're essential to guarantee the ACID nature of RDBMSs. There are situations when a business can't wait for the backup to restore and the journal files to be played. In these situations, the data can immediately be written not only to the master database but also to a copy (or mirror) of the original database. Figure 3.8 demonstrates how mirroring is applied in RDBMSs.

In a mirrored database, when the master database crashes, the mirrored system (slave) takes over the primary system's operations. When additional redundancy is required, more than one mirror system is created, as the likelihood of two or more systems all crashing at the same time is slim and generally sufficient security for most business processes.

The replication process solves some of the challenges associated with creating high-availably systems. If one of the master systems goes down, the slave can step in to take its place. With that being said, it introduces database administration staff to the challenges of distributed computing. For example, what if one of the slave systems crashes for a while? Should the master system stop accepting transactions while it waits for the slave system to come back online? How does one system get "caught up" on the

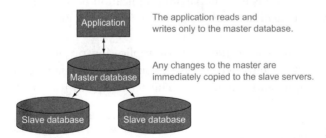

Figure 3.8 Replication and mirroring—how applications are configured to read and write all their data to a single master database. Any change in the master database immediately triggers a process that copies the transaction information (inserts, updates, deletes) to one or more slave systems that mirror the master database. These slave servers can quickly take over the load of the master if the master database becomes unavailable. This configuration allows the database to provide high availability data services.

transactions that occurred while it was down? Who should store these transactions and where should they be stored? These questions led to a new class of products that specialize in database replication and synchronization.

Replication is different than sharding, which we discussed in chapter 2. Sharding stores each record on different processors but doesn't duplicate the data. In addition, sharding allows reads and writes to be distributed to multiple systems but doesn't increase system availability. On the other hand, replication can increase availability and read access speeds by allowing read requests to be performed by slave systems. In general, replication doesn't increase the performance of write operations to a database. Since data has to be copied to multiple systems, it sometimes slows down total write throughput rates. In the end, replication and sharding are independent processes and in appropriate situations can be used together.

So what should happen if the slave systems crash? It doesn't make sense to have the master reject all transactions, since it would render the system unavailable for writes if any slave system crashed. If you allow the master to continue accepting updates, you'll need a process to resync the slave system when it comes back online.

One common solution to the slave resync problem is to use a completely separate piece of software called a *reliable messaging system* or *message store,* as shown in figure 3.9.

Reliable messaging systems accept messages even if a remote system isn't responding. When used in a master/slave configuration, these systems queue all update messages when one or more slave systems are down, and send them on when the slave system is online, allowing all messages to be posted so that the master and slave remain in sync.

Replication is a complex problem when one or more systems go offline, even if only for a short period of time. Knowing exactly what information has changed and resyncing the changed data is critical for reliability. Without some way of breaking large databases into smaller subsets for comparison, replication becomes impractical. This is why using consistent caching NoSQL databases (discussed in chapter 2) may be a better solution.

NoSQL systems also need to solve the database replication problem, but unlike relational databases, NoSQL systems need to synchronize not only tables, but other structures as well, like graphs and documents. The technologies used to replicate

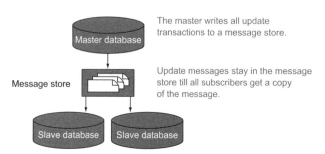

The master writes all update transactions to a message store.

Update messages stay in the message store till all subscribers get a copy of the message.

Figure 3.9 Using message stores for reliable data replication—how message stores can be used to increase the reliability of the data on each slave database, even if the slave systems are unavailable for a period of time. When slave systems restart, they can access an external message store to retrieve the transactions they missed when they were unavailable.

these structures will at times be similar to message stores and other times will need more specialized structures.

Now that we've taken a tour of the main features of RDBMS systems typically used in online transaction systems, let's see how similar systems solve the problem of delivering large complex reports using millions of records of historical transactions without sacrificing transactional system performance by creating and using data warehouse and business intelligence systems.

3.5 *Analyzing historical data with OLAP, data warehouse, and business intelligence systems*

Most RDBMSs are used to handle real-time transactions such as online sales orders or banking transactions. Collectively, these systems are known as *online transaction processing (OLTP)* systems. In this section, we'll shift our focus away from real-time OLTP and look at a different class of data patterns associated with creating detailed, ad hoc reports using historical transactions. Instead of using records that are constantly changing, the records used in these analyses are written once but read many times. We call these systems *online analytical processing (OLAP)*.

OLAP systems empower nonprogrammers to quickly generate ad hoc reports on large datasets. The data architecture patterns used in OLAP are significantly different from transactional systems, even though they rely on tables to store their data. OLAP systems are usually associated with front-end business intelligence software applications that generate graphical outputs used to show trends and help business analysts understand and define their business rules. OLAP systems are frequently used to feed data mining software to automatically look for patterns in data and detect errors or cases of fraud.

Understanding what OLAP systems are, what concepts are used, and the types of problems they solve will help you determine when each should be used. You'll be able to see how these differences are critical when you're performing software selection and architectural trade-off analysis.

Table 3.3 summarizes the differences between OLTP and OLAP systems with respect to their impact on the categories of business focus, type of updates, key structure, and criteria for success.

Table 3.3   A comparison of OLTP and OLAP systems

	Online transaction processing (OLTP)	**Online analytical processing (OLAP)**
Business focus	Managing accurate real-time transactions with ACID constraints	Rapid ad hoc analysis of historical event data by nonprogrammers even if there are millions or billions of records
Type of updates	Mix of reads, writes, and updates by many concurrent users	Daily batch loads of new data and many reads. Concurrency is not a concern.

Table 3.3   A comparison of OLTP and OLAP systems *(continued)*

	Online transaction processing (OLTP)	Online analytical processing (OLAP)
Key structures	Tables with multiple levels of joins	Star or snowflake designs with a large central fact table and dimension tables to categorize facts. Aggregate structures with summary data are precomputed.
Typical criteria for success	Handles many concurrent users constantly making changes without any bottlenecks	Analysts can easily generate new reports on millions of records, quickly get key insights into trends, and spot new business opportunities.

In this chapter, we've focused on general-purpose transactional database systems that interact in a real-time environment, on an event-by-event basis. These real-time systems are designed to store and protect records of events such as sales transactions, button-clicks on a web page, and transfers of funds between accounts. The class of systems we turn to now isn't concerned with button-clicks, but rather with analyzing past events and drawing conclusions based on that information.

3.5.1   *How data flows from operational systems to analytical systems*

OLAP systems, frequently used in data warehouse/business intelligence (DW/BI) applications, aren't concerned with new data, but rather focus on the rapid analysis of events in the past to make predictions about future events.

In OLAP systems, data flows from real-time operational systems into downstream analytical systems as a way to separate daily transactions from the job of doing analysis on historical data. This separation of concerns is important when designing NoSQL systems, as the requirements of operational systems are dramatically different than the requirements of analytical systems.

BI systems evolved because running summary reports on production databases while traversing millions of rows of information was inefficient and slowed production systems during peak workloads. Running reports on a mirrored system was an option, but the reports still took a long time to run and were inefficient from an employee productivity perspective. Sometime in the '80s a new class of databases emerged, specifically designed to focus on rapid ad hoc analysis of data even if there were millions or billions of rows. The pioneers in these systems came, not from web companies, but from firms that needed to understand retail store sales patterns and predict what items should be in the store and when.

Let's look at a data flow diagram of how this works. Figure 3.10 shows the typical data flow and some of the names associated with different regions of the business intelligence and data warehouse data flow.

Each region in this diagram is responsible for specific tasks. Data that's constantly changing during daily operations is stored on the left side of the diagram inside

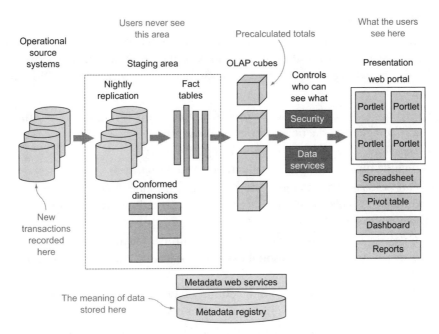

Figure 3.10 Business intelligence and data warehouse (BI/DW) data flow—how data flows into a typical OLAP data warehouse system. In the first step, new transactions are copied from the operational source systems and loaded into a temporary staging area. Data in the staging area is then transformed to create fact and dimension tables that are used to build OLAP cube structures. These cubes contain precalculated aggregate structures that contain summary information which must be updated as new facts are added to the fact tables. The information in the OLAP cubes is then accessed from a graphical front-end tool through the security and data services layers. The precise meaning of data in any part of the system is stored in a separate metadata registry database that ensures data is used and interpreted consistently despite the many layers of transformation.

computers that track daily transactions. These computers are called the *operational source systems*. At regular intervals new data is extracted from these source systems and stored in the temporary staging area, as shown in the dashed-line box in the center.

The staging area is a series of computers that contain more RDBMS tables where the data is massaged using *extract, transform, and load (ETL)* tools. ETL tools are designed to extract data in tables from one RDBMS and move the data, after transformation, into another set of RDBMS tables. Eventually, the new data is added to fact tables that store the fine-grained events of the system. Once the fact tables have been updated, new sums and totals are created that include this new information. These are called *aggregate tables*.

Generally, NoSQL systems aren't intended to replace all components in a data warehouse application. They target areas where scalability and reliability are important. For example, many ETL systems can be replaced by MapReduce-style transforms that have better scale-out properties.

3.5.2 Getting familiar with OLAP concepts

Generally, OLAP systems have the same row-store pattern as OLTP systems, but the concepts and constructs are different. Let's look at the core OLAP concepts to see how they're combined to generate sub-second transactional reports using millions of transactions:

- *Fact table*—A central table of events that contains foreign keys to other tables and integer and decimal values called *measures.*
- *Dimension table*—A table used to categorize every fact. Examples of dimensions include time, geography, product, or promotion.
- *Star schema*—An arrangement of tables with one fact table surrounded by dimension tables. Each transaction is represented by a single row in the central fact table.
- *Categories*—A way to divide all the facts into two or more classes. For example, products may have a Seasonal category indicating they're only stocked part of the year.
- *Measures*—A number used in a column of a fact table that you can sum or average. Measures are usually things like sales counts or prices.
- *Aggregates*—Precomputed sums used by OLAP systems to quickly display results to users.
- *MDX*—A query language that's used to extract data from cubes. MDX looks similar to SQL in some ways, but is customized to select data into pivot-table displays.

For a comparison of MDX with SQL, see figure 3.11.

In this example, we're placing the total of each of the store sales in Minnesota (WHERE STORE.USA.MN) in each of the columns and placing each of the sales quarters (Q1, Q2, Q3, and Q4) in the rows. The result would be a grid that has the stores on one axis and dates on the other axis. Each grid has the total of sales for that store for that quarter. The SELECT and WHERE statements are identical to SQL, but ON COLUMNS and ON ROWS are unique to MDX. The output of this query might be viewed in a chart, like in figure 3.12.

Note that this chart would typically be displayed by an OLAP system in less than a second. The software doesn't have to recompute sales totals to generate the chart.

Figure 3.11   A sample of an MDX query—like SQL, MDX uses the same keywords of SELECT, FROM, and WHERE. MDX is distinct from SQL in that it always returns a two-dimensional grid of values for both column and row categories. The ON COLUMNS and ON ROWS keywords show this difference.

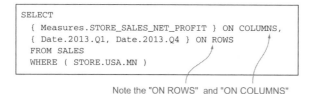

```
SELECT
   { Measures.STORE_SALES_NET_PROFIT } ON COLUMNS,
   { Date.2013.Q1, Date.2013.Q4 } ON ROWS
   FROM SALES
   WHERE ( STORE.USA.MN )
```

Note the "ON ROWS" and "ON COLUMNS"

The OLAP process creates precomputed structures called *aggregates* for the monthly store sales as the new transactions are loaded into the system. The only calculation needed is to add the monthly totals associated with each quarter to generate quarterly figures.

3.5.3   Ad hoc reporting using aggregates

Why is it important for users to create ad hoc reports using prebuilt summary data created by OLAP systems? Ad hoc reporting is important for organizations that rely on analyzing patterns and trends in their data to make business decisions. As you'll see here, NoSQL systems can be combined with other SQL and NoSQL systems to feed data directly into OLAP reporting tools.

Many organizations find OLAP a cost-effective way to perform detailed analyses of a large number of past events. Their

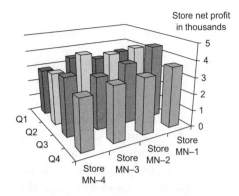

Figure 3.12   Sample business intelligence report that leverages summary information— the result of a typical MDX query that places *measures* **(the vertical axis) within** *categories* **(store axis) to create graphical reports. The report doesn't have to create results by directly using each individual sales transaction. The results are created by accessing precomputed summary information in aggregate structures. Even new reports that derive data from millions of transactions can be generated on an ad hoc basis in less than a second.**

strength comes in allowing nonprogrammers to quickly analyze large datasets or big data. To generate reports, all you need is to understand how categories and measures are combined. This empowerment of the nonprogramming staff in the purchasing department of retail stores has been one of the key factors driving down retail costs for consumers. Stores are filled with what people want, when they want it.

Although this data may represent millions or billions of transactions spread out over the last 10 years, the results are usually returned to the screen in less than a second. OLAP systems are able to do this by precomputing the sums of measures in the fact tables using categories such as time, store number, or product category code. Does it sound like you'll need a lot of disk to store all of this information? You might, but remember disk is cheap these days and the more disk space you assign to your OLAP systems, the more precomputed sums you can create. The more information you have, the easier it might be to make the right business decision.

One of the nice things about using OLAP systems is that as a user you don't need to know the process of how aggregates are created and what they contain. You only need to understand your data and how it's most appropriately totaled, averaged, or studied. In addition, system designers don't need to understand how the aggregates are created; their focus is on defining cube categories and measures, and mapping the data from the fact and dimension tables into the cube. The OLAP software does the rest.

When you go to your favorite retailer and find the shelves stocked with your favorite items, you'll understand the benefits of OLAP. Tens of thousands of buyers and inventory specialists use these tools every day to track retail trends and make adjustments to their inventory and deliveries. Due to the popularity of OLAP systems and their empowerment of nonprogammers to create ad hoc queries, the probability is low that the fundamental structures of OLAP and data warehouses systems will be quickly displaced by NoSQL solutions. What will change is how tools such as Map-Reduce will be used to create the aggregates used by the cubes. To be effective, OLAP systems need tools that efficiently create the precomputed sums and totals. In a later chapter, we'll talk about how NoSQL components are appropriate for performing analysis on large datasets.

In the past 10 years, the use of open source OLAP tools such as Mondrian and Pentaho has allowed organizations to dramatically cut their data warehouse costs. In order to be a viable ad hoc analysis tool, NoSQL systems must be as low-cost and as easy to use as these systems. They must have the performance and scalability benefits that current systems lack, and they must have the tools and interfaces that facilitate integration with existing OLAP systems.

Despite the fact that OLAP systems have now become commodity products, the cost of setting up and maintaining OLAP systems can still be a hefty part of an organization's IT budget. The ETL tools to move data between operational and analytical systems still usually run on single processors, perform costly join operations, and limit the amount of data that can be moved each night between the operational and analytical systems. These challenges and costs are even greater when organizations lack strong data governance policies or have inconsistent category definitions. Though not necessarily data architecture issues, they fall under enterprise semantics and standards concerns, and should be taken to heart in both RDBMS and NoSQL solutions.

Standards watch: standards for OLAP

Several XML standards are associated with OLAP systems that promote portability of your MDX applications between OLAP systems. These standards include *XML for Analysis (XMLA)* and the *Common Warehouse Metamodel (CWM)*.

The XMLA standard is an XML wrapper standard for exchanging MDX statements between various OLAP servers and clients. XMLA systems allow users to use many different MDX clients such as JPivot against many different OLAP servers.

CWM is an XML standard for describing all components you might find in an OLAP system including cubes, dimensions, measures, tables, and aggregates. CWM systems allow you to define your OLAP cubes in terms of a standardized and portable XML file so that your cube definition can be exchanged between multiple systems.

In general, commercial vendors make it easy to import CWM data, but frequently make it difficult to export this data. This makes it easy to start to use their products but difficult to leave them. Third-party vendor products are frequently needed to provide high-quality translation from one system to another.

OLAP systems are unique in that once event records are written to a central fact table, they're usually not modified. This write-once, read-many pattern is also common in log file and web usage statistics processing, as we'll see next.

3.6 Incorporating high availability and read-mostly systems

Read-mostly non-RDBMSs such as Directory Services and DNS are used to provide high availability for systems where the data is written once and read often. You use these high-availability systems to guarantee that data services are always available and your productivity isn't lost when your login and password information isn't available on the local area network. These systems use many of the same replication features that you see in NoSQL systems to provide high-availability data services. Studying these systems carefully gives you an appreciation for their complexity and helps you to understand how NoSQL systems can be enhanced to benefit from these same replication techniques.

If you've ever set up a local area network (LAN), you might be familiar with the concept of *directory services*. When you create a LAN, you select one or more computers to store the data that's common to all computers on the network. This information is stored in a highly specialized database called a *directory server*. Generally, directory servers have a small amount of read data; write operations are rare. Directory services don't have the same capabilities as RDBMSs and don't use a query language. They're not designed to handle complex transactions and don't provide ACID guarantees and rollback operations. What they do provide is a fast and ultra-reliable way to look up a username and password and authenticate a user.

Directory services need to be highly available. If you can't authenticate a user, they can't log in to the network and no work gets done. In order to provide a high-availability service directory, services are replicated across the network on two, three, or four different servers. If any of the servers becomes unavailable, the remaining servers can provide the data you need. You see that by replicating their data, directory services can provide high service levels to applications that need high availability.

Another reference point for high availability systems is the topic of *Domain Name System (DNS)*. DNS servers provide a simple lookup service that translates a logical human-readable domain name like *danmccreary.com* into a numeric Internet Protocol (IP) address associated with a remote host, such as 66.96.132.92. DNS servers, like directory servers, need to be reliable; if they're not working properly, people can't get to the websites they need, unless they know the server IP address.

We mention directory services and DNS-type systems because they're true database systems and are critical for solving highly specialized business problems where high availability can only be solved by eliminating single points of failure. They also do this better than a general RDBMS.

Directory services and DNSs are great examples of how different data architecture patterns are used in conjunction with RDBMSs to provide specialized data services. Because their data is relatively simple, they don't need complex query languages to be effective. These highly distributed systems sit at different points in the CAP triangle to meet different business objectives. NoSQL systems frequently incorporate techniques used in these distributed systems to achieve different availability and performance objectives.

In our last section, we'll look at how document revision control systems provide a unique set of services that NoSQL systems also share.

3.7 *Using hash trees in revision control systems and database synchronization*

As we come to our last section, we'll look at some innovations in revision control systems for software engineering to see how these innovations are being used in NoSQL systems. We'll touch on how innovations in distributed revision control systems like Subversion and Git make the job of distributed software development much easier. Finally, we'll see how revision control systems use hashes and delta mods to synchronize complex documents.

> **Is it "version" or "revision" control?**
>
> The terms *version control* and *revision control* are both commonly used to describe how you manage the history of a document. Although there are many definitions, version control is a general term applied to any method that tracks the history of a document. This would include tools that store multiple binaries of your Microsoft Word documents in a document management system like SharePoint. Revision control is a more specific term that describes a set of features found in tools like Subversion and Git. Revision control systems include features such as adding release labels (tags), branching, merging, and storing the differences between text documents. We'll use the term *revision control*, as it's more specific to our context.

Revision control systems are critical for projects that involve distributed teams of developers. For these types of projects, losing code or using the wrong code means lost time and money. These systems use many of the same patterns you see in NoSQL systems, such as distributed systems, document hashing, and tree hashing, to quickly determine whether things are in sync.

Early revision control systems (RCSs) weren't distributed. There was a single hard drive that stored all source code, and all developers used a networked filesystem to mount that drive on their local computer. There was a single master copy that everyone used, and no tools were in place to quickly find differences between two revisions, making it easy to inadvertently overwrite code. As organizations began to realize that talented development staff didn't necessarily live in their city, developers were recruited from remote locations and a new generation of distributed revision control systems was needed.

In response to the demand of distributed development, a new class of *distributed revision control systems (DRCs)* emerged. Systems like Subversion, Git, and Mercurial have the ability to store local copies of a revisioned database and quickly sync up to a master copy when needed. They do this by calculating a hash of each of the revision objects (directories as well as files) in the system. When remote systems need to be synced, they compare the hashes, not the individual files, which allows syncing even on large and deep trees of data to occur quickly.

The data structure used to detect if two trees are the same is called a *hash tree* or *Merkle tree.* Hash trees work by calculating the hash values of each leaf of a tree, and then using these hash values to create a *node object.* Node objects can then be hashed and result in a new hash value for the entire directory. An example of this is shown in figure 3.13.

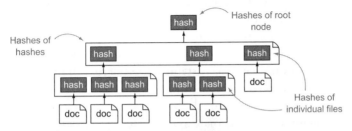

Figure 3.13 A hash tree, or Merkle tree, is created by calculating the hash of all of the leaf structures in a tree. Once the leaf structures have been hashed, all the nodes within a directory combine their hash values to create a new document that can also be hashed. This "hash of hashes" becomes the hash of the directory. This hash value can in turn be used to create a hash of the parent node. In this way you can compare the hashes of any point in two trees and immediately know if all of the structures below a particular node are the same.

Hash trees are used in most distributed revision control systems. If you make a copy of your current project's software and store it on your laptop and head to the North Woods for a week to write code, when you return you simply reconnect to the network and merge your changes with all the updates that occurred while you were gone. The software doesn't need to do a byte-by-byte comparison to figure out what revision to use. If your system has a directory with the same hash value as the base system, the software instantly knows they're the same by comparing the hash values.

The "gone to the North Woods for a week" synchronization scenario is similar to the problem of what happens when any node on a distributed database is disconnected from other nodes for a period of time. You can use the same data structures and algorithms to keep NoSQL databases in sync as in revision control systems.

Say you need to upgrade some RAM on one of your six servers, and it provides replication for a master node. You shut down the server, install the RAM, and restart the server. While the slave server was down, additional transactions were processed and now need to be replicated. Copying the entire dataset would be inefficient. Using hash trees allows you to simply check what directories and files have new hash values and synchronize those files—you're done.

As you've seen, distributed revision control systems are important in today's work environment for database as well as software development scenarios. The ability to synchronize data by reconnecting to a network and merging changes saves valuable time and money for organizations and allows them to focus on other business concerns.

3.8   *Apply your knowledge*

Sally is working on a project that uses a NoSQL document database to store product reviews for hundreds of thousands of products. Since products and product reviews have many different types of attributes, Sally agrees that a document store is ideal for storing this high-variability data. In addition, the business unit needs full-text search capability also provided by the document store.

The business unit has come to Sally: they want to perform aggregate analysis on a subset of all the properties that have been standardized across the product reviews. The analysis needs to show total counts and averages for different categories of products. Sally has two choices. She can use the aggregate functions supplied by the NoSQL document database or she can create a MapReduce job to summarize the data and then use existing OLAP software to do the analysis.

Sally realizes that both options require about the same amount of programming effort. But the OLAP solution allows more flexible ad hoc query analysis using a pivot-table-like interface. She decides to use a MapReduce transform to create a fact table and dimension tables, and then builds an OLAP cube from the star schema. In the end, product managers can create ad hoc reports on product reviews using the same tools they use for product sales.

This example shows that NoSQL systems may be ideal for some data tasks, but they may not have the same features of a traditional table-centric OLAP system for some analyses. Here, Sally combined parts of a new NoSQL approach with a traditional OLAP tool to get the best of both worlds.

3.9   *Summary*

In this chapter, we reviewed many of the existing features of RDBMSs, as well as their strengths and weaknesses. We looked at how relational databases use the concept of joins between tables and the challenge this can present when scalability across multiple systems is desired.

We reviewed how the large integration costs of siloed systems drove RDBMS vendors to create larger centralized systems that allowed up-to-date integrated reporting with fine-grained access control. We also reviewed how online analytical systems allow nonprogrammers to quickly create reports that slice and dice sales into the categories they need. We then took a short look at how specific non-RDBMS database systems like directory services and DNS are used for high availability. Lastly, we showed how distributed document revisioning systems have developed rapid ways to compare document trees and how these same techniques can be used in distributed NoSQL systems.

There are several take-away points from this chapter. First, RDBMSs continue to be the appropriate solution for many business problems, and organizations will continue to use them for the foreseeable future. Second, RDBMSs are continuing to evolve and are making it possible to relax ACID requirements and manage document-oriented structures. For example, IBM, Microsoft, and Oracle now support XML column types and limited forms of XQuery.

Reflecting on how RDBMSs were impacted by the needs of ERP systems, we should remember that even if NoSQL systems have cool new features, organizations must include integration costs when calculating their total cost of ownership.

One of the primary lessons of this chapter is how critical cross-vendor and cross-product query languages are in the creation of software platforms. NoSQL systems will almost certainly stay in small niche areas until universal query standards are adopted. The fact that object-oriented databases still have no common query language despite being around for 15 years is a clear example of the role of standards. Only after application portability is achieved will software vendors consider large-scale migration away from SQL to NoSQL systems.

The data architecture patterns reviewed in this chapter provide the foundation for our next chapter, where we'll look at a new set of patterns called NoSQL patterns. We'll see how NoSQL patterns fit into new and existing infrastructures to assist organizations in solving business problems in different ways.

3.10 *Further reading*

- "Database transaction." Wikipedia. http://mng.bz/1m55.
- "Hash tree." Wikipedia. http://mng.bz/zQbT
- "Isolation (database systems)." Wikipedia. http://mng.bz/76AF.
- PostgreSQL. "Table 8-1. Data Types."http://mng.bz/FAtT.
- "Replication (computing)." Wikipedia. http://mng.bz/5xuQ.

NoSQL data architecture patterns

4

This chapter covers

- Key-value stores
- Graph stores
- Column family stores
- Document stores
- Variations of NoSQL architecture patterns

...no pattern is an isolated entity. Each pattern can exist in the world only to the extent that is supported by other patterns: the larger patterns in which it is embedded, the patterns of the same size that surround it, and the smaller patterns which are embedded in it.

—Christopher Alexander, *A Timeless Way of Building*

One of the challenges for users of NoSQL systems is there are many different architectural patterns from which to choose. In this chapter, we'll introduce the most common high-level NoSQL data architecture patterns, show you how to use them, and give you some real-world examples of their use. We'll close out the chapter by looking at some NoSQL pattern variations such as RAM and distributed stores.

Table 4.1 NoSQL data architecture patterns—the most important patterns introduced by the NoSQL movement, brief descriptions, and examples of where these patterns are typically used

Pattern name	Description	Typical uses
Key-value store	A simple way to associate a large data file with a simple text string	Dictionary, image store, document/file store, query cache, lookup tables
Graph store	A way to store nodes and arcs of a graph	Social network queries, friend-of-friends queries, inference, rules system, and pattern matching
Column family (Bigtable) store	A way to store sparse matrix data using a row and a column as the key	Web crawling, large sparsely populated tables, highly-adaptable systems, systems that have high variance
Document store	A way to store tree-structured hierarchical information in a single unit	Any data that has a natural container structure including office documents, sales orders, invoices, product descriptions, forms, and web pages; popular in publishing, document exchange, and document search

Table 4.1 lists the significant data architecture patterns associated with the NoSQL movement.

After reading this chapter, you'll know the main NoSQL data architectural patterns, how to classify the associated NoSQL products and services with a pattern, and the types of applications that use each pattern. When confronted with a new business problem, you'll have a better understanding of which NoSQL pattern might help provide a solution.

We talked about data architecture patterns in chapter 3; to refresh your memory, a *data architecture pattern* is a consistent way of representing data in a structure. This is true for SQL as well as NoSQL patterns. In this chapter, we'll focus on the architectural patterns associated with NoSQL. We'll begin with the simplest NoSQL pattern, the key-value store, and then look at graph stores, column family stores, document stores, and some variations on the NoSQL theme.

4.1 *Key-value stores*

Let's begin with the *key-value store* and then move on to its variants, and how this pattern is used to cost-effectively solve a variety of business problems. We'll talk about

- What a key-value store is
- Benefits of using a key-value store
- How to use a key-value store in an application
- Key-value store use cases

We'll start by giving you a clear definition.

4.1.1   *What is a key-value store?*

A *key-value store* is a simple database that when presented with a simple string (the key) returns an arbitrary large BLOB of data (the value). Key-value stores have no query language; they provide a way to add and remove key-value pairs (a combination of key and value where the key is bound to the value until a new value is assigned) into/from a database.

A key-value store is like a dictionary. A dictionary has a list of words and each word has one or more definitions, as shown in figure 4.1.

The dictionary is a simple key-value store where word entries represent keys and definitions represent values. Inasmuch as dictionary entries are sorted alphabetically by word, retrieval is quick; it's not necessary to scan the entire dictionary to find what you're looking for. Like the dictionary, a key-value store is also indexed by the key; the key points directly to the value, resulting in rapid retrieval, regardless of the number of items in your store.

One of the benefits of not specifying a data type for the value of a key-value store is that you can store any data type that you want in the value. The system will store the information as a BLOB and return the same BLOB when a GET (retrieval) request is made. It's up to the application to determine what type of data is being used, such as a string, XML file, or binary image.

The key in a key-value store is flexible and can be represented by many formats:

- Logical path names to images or files
- Artificially generated strings created from a hash of the value
- REST web service calls
- SQL queries

Values, like keys, are also flexible and can be any BLOB of data, such as images, web pages, documents, or videos. See figure 4.2 for an example of a common key-value store.

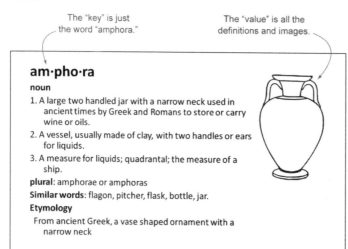

The "key" is just the word "amphora."

The "value" is all the definitions and images.

am·pho·ra

noun

1. A large two handled jar with a narrow neck used in ancient times by Greek and Romans to store or carry wine or oils.
2. A vessel, usually made of clay, with two handles or ears for liquids.
3. A measure for liquids; quadrantal; the measure of a ship.

plural: amphorae or amphoras

Similar words: flagon, pitcher, flask, bottle, jar.

Etymology

From ancient Greek, a vase shaped ornament with a narrow neck

Figure 4.1   A sample dictionary entry showing how a dictionary is similar to a key-value store. In this case, the word you're looking up (amphora) is called the *key* and the definitions are the *values*.

	Key	Value
Image name →	image-12345.jpg	Binary image file
Web page URL →	http://www.example.com/my-web-page.html	HTML of a web page
File path name →	N:/folder/subfolder/myfile.pdf	PDF document
MD5 hash →	9e107d9d372bb6826bd81d3542a419d6	The quick brown fox jumps over the lazy dog
REST web service call →	view-person?person-id=12345&format=xml	<Person><id>12345</id .</Person>
SQL query →	SELECT PERSON FROM PEOPLE WHERE PID="12345"	<Person><id>12345</id .</Person>

Figure 4.2 Sample items in a key-value store. A key-value store has a key that's associated with a value. Keys and values are flexible. Keys can be image names, web page URLs, or file path names that point to values like binary images, HTML web pages, and PDF documents.

The many names of a key-value store

A key-value store has different names depending on what system or programming language you're using. The process of looking up a stored value using an indexed key for data retrieval is a core-data access pattern that goes back to the earliest days of computing. A key-value store is used in many different computing systems but wasn't formalized as a data architecture pattern until the early 1990s. Popularity increased in 1992, when the open source Berkley DB libraries popularized it by including the key-value store pattern in the free UNIX distribution. Key-value store systems are sometimes referred to as *key-data stores*, since any type of byte-oriented data can be stored as the value. For the application programmer, a structure of an array with two columns is generally called an *associative array* or *map*, and each programming language may call it something slightly different—a hash, a dictionary, or even an object. The current convention, and this text, uses the term key-value store. For more on the history of Berkeley DB, see http://mng.bz/kG9c.

4.1.2 Benefits of using a key-value store

Why are key-value stores so powerful, and why are they used for so many different purposes? To sum it up: their simplicity and generality save you time and money by moving your focus from architectural design to reducing your data services costs through

- Precision service levels
- Precision service monitoring and notification
- Scalability and reliability
- Portability and lower operational costs

PRECISION SERVICE LEVELS

When you have a simple data service interface that's used across multiple applications, you can focus on things like creating precise service levels for data services. A service level doesn't change the API; it only puts precise specifications on how quickly or reliably the service will perform under various load conditions. For example, for any data service you might specify

- The maximum read time to return a value
- The maximum write time to store a new key-value pair
- How many reads per second the service must support
- How many writes per second the service must support
- How many duplicate copies of the data should be created for enhanced reliability
- Whether the data should be duplicated across multiple geographic regions if some data centers experience failures
- Whether to use transaction guarantees for consistency of data or whether eventual consistency is adequate

One of the best ways to visualize how developers control this is to think of a series of knobs and controls similar to what you'd see on a radio tuner, as shown in figure 4.3.

Each input knob can be adjusted to tune the service level that your business needs. Note that as the knobs are adjusted, the estimated monthly cost of providing this data service will change. It can be difficult to precisely estimate the total cost, since the actual cost of running the service is driven by market conditions and other factors, such as the cost for moving data into and out of the service.

You can configure your system to use a simple input form for setting up and allocating resources to new data services. By changing the information using the form, you can quickly change the number of resources allocated to the service. This simple interface allows you to set up new data services and reconfigure data services quickly without the additional overhead of operations staff. Because service levels can be tuned to an application requirement, you can rapidly allocate the appropriate reliability and performance resources to the system.

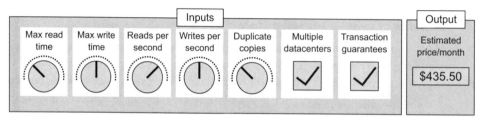

Figure 4.3   NoSQL data services can be adjusted like the tuning knobs on a radio. Each knob can individually be adjusted to control how many resources are used to provide service guarantees. The more resources you use, the higher the cost will be.

PRECISION SERVICE MONITORING AND NOTIFICATION

In addition to specifying service levels, you can also invest in tools to monitor your service level. When you configure the number of reads per second a service performs, setting the parameter too low may mean the user would experience a delay during peak times. By using a simple API, detailed reports showing the expected versus actual loads can point you to system bottlenecks that may need additional resource adjustments.

Automatic notification systems can also trigger email messages when the volume of reads or writes exceeds a threshold within a specified period of time. For example, you may want to send an email notification if the number of reads per second exceeds 80% of some predefined number within a 30-minute period. The email message could contain a link to the monitoring tools as well as links that would allow you to add more servers if the service level was critical to your users.

SCALABILITY AND RELIABILITY

When a database interface is simple, the resulting systems can have higher scalability and reliability. This means you can tune any solution to the desired requirements. Keeping an interface simple allows novice as well as advanced data modelers to build systems that utilize this power. Your only responsibility is to understand how to put this power to work solving business problems.

A simple interface allows you to focus on load and stress testing and monitoring of service levels. Because a key-value store is simple to set up, you can spend more time looking at how long it takes to put or get 10,000 items. It also allows you to share these load- and stress-testing tools with other members of your development team.

PORTABILITY AND LOWER OPERATIONAL COSTS

One of the challenges for information systems managers is to continually look for ways to lower their operational costs of deploying systems. It's unlikely that a single vendor or solution will have the lowest cost for all of your business problems. Ideally, information systems managers would like to annually request data service bids from their database vendors. In the traditional relational database world, this is impractical since porting applications between systems is too expensive compared to the relative savings of hosting your data on a new vendor's system. The more complicated and nonstandardized they are, the less portable they can be and the more difficult moving them to the lowest cost operator is (see figure 4.4).

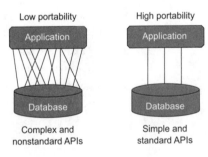

Figure 4.4 Portability of any application depends on database interface complexity. The low-portability system on the left has many complex interfaces between the application and the database, and porting the application between two databases might be a complex process requiring a large testing effort. In contrast, the high-portability application on the right only uses a few standardized interfaces, such as put, get, and delete, and could be quickly ported to a new database with lower testing cost.

> **Standards watch: complex APIs can still be portable if they're standardized and have portability tests**
>
> It's important to note that complex interfaces can still permit high portability. For example, XQuery, a query language used in XML systems, has hundreds of functions, which can be considered a complex application-database interface. But these functions have been standardized by the World Wide Web (W3C) and are still considered to be a low-cost and highly portable application-database interface layer. The W3C provides a comprehensive XQuery test suite to verify if the XQuery interfaces are consistent between implementations. Any XQuery implementation that has over a 99% pass rate allows applications to be ported without significant change.

4.1.3   Using a key-value store

Let's take a look at how an application developer might use a key-value store within an application. The best way to think about using a key-value store is to visualize a single table with two columns. The first column is called the *key* and the second column is called the *value*. There are three operations performed on a key-value store: put, get, and delete. These three operations form the basis of how programmers interface with the key-value store. We call this set of programmer interfaces the *application program interface* or *API*. The key-value interface is summarized in figure 4.5.

Instead of using a query language, application developers access and manipulate a key-value store with the `put`, `get`, and `delete` functions, as shown here:

1 `put($key as xs:string, $value as item())` adds a new key-value pair to the table and will update a value if this key is already present.

2 `get($key as xs:string) as item()` returns the value for any given key, or it may return an error message if there's no key in the key-value store.

3 `delete($key as xs:string)` removes a key and its value from the table, or it many return an error message if there's no key in the key-value store.

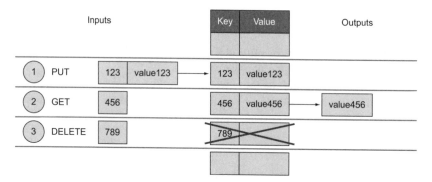

Figure 4.5   The key-value store API has three simple commands: `put`, `get`, and `delete`. This diagram shows how the `put` command inserts the input key `"123"` and value `"value123"` into a new key-value pair; the `get` command presents the key `"456"` and retrieves the value `"value456"`; and the `delete` command presents the key `"789"` and removes the key-value pair.

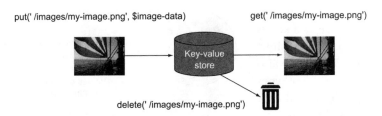

put(' /images/my-image.png', $image-data)   get(' /images/my-image.png')

delete(' /images/my-image.png')

Figure 4.6   The code and result of using the commands associated with a key-value store. To add a new key, you use the put command, as shown on the left; to remove, you use the delete command, as shown in the middle; and to retrieve, you use the get command, as shown on the right.

Figure 4.6 shows how an application would store (put), retrieve (get), and remove (delete) an image from a key-value store.

Standards watch: REST API

Note that we use the verb put instead of add in a key-value store to align with the standard Representational State Transfer (REST) protocol, a style of software architecture for distributed systems that uses clients to initiate requests and servers to process requests and return responses. The use of as xs:string indicates that the key can be any valid string of characters with the exception of binary structures. The item() references a single structure that may be a binary file. The xs: prefix indicates that the format follows the W3C definition of data types that's consistent with the XML Schema and the closely related XPath and XQuery standards.

In addition to the put, get, and delete API, a key-value store has two rules: distinct keys and no queries on values:

1 *Distinct keys*—You can never have two rows with the same key-value. This means that all the keys in any given key-value store are unique.

2 *No queries on values*—You can't perform queries on the values of the table.

The first rule, distinct keys, is straightforward: if you can't uniquely identify a key-value pair, you can't return a single result. The second rule requires some additional thought if your knowledge base is grounded in traditional relational databases. In a relational database, you can constrain a result set using the where clause, as shown in figure 4.7.

A key-value store prohibits this type of operation, as you can't select a key-value pair using the value. The key-value store resolves the issues of indexing and retrieval in large datasets by transferring the association of the key with the value to the application layer, allowing the key-value store to retain a simple and flexible structure. This is an example of the trade-offs between application and database layer complexity we discussed in chapter 2.

There are few restrictions about what you can use as a key as long as it's a reasonably short string of characters. There are also few restrictions about what types of data you can put in the value of a key-value store. As long as your storage system can hold it, you can store it in a key-value store, making this structure ideal for multimedia: images, sounds, and even full-length movies.

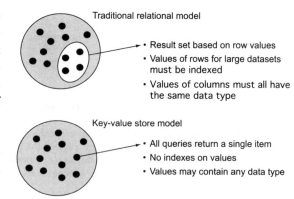

Figure 4.7   **The trade-offs associated with traditional relational models (which focus on the database layer) versus key-value store models (which focus on the application layer).**

GENERAL PURPOSE

In addition to being simple, a key-value store is a general-purpose tool for solving business problems. It's the Swiss Army knife of databases. What enables the generality is the ability for the application programmer to define what their key structures will be and what type of data they're going to store in the values.

Now that we've looked at the benefits and uses of a key-value store, we'll look at two use case examples. The first, storing web pages in a key-value store, shows how web search engines such as Google easily store entire websites in a key-value store. So if you want to store external websites in your own local database, this type of key-value store is for you.

The second use case, Amazon simple storage service (S3), shows how you can use a key-value store like S3 as a repository for your content in the cloud. If you have digital media assets such as images, music, or video, you should consider using a key-value store to increase the reliability and performance for a fraction of the cost.

4.1.4   *Use case: storing web pages in a key-value store*

We're all familiar with web search engines, but you may not realize how they work. Search engines like Google use a tool called a *web crawler* to automatically visit a website to extract and store the content of each web page. The words in each web page are then indexed for fast keyword search.

When you use your web browser, you usually enter a web address such as http://www.example.com/hello.html. This *uniform resource locator*, or *URL*, represents the *key* of a website or a web page. You can think of the web as a single large table with two columns, as depicted in figure 4.8.

The URL is the key, and the value is the web page or resource located at that key. If

Key	Value
http://www.example.com/index.html	<html>...
http://www.example.com/about.html	<html>...
http://www.example.com/products.html	<html>...
http://www.example.com/logo.png	Binary...

Figure 4.8   **How you can use URLs as a key in a key-value store. Since each web page has a unique URL, you can be assured that no two web pages have the same URL.**

all the web pages in only part of the web were stored in a single key-value store system, there might be billions or trillions of key-value pairs. But each key would be unique, like a URL to a web page is unique.

The ability to use a URL as a key allows you to store all of the static or unchanging components of your website in a key-value store. This includes images, static HTML pages, CSS, and JavaScript code. Many websites use this approach, and only the dynamic portions of a site where pages are generated by scripts are *not* stored in the key-value store.

4.1.5 Use case: Amazon simple storage service (S3)

Many organizations have thousands or millions of digital assets they want to store. These assets can include images, sound files, and videos. By using Amazon Simple Storage Service, which is really a key-value store, a new customer can quickly set up a secure web service accessible to anyone as long as they have a credit card.

Amazon S3, launched in the U.S. in March 2006, is an online storage web service that uses a simple REST API interface for storing and retrieving your data, at any time, from anywhere on the web.

At its core, S3 is a simple key-value store with some enhanced features:

- It allows an owner to attach metadata tags to an object, which provides additional information about the object; for example, content type, content length, cache control, and object expiration.
- It has an access control module to allow a bucket/object owner to grant rights to individuals, groups, or everyone to perform put, get, and delete operations on an object, group of objects, or bucket.

At the heart of S3 is the *bucket.* All objects you store in S3 will be in buckets. Buckets store key/object pairs, where the key is a string and the object is whatever type of data you have (like images, XML files, digital music). Keys are unique within a bucket, meaning no two objects will have the same key-value pair. S3 uses the same HTTP REST verbs (PUT, GET, and DELETE) discussed earlier in this section to manipulate objects:

- New objects are added to a bucket using the HTTP PUT message.
- Objects are retrieved from a bucket using the HTTP GET message.
- Objects are removed from a bucket using the HTTP DELETE message.

To access an object, you can generate a URL from the bucket/key combination; for example, to retrieve an object with a key of gray-bucket in a bucket called *testbucket*, the URL would be http://testbucket.s3.amazonws.com/gray-bucket .png.

The result on your screen would be the image shown in figure 4.9.

In this section, we looked at key-value store systems and how they can benefit an organization, saving them time and money by moving the focus from archi-

Figure 4.9 This image is the result of performing the http://testbucket.s3 .amazonws.com/gray-bucket .png GET request from an Amazon S3 bucket.

tectural design to reducing data services costs. We've demonstrated how these simple and versatile structures can and are used to solve a broad range of business problems for organizations having similar as well as different business requirements. As you attack your next business problem, you'll be able to determine whether a key-value store is the right solution.

Now that you understand the key-value store, let's move to a similar and more complex data architecture pattern: the graph store. As you move through the graph store section, you'll see some similarities to the key-value store as well as different business situations where a using a graph store is the more appropriate solution.

4.2   Graph stores

Graph stores are important in applications that need to analyze relationships between objects or visit all nodes in a graph in a particular manner (graph traversal). Graph stores are highly optimized to efficiently store graph nodes and links, and allow you to query these graphs. Graph databases are useful for any business problem that has complex relationships between objects such as social networking, rules-based engines, creating mashups, and graph systems that can quickly analyze complex network structures and find patterns within these structures.

By the end of this section, you'll be able to identify the key features of a graph store and understand how graph stores are used to solve specific business problems. You'll become familiar with graph terms such as nodes, relationships, and properties, and you'll know about the published W3C standards for graph data. You'll also see how graph stores have been effectively implemented by companies to perform link analysis, use with rules and inference engines, and integrate linked data.

4.2.1   Overview of a graph store

A *graph store* is a system that contains a sequence of nodes and relationships that, when combined, create a graph. You know that in a key-value store there two data fields: the key and the value. In contrast, a graph store has three data fields: *nodes, relationships,* and *properties.* Some types of graph stores are referred to as *triple stores* because of their node-relationship-node structure (see figure 4.10).

In the last section, you saw how the structure of a key-value store is general and can be applied to many different situations. This is also true of the basic node-relationship-node structure of a graph store. Graph stores are ideal when you have many items that are related to each other in complex ways and these relationships have properties (like a sister/brother of). Graph stores allow you to do simple queries that show you the nearest neighboring nodes as well as queries that look deep into networks and quickly find patterns. For example, if you use a

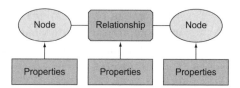

Figure 4.10   A graph store consists of many node-relationship-node structures. Properties are used to describe both the nodes and relationships.

relational database to store your list of friends, you can produce a list of your friends sorted by their last name. But if you use a graph store, you can not only get a list of your friends by their last name, you can also get a list of which friends are most likely to buy you a beer! Graph stores don't just tell you there's a relationship—they can give you detailed reports about each of your relationships.

Graph nodes are usually representations of real-world objects like nouns. Nodes can be people, organizations, telephone numbers, web pages, computers on a network, or even biological cells in a living organism. The relationships can be thought of as connections between these objects and are typically represented as arcs (lines that connect) between circles in diagrams.

Graph queries are similar to traversing nodes in a graph. You can query to ask things like these:

- What's the shortest path between two nodes in a graph?
- What nodes have neighboring nodes that have specific properties?
- Given any two nodes in a graph, how similar are their neighboring nodes?
- What's the average connectedness of various points on a graph with each other?

As you saw in chapter 2, RDBMSs use artificial numbers as primary and foreign keys to relate rows in tables that are stored on different sections of a single hard drive. Performing a join operation in RDBMSs is expensive in terms of latency as well as disk input and output. Graph stores relate nodes together, understanding that two nodes with the same identifiers are the same node. Graph stores assign internal identifiers to nodes and use those identifiers to join networks together. But unlike RDBMSs, graph store joins are computationally lightweight and fast. This speed is attributed to the small nature of each node and the ability to keep graph data in RAM, which means once the graph is loaded into memory, retrieving the data doesn't require disk input and output operations.

Unlike other NoSQL patterns we'll discuss in this chapter, graph stores are difficult to scale out on multiple servers due to the close connectedness of each node in a graph. Data can be replicated on multiple servers to enhance read and query performance, but writes to multiple servers and graph queries that span multiple nodes can be complex to implement.

Although graph stores are built around the simple and general-purpose node-relationship-node data structure, graph stores come with their own complex and inconsistent jargon when they're used in different ways. You'll find that you interact with graph stores in much the same way you do other types of databases. For example, you'll load, query, update, and delete data. The difference is found in the types of queries you use. A graph query will return a set of nodes that are used to create a graph image on the screen to show you the relationship between your data.

Let's take a look and see the variations on terms used to describe different types of graphs.

As you use the web, you'll often see links on a page that take you to another page; these links can be represented by a graph or triple. The current web page is the first or source node, the link is the arc that "points to" the second page, and the second or destination page is the second node. In this example, the first node is represented by the URL of the source page and the second node or destination is the URL of the destination page. This linking process can be found in many places on the web, from page links to wiki sites, where each source and destination node is a page URL. Figure 4.11 is an example of a graph store that has a web page that links to other web pages.

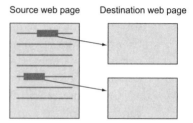

Source web page   Destination web page

Figure 4.11 An example of using a graph store to represent a web page that contains links to two other web pages. The URL of the source web page is stored as a URL property and each link is a relationship that has a "points to" property. Each link is represented as another node with a property that contains the destination page's URL.

The concept of using URLs to identify nodes is appealing since it's human readable and provides a structure within the URL. The W3C generalized this structure to store the information about the links between pages as well as the links between objects into a standard called *Resource Description Format*, more commonly known as *RDF*.

4.2.2 *Linking external data with the RDF standard*

In a general-purpose graph store, you can create your own method to determine whether two nodes reference the same point in a graph. Most graph stores will assign internal IDs to each node as they load these nodes into RAM. The W3C has focused on a process of using URL-like identifiers called *uniform resource identifiers (URIs)* to create explicit node identifiers for each node. This standard is called the W3C *Resource Description Format (RDF)*.

RDF was specifically created to join together external datasets created by different organizations. Conceptually, you can load two external datasets into one graph store and then perform graph queries on this joined database. The trick is knowing when two nodes reference the same object. RDF uses directed graphs, where the relationship specifically points from a source node to a destination node. The terminology for the source, link, and destination may vary based on your situation, but in general the terms *subject*, *predicate*, and *object* are used, as shown in figure 4.12.

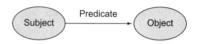

Subject ────Predicate────▶ Object

Figure 4.12 How RDF uses specific names for the general node-relationship-node structure. The source node is the subject, and the destination node is the object. The relationship that connects them together is the predicate. The entire structure is called an assertion.

These terms come from formal logic systems and language. This terminology for describing how nodes are identified has been standardized by the W3C in their RDF standard. In RDF each node-arc-node relationship is called a *triple* and is associated with an assertion of fact. In figure 4.13 the first assertion is (book, has-author, Person123), and the second assertion is (Person123, has-name, "Dan").

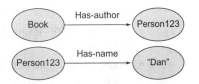

When stored in a graph store, the two statements are independent and may even be stored on different systems around the world. But if the URI of the Person123 structure is the same in both assertions, your application can figure out that the author of the book has a name of "Dan", as shown in figure 4.14.

Figure 4.13   Two distinct RDF assertions. The first assertion states that a book has a person as its author. The second assertion shows that this person has a name of Dan. Since the object of the first and the subject of the second have the same URI, they can be joined together.

Figure 4.14   How two distinct RDF assertions can be joined together to create a new assertion. From this graph you can answer yes to the question, "Does this book have any author that has the name "Dan"?"

The ability to traverse a graph relies on the fact that two nodes in different groups reference the same physical object. In this example, the Person123 node needs to globally refer to the same item. Once you determine they're the same, you can join the graphs together. This process is useful in areas like logic inference and complex pattern matching.

As you can imagine, the W3C, who created the RDF standard, is highly motivated to be consistent across all of their standards. Since they already have a method for identifying an HTML page anywhere in the world using a uniform resource locator structure, it makes sense to repurpose these structures whenever possible. The major difference is that, unlike a URL, a URI doesn't have to point to any actual website or web page. The only criteria is that you must have a way to make them globally consistent across the entire web and match exactly when you compare two nodes.

While a pure triple store is the ideal, in the real world triple stores frequently associate other information with each triple. For example, they might include what group ID the graph belongs to, the date and time the node was created or last updated, or what security groups are associated with the graph. These attributes are frequently called *link metadata* because they describe information about the link itself. Storing this metadata with every node does take more disk space, but it makes the data much easier to audit and manage.

4.2.3   Use cases for graph stores

In this section, we'll look at situations where a graph store can be used to effectively solve a particular business problem:

- *Link analysis* is used when you want to perform searches and look for patterns and relationships in situations such as social networking, telephone, or email records.
- *Rules and inference* are used when you want to run queries on complex structures such as class libraries, taxonomies, and rule-based systems.
- *Integrating linked data* is used with large amounts of open linked data to do real-time integration and build mashups without storing data.

LINK ANALYSIS

Sometimes the best way to solve a business problem is to traverse graph data—a good example of this is social networking. An example of a social network graph is shown in figure 4.15.

As you add new contacts to your friends list, you might want to know if you have any mutual friends. To get this information, you'd first need to get a list of your friends, and for each one of them get a list of their friends (friends-of-friends). Though you can do this type of search against a relational database, after the initial pass of listing out your friends, the system performance drops dramatically.

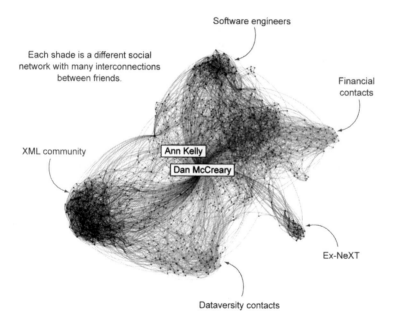

Figure 4.15   A social network graph generated by the LinkedIn InMap system. Each person is represented by a circle, and a line is drawn between two people that have a relationship. People are placed on the graph based on the number of connections they have with all the other people in the graph. People and relationships are shaded the same when there's a high degree of connectivity between the people. Calculating the placement of each person in a social network map is best performed by an in-memory graph traversal program.

Doing this type of analysis using an RDBMS would be slow. In the social networking scenario, you can create a "friends" table for each person with three columns: the ID of the first person, the ID of the second person, and the relationship type (family, close friend, or acquaintance). You can then index that table on both the first and second person, and an RDBMS will quickly return a list of your friends and your friends-of-friends. But in order to determine the next level of relationships, another SQL query is required. As you continue to build out the relationships, the size of each query grows quickly. If you have 100 friends who each have 100 friends, the friends-of-friends query or the second-level friends returns 10,000 (100 x 100) rows. As you might guess, doing this type of query in SQL could be complex.

Graph stores can perform these operations much faster by using techniques that consolidate and remove unwanted nodes from memory. Though graph stores would clearly be much faster for link analysis tasks, they usually require enough RAM to store all the links during analysis.

Graph stores are used for things beyond social networking—they're appropriate for identifying distinct patterns of connections between nodes. For example, creating a graph of all incoming and outgoing phone calls between people in a prison might show a concentration of calls (patterns) associated with organized crime. Analyzing the movement of funds between bank accounts might show patterns of money laundering or credit card fraud. Companies that are under criminal investigation might have all of their email messages analyzed using graph software to see who sent who what information and when. Law firms, law enforcement agencies, intelligence agencies, and banks are the most frequent users of graph store systems to detect legitimate activities as well as for fraud detection.

Graph stores are also useful for linking together data and searching for patterns within large collections of text documents. *Entity extraction* is the process of identifying the most important items (entities) in a document. Entities are usually the nouns in a document like people, dates, places, and products. Once the key entities have been identified, they're used to perform advanced search functions. For example, if you know all the dates and people mentioned in a document, you can create a report that shows which documents mention what people and when.

This entity extraction process (a type of *natural language processing* or *NLP*) can be combined with other tools to extract simple facts or assertions made within a document. For example, the sentence "John Adams was born on October 19, 1735" can be broken into the following assertions:

1. A person record was found with the name of John Adams and is a subject.
2. The born-on relationship links the subject to the object.
3. A date object record was found that has the value of October 19, 1735.

Although simple assertions can be easy to find using simple NLP processing, the process of fully understanding every sentence can be complex and dependant on the context of the situation. Our key takeaway is that if assertions are found in text, they can best be represented in graph structures.

GRAPHS, RULES, AND INFERENCE

The term *rules* can have multiple meanings that depend on where you're coming from and the context of the situation. Here, we use the term to define abstract rules that relate to an understanding of objects in a system, and how the object properties allow you to gain insight into and better use large datasets.

RDF was designed to be a standard way to represent many types of problems in the structure of a graph. A primary use for RDF is to store logic and rules. Once you've set these rules up, you can use an inference or rules engine to discover other facts about a system.

In our section on link analysis, we looked at how text can be encoded with entities such as people and dates to help you find facts. We can now take things a step further to get additional information from the facts that will help you solve business problems.

Let's start with trust, since it's an important aspect for businesses who want to attract and retain customers. Suppose you have a website that allows anyone to post restaurant reviews. Would there be value in allowing you to indicate which reviewers you trust? You're going out to dinner and you're considering two restaurants. Each restaurant has positive and negative reviews. Can you use simple inference to help you decide which restaurant to visit?

As a first test, you could see if your friends reviewed the restaurants. But a more powerful test would be to see if any of your friends-of-friends also reviewed the restaurants. If you trust John and John trusts Sue, what can you infer about your ability to trust Sue's restaurant recommendations? Chances are that your social network will help you use inference to calculate what reviews should have more weight. This is a simple example of using networks, graphs, and inference to gain additional knowledge on a topic. The use of RDF and inference isn't limited to social networks and product reviews. RDF is a general-purpose structure that can be used to store many forms of business logic.

The W3C does more than define RDF; it has an entire framework of standards for using RDF to solve business problems. This framework is frequently referred to as the *Semantic Web Stack*. Some of these are described in figure 4.16.

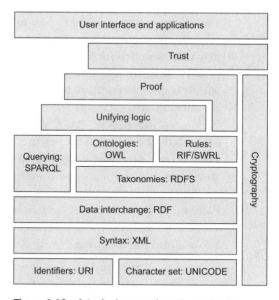

Figure 4.16   A typical semantic web stack with common low-level standards like URI, XML, and RDF at the bottom of the stack. The middle layer includes standards for querying (SPARQL) and standards for rules (RIF/SWRL). At the top of the stack are user interface and application layers above abstract layers of logic, proof, and trust building.

At the bottom of the stack, you see standards that are used in many areas, such as standardized character sets (Unicode) and standards that represent identifiers to objects in a URI-like format. Above that, you see that RDF is stored in XML files, a good example of using the XML tree-like document structure to contain graphs. Above the XML layer you see ways that items are classified using a taxonomy (RDFS) and above this you see the standards for ontologies (OWL) and rules (RIF/SWRL). The SPARQL query language also sits above the RDF layer. Above these areas, you see some of the areas that are still not standardized: logic, proof, and trust. This is where much of the research and development in the Semantic Web is focused. At the top, the user interface layer is similar to the application layers we talked about in chapter 2. Finally, along the side and to the right are cryptography standards that are used to securely exchange data over the public internet.

Many of the tools and languages associated with the upper layers of the Semantic Web Stack are still in research and development, and the number of investment case studies showing a significant ROI remain few and far between. A more practical step is to store original source documents with their extracted entities (annotations) directly in a document store that supports mixed content. We'll discuss these concepts and techniques later in the next chapter when we look at XML data stores.

In the next section, we'll look at how organizations are combining publicly available datasets (linked open data) from domain areas such as media, medical and environmental science, and publications to perform real-time extract, transform, and display operations.

USING GRAPHS TO PROCESS PUBLIC DATASETS

Graph stores are also useful for doing analysis on data that hasn't been created by your organization. What if you need to do analysis with three different datasets that were created by three different organizations? These organizations may not even know each other exists! So how can you automatically join their datasets together to get the information you need? How do you create mashups or recombinations of this data in an efficient way? One answer is by using a set of tools referred to as *linked open data* or *LOD*. You can think of it as an integration technique for doing joins between disparate datasets to create new applications and new insights.

LOD strategies are important for anyone doing research or analysis using publicly available datasets. This research includes topics such as customer targeting, trend analysis, sentiment analysis (the application of NLP, computational linguistics, and text analytics to identify and extract subjective information in source materials), or the creation of new information services. Recombining data into new forms provides opportunities for new businesses. As the amount of LOD grows, there are often new opportunities for new business ventures that combine and enrich this information.

LOD integration creates new datasets by combining information from two or more publicly available datasets that conform to the LOD structures such as RDF and URIs. A figure of some of the popular LOD sites called an *LOD cloud* diagram is shown in figure 4.17.

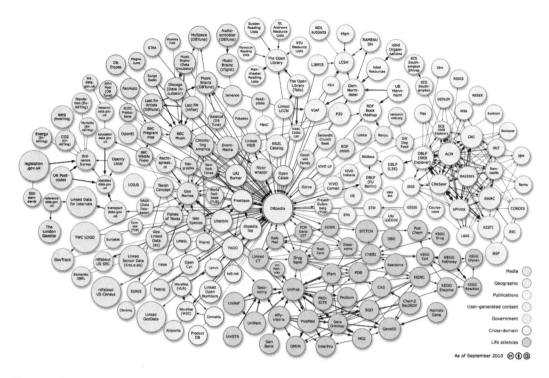

Figure 4.17   The linked open data cloud is a series of shaded circles that are connected by lines. The shades indicate the domain—for example, darker for geographic datasets, lighter for life sciences. (Diagram by Richard Cyganiak and Anja Jentzsch: http://lod-cloud.net)

At the center of LOD cloud diagrams you'll see sites that contain a large number of general-purpose datasets. These sites include LOD hub sites such as DBPedia or Free-base. DBPedia is a website that attempts to harvest facts from Wikipedia and convert them into RDF assertions. The data in the info boxes in Wikipedia is a good example of a source of consistent data in wiki format. Due to the diversity of data in DBPedia, it's frequently used as a hub to connect different datasets together.

Once you find a site that has the RDF information you're looking for, you can pro-ceed in two ways. The first is to download *all* the RDF data on the site and load it into your graph store. For large RDF collections like DBPedia that have billions of triples, this can be impracticable. The second and more efficient method is to find a web ser-vice for the RDF site called a *SPARQL endpoint*. This service allows you to submit SPARQL queries to extract the data from each of the websites you need in an RDF form that can then be joined with other RDF datasets. By combining the data from SPARQL queries, you can create new data mashups that join data together in the same way joins combine data from two different tables in an RDBMS.

The key difference between a SPARQL query and an RDBMS is the process that cre-ates the primary/foreign keys. In the RDBMS, all of the keys are in the same domain, but in the LOD the data was created by different organizations, so the only way to join the data is to use consistent URIs to identify nodes.

The number of datasets that participate in the LOD community is large and growing, but as you might guess, there are few ways to guarantee the quality and consistency of public data. If you find inconsistencies and missing data, there's no easy way to create bulk updates to correct the source data. This means you may need to manually edit hundreds of Wiki pages in order to add or correct data. After this is done, you may need to wait till the next time the pages get indexed by the RDF extraction tools. These are challenges that have led to the concept of curated datasets that are based on public data but then undergo a postprocessing cleanup and normalization phase to make the data more usable by organizations.

In this section, we've covered graph representations and shown how organizations are using graph stores to solve business problems. We now move on to our third NoSQL data architecture pattern.

4.3 *Column family (Bigtable) stores*

As you've seen, key-value stores and graph stores have simple structures that are useful for solving a variety of business problems. Now let's look at how you can combine a row and column from a table to use as the key.

Column family systems are important NoSQL data architecture patterns because they can scale to manage large volumes of data. They're also known to be closely tied with many MapReduce systems. As you may recall from our discussion of MapReduce in chapter 2, MapReduce is a framework for performing parallel processing on large datasets across multiple computers (nodes). In the MapReduce framework, the *map* operation has a master node which breaks up an operation into subparts and distributes each operation to another node for processing, and *reduce* is the process where the master node collects the results from the other nodes and combines them into the answer to the original problem.

Column family stores use row and column identifiers as general purposes keys for data lookup. They're sometimes referred to as *data stores* rather than *databases*, since they lack features you may expect to find in traditional databases. For example, they lack typed columns, secondary indexes, triggers, and query languages. Almost all column family stores have been heavily influenced by the original Google Bigtable paper. HBase, Hypertable, and Cassandra are good examples of systems that have Bigtable-like interfaces, although how they're implemented varies.

We should note that the term *column family* is distinct from a *column store*. A column-store database stores all information within a column of a table at the same location on disk in the same way a row-store keeps row data together. Column stores are used in many OLAP systems because their strength is rapid column aggregate calculation. *MonetDB, SybaseIQ,* and *Vertica* are examples of column-store systems. Column-store databases provide a SQL interface to access their data.

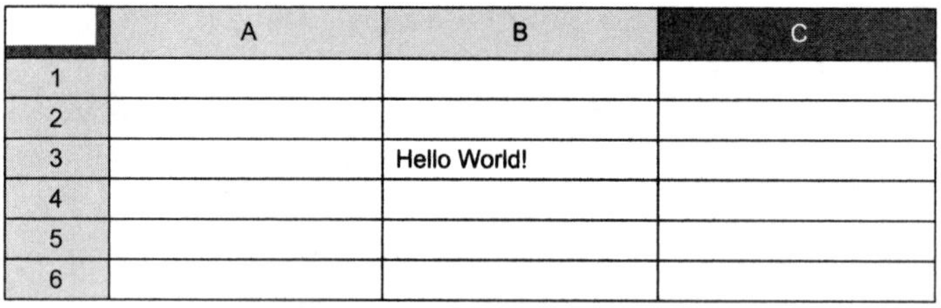

	A	B	C
1			
2			
3		Hello World!	
4			
5			
6			

Figure 4.18   Using a row and column to address a cell. The cell has an address of 3B and can be thought of as the lookup key in a sparse matrix system.

4.3.1   Column family basics

Our first example of using rows and columns as a key is the spreadsheet. Though most of us don't think of spreadsheets as a NoSQL technology, they serve as an ideal way to visualize how keys can be built up from more than one value. Figure 4.18 shows a spreadsheet with a single cell at row 3 and column 2 (the B column) that contains the text "Hello World!"

In a spreadsheet, you use the combination of a row number and a column letter as an address to "look up" the value of any cell. For example, the third column in the second row in the figure is identified by the key C2. In contrast to the key-value store, which has a single key that identifies the value, a spreadsheet has row and column identifiers that make up the key. But like the key-value store, you can put many different items in a cell. A cell can contain data, a formula, or even an image. The model for this is shown in figure 4.19.

This is roughly the same concept in column family systems. Each item of data can only be found by knowing information about the row and column identifiers. And, like a spreadsheet, you can insert data into any cell at any time. Unlike an RDBMS, you don't have to insert all the column's data for each row.

Figure 4.19   Spreadsheets use a row-column pair as a key to look up the value of a cell. This is similar to using a key-value system where the key has two parts. Like a key-value store, the value in a cell may take on many types such as strings, numbers, or formulas.

4.3.2   Understanding column family keys

Now that you're comfortable with slightly more complex keys, we'll add two additional fields to the keys from the spreadsheet example. In figure 4.20 you can see we've added a column family and timestamp to the key.

Figure 4.20   The key structure in column family stores is similar to a spreadsheet but has two additional attributes. In addition to the column name, a column family is used to group similar column names together. The addition of a timestamp in the key also allows each cell in the table to store multiple versions of a value over time.

The key in the figure is typical of column stores. Unlike the typical spreadsheet, which might have 100 rows and 100 columns, column family stores are designed to be...well...very big. How big? Systems with billions of rows and hundreds or thousands of columns are not unheard of. For example, a Geographic Information System (GIS) like Google Earth might have a row ID for the longitude portion of a map and use the column name for the latitude of the map. If you have one map for each square mile on Earth, you could have 15,000 distinct row IDs and 15,000 distinct column IDs.

What's unusual about these large implementations is that if you viewed them in a spreadsheet, you'd see that few cells contain data. This *sparse matrix* implementation is a grid of values where only a small percent of cells contain values. Unfortunately, relational databases aren't efficient at storing sparse data, but column stores are designed exactly for this purpose.

With a traditional relational database, you can use a simple SQL query to find all the columns in any table; when querying sparse matrix systems, you must look for every element in the database to get a full listing of all column names. One problem that may occur with many columns is that running reports that list columns and related columns can be tricky unless you use a column family (a high-level category of data also known as an *upper level ontology*). For example, you may have groups of columns that describe a website, a person, a geographical location, and products for sale. In order to view these columns together, you'd group them in the same column family to make retrieval easier.

Not all column family stores use a column family as part of their key. If they do, you'll need to take this into account when storing an item key, since the column family is part of the key, and retrieval of data can't occur without it. In as much as the API is simple, NoSQL products can scale to manage large volumes of data, adding new rows and columns without needing to modify a data definition language.

4.3.3 Benefits of column family systems

The column family approach of using a row ID and column name as a lookup key is a flexible way to store data, gives you benefits of higher scalability and availability, and saves you time and hassles when adding new data to your system. As you read through these benefits, think about the data your organization collects to see if a column family store would help you gain a competitive advantage in your market.

Since column family systems don't rely on joins, they tend to scale well on distributed systems. Although you can start your development on a single laptop, in production column family systems are usually configured to store data in three distinct nodes in possibly different geographic regions (geographically distinct data centers) to ensure high availability. Column family systems have automatic failover built in to detect failing nodes and algorithms to identify corrupt data. They leverage advanced hashing and indexing tools such as Bloom filters to perform probabilistic analysis on large data sets. The larger the dataset, the better these tools perform. Finally, column family implementations are designed to work with distributed filesystems (such as the

Hadoop distributed filesystem) and MapReduce transforms for getting data into or out of the systems. So be sure to consider these factors before you select a column family implementation.

HIGHER SCALABILITY

The world *Big* in the title of the original Google paper tells us that Bigtable-inspired column family systems are designed to scale beyond a single processor. At the core, column family systems are noted for their scalable nature, which means that as you add more data to your system, your investment will be in the new nodes added to the computing cluster. With careful design, you can achieve a linear relationship between the way data grows and the number of processors you require.

The principal reason for this relationship is the simple way that row IDs and column names are used to identify a cell. By keeping the interface simple, the back-end system can distribute queries over a large number of processing nodes without performing any join operations. With careful design of row IDs and columns, you give the system enough hints to tell it where to get related data and avoid unnecessary network traffic crucial to system performance.

HIGHER AVAILABILITY

By building a system that scales on distributed networks, you gain the ability to replicate data on multiple nodes in a network. Because column family systems use efficient communication, the cost of replication is lower. In addition, the lack of join operations allows you to store any portion of a column family matrix on remote computers. This means that if the server that holds part of the sparse matrix crashes, other computers are standing by to provide the data service for those cells.

EASY TO ADD NEW DATA

Like the key-value and graph stores, a key feature of the column family store is that you don't need to fully design your data model before you begin inserting data. But there are a couple constraints that you should know before you begin. Your groupings of column families should be known in advance, but row IDs and column names can be created at any time.

For all the good things that you can do with column family systems, be warned that they're designed to work on distributed clusters of computers and may not be appropriate for small datasets. You usually need at least five processors to justify a column family cluster, since many systems are designed to store data on three different nodes for replication. Column family systems also don't support standard SQL queries for real-time data access. They may have higher-level query languages, but these systems often are used to generate batch MapReduce jobs. For fast data access, you'll use a custom API written in a procedural language like Java or Python.

In the next three sections, we'll look at how column family implementations have been efficiently used by companies like Google to manage analytics, maps, and user preferences.

4.3.4 *Case study: storing analytical information in Bigtable*

In Google's Bigtable paper, they described how Bigtable is used to store website usage information in Google Analytics. The Google Analytics service allows you to track who's visiting your website. Every time a user clicks on a web page, the hit is stored in a single row-column entry that has the URL and a timestamp as the row ID. The row IDs are constructed so that all page hits for a specific user session are together.

As you can guess, viewing a detailed log of all the individual hits on your site would be a long process. Google Analytics makes it simple by summarizing the data at regular intervals (such as once a day) and creating reports that allow you to see the total number of visits and most popular pages that were requested on any given day.

Google Analytics is a good example of a large database that scales in a linear fashion as the number of users increases. As each transaction occurs, new hit data is immediately added to the tables even if a report is running. The data in Google Analytics, like other logging-type applications, is generally written once and never updated. This means that once the data is extracted and summarized, the original data is compressed and put into an intermediate store until archived.

This pattern of storing write-once data is the same pattern we discussed in the data warehouse and business intelligence section in chapter 3. In that section, we looked at sales fact tables and how business intelligence/data warehouse (BI/DW) problems can be cost-effectively solved by Bigtable implementations. Once the data from event logs is summarized, tools like pivot tables can use the aggregated data. The events can be web hits, sales transactions, or any type of event-monitoring system. The last step will be to use an external tool to generate the summary reports.

In the case of using HBase as a Bigtable store, you'll need to store the results in the Hadoop distributed filesystem (HDFS) and use a reporting tool such as Hadoop Hive to generate the summary reports. Hadoop Hive has a query language that looks similar to SQL in many ways, but it also requires you to write a MapReduce function to move data into and out of HBase.

4.3.5 *Case study: Google Maps stores geographic information in Bigtable*

Another example of using Bigtable to store large amounts of information is in the area of geographic information systems (GIS). GIS systems, like Google Maps, store geographic points on Earth, the moon, or other planets by identifying each location using its longitude and latitude coordinates. The system allows users to travel around the globe and zoom into and out of places using a 3D-like graphical interface.

When viewing the satellite maps, you can then choose to display the map layers or points of interest within a specific region of a map. For example, if you post vacation photos from your trip to the Grand Canyon on the web, you can identify each photo's location. Later, when your neighbor, who heard about your awesome vacation, is searching for images of the Grand Canyon, they'll see your photo as well as other photos with the same general location.

GIS systems store items once and then provide multiple access paths (queries) to let you view the data. They're designed to cluster similar row IDs together and result in rapid retrieval of all images/points that are near each other on the map.

4.3.6   *Case study: using a column family to store user preferences*

Many websites allow users to store preference information as part of their profile. This account-specific information can store privacy settings, contact information, and how they want to be notified about key events. Typically the size of this user preference page for a social networking site is under 100 fields or about 1 KB in size, which is reasonable as long as there's not a photo associated with it.

There are some things about user preference files that make them unique. They have minimal transactional requirements, and only the individual associated with the account makes changes. As a result, ensuring an ACID transaction isn't as important as making sure the transaction occurs when a user attempts to save or update their preference information.

Other factors to consider are the number of user preferences you have and system reliability. It's important that these read-mostly events are fast and scalable so that when a user logs in, you can access the preferences and customize their screen regardless of the number of concurrent system users.

Column family systems can provide the ideal match for storing user preferences when combined with an external reporting system. These reporting systems can be set up to provide high availability through redundancy, and yet still allow reporting to be done on the user preference data. In addition, as the number of users increases, the size of the database can expand by the addition of new nodes to your system without changing the architecture. If you have large datasets, big data stores may provide an ideal way to create reliable yet scalable data services.

Column family systems are known for their ability to scale to large datasets but they're not alone in this regard; document stores with their general and flexible nature are also a good pattern to consider when scalability is a requirement.

4.4   *Document stores*

Our coverage of NoSQL data patterns wouldn't be complete without talking about the most general, flexible, powerful, and popular area of the NoSQL movement: the document store. After reading this section, you'll have a clear idea of what document stores are and how they're used to solve typical business problems. We'll also look at some case studies where document stores have been successfully implemented.

As you may recall, key-value and Bigtable stores, when presented with a key, return the value (a BLOB of data) associated with that key. The key-value store and Bigtable values lack a formal structure and aren't indexed or searchable. Document stores work in the opposite manner: the key may be a simple ID which is never used or seen. But you can get almost any item out of a document store by querying any value or content within the document. For example, if you queried 500 documents associated with the Civil War, you could search for those documents that referenced General Robert E. Lee. The query would return a list of documents that contained his name.

A consequence of using a document store is everything inside a document is automatically indexed when a new document is added. Though the indexes are large, everything is searchable. This means that if you know any property of a document, you can quickly find all documents with the same property. Document stores can tell not only that your search item is in the document, but also the search item's exact location by using the *document path*, a type of key, to access the leaf values of a tree structure, as illustrated in figure 4.21.

Even if a document structure is complex, a document store search API can remain simple and provides an easy way to select a document or subset of a document. A key-value store can store an entire document in the value portion of the key-value store, but a document store can quickly extract subsections of a large number of documents without loading each document into memory. If you want to display a single paragraph of a book, you don't need to load the entire book into RAM.

We'll begin our document store learning by visualizing something familiar: a tree with roots, branches, and leaves. We'll then look at how document and application collections use the document store concept and the document store API. Finally, we'll look at some case studies and popular software implementations that use document stores.

4.4.1 Document store basics

Think of a document store as a tree-like structure, as shown in figure 4.21.

Document trees have a single root element (or sometimes multiple root elements). Beneath the root element there is a sequence of branches, sub-branches, and values. Each branch has a related path expression that shows you how to navigate from the root of the tree to any given branch, sub-branch, or value. Each branch may have a value associated with that branch. Sometimes the existence of a branch in the tree has specific meaning, and sometimes a branch must have a given value to be interpreted correctly.

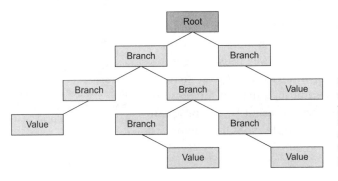

Figure 4.21 Document stores use a tree structure that begins with a root node, and have sub-branches that can also contain sub-branches. The actual data values are usually stored at the leaf levels of a tree.

4.4.2   *Document collections*

Most document stores group documents together in *collections*. These collections look like a directory structure you might find in a Windows or UNIX filesystem. Document collections can be used in many ways to manage large document stores. They can serve as ways to navigate document hierarchies, logically group similar documents, and store business rules such as permissions, indexes, and triggers. Collections can contain other collections and trees can contain subtrees.

If you're familiar with RDBMSs, you might think it natural to visualize document collections as an RDBMS. It might seem natural because you've used an XML column data type within your system. In this example, the RDBMS is a single table that contains XML documents. The problem with this view is that in the relational world, RDBMSs don't contain other tables, and you'd be missing the power and flexibility that comes with using a document store: allowing collections to have collections.

Document collections can also be used as application collections, which are containers for the data, scripts, views, and transforms of a software application. Let's see how an application collection (package) is used to load software applications into a native XML database like eXist.

4.4.3   *Application collections*

In some situations, the collection in a document store is used as a container for a web application package, as shown in figure 4.22.

This packaging format, called a *xar* file, is similar to a Java JAR file or a WAR file on Java web servers. Packaged applications can contain scripts as well as data. They're loaded into the document store and use packaging tools (scripts) to load the data if it's not already there. These packaging features make document stores more versatile, expanding their functionality to become application servers as well as document stores.

The use of collection structures to store application packages shows that a document store can be used as a container of high-level reusable components that can run on multiple NoSQL systems. If these developments continue, a market for reusable applications that are easy to install by nonprogrammers and can run on multiple NoSQL systems will soon be a reality.

Figure 4.22   Document store collections can contain many objects, including other collections and application packages. This is an example of a package repository that's used to load application packages into the eXist native XML database.

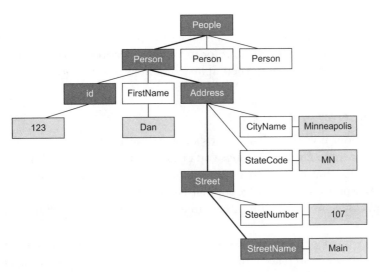

Figure 4.23 How a document path is used like a key to get the value out of a specific cell in a document. In this example, the path to the street name is
`People/Person[id='123']/Address/Street/StreetName/text()`.

4.4.4 Document store APIs

Each document store has an API or query language that specifies the path or path expression to any node or group of nodes. Generally, nodes don't need to have distinct names; instead, a position number can be used to specify any given node in the tree. For example, to select the seventh person in a list of people, you might specify this query: `Person[7]`. Figure 4.23 is a more complex example of a complete path expression.

In figure 4.23 you begin by selecting a subset of all people records that have the identifier 123. Often this points to a single person. Next you look in the Address section of the record and select the text from the Address street name. The full path name to the street name is the following: `People/Person[id='123']/Address/Street/StreetName/text()`. If you think this seems complicated, know that path expressions are simple and easy to learn. When looking for something, you specify the correct child element down a path of the tree structure, or you can use a where clause, called a *predicate*, at any point in the path expression to narrow down the items selected.

We'll discuss more on using the World Wide Web standard for selecting a path using the XPath language in the next chapter.

4.4.5 Document store implementations

A document store can come in many varieties. Some are based on simple serialized object trees and some are more complex, containing content that might be found in web pages with text markup. Simpler document structures are often associated with serialized objects and may use the *JavaScript Object Notation (JSON)* format. JSON allows arbitrary deep nesting of tree structures, but doesn't support the ability to store and query document attributes such as bold, italics, or hyperlinks within the text. We call this *complex content*. In our context we refer to JSON data stores as *serialized object stores* and to document stores that support complex content as *true document stores* with XML as the native format.

4.4.6 *Case study: ad server with MongoDB*

Do you ever wonder how those banner ads show up on the web pages you browse or how they really seem to target the things you like or are interested in? It's not a coincidence that they match your interests: they're tailored to you. It's done with ad serving. The original reason for MongoDB, a popular NoSQL product, was to create a service that would quickly send a banner ad to an area on a web page for millions of users at the same time.

The primary purpose behind ad serving is to quickly select the most appropriate ad for a particular user and place it on the page in the time it takes a web page to load. Ad servers should be highly available and run 24/7 with no downtime. They use complex business rules to find the most appropriate ad to send to a web page. Ads are selected from a database of ad promotions of paid advertisers that best match the person's interest. There are millions of potential ads that could be matched to any one user. Ad servers can't send the same ad repeatedly; they must be able to send ads of a specific type (page area, animation, and so on) in a specific order. Finally, ad systems need accurate reporting that shows what ads were sent to which user and which ads the user found interesting enough to click on.

The business problem 10gen (creators of MongoDB) was presented with was that no RDBMSs could support the complex real-time needs of the ad service market. MongoDB proved that it could meet all of the requirements at its inception. It has built-in autopartitioning, replication, load balancing, file storage, and data aggregation. It uses a document store structure that avoids the performance problems associated with most object-relational systems. In short, it was custom designed to meet the needs and demands of the ever-growing ad serving business and in the process turned out to be a good strategy for other problems that don't have real-time requirements, but want the ability to avoid the complex and slow object-relational mapping problems of traditional systems.

As well as being used as a basis for banner ad serving, MongoDB can be used in some of the following use cases:

- *Content management*—Store web content and photos and use tools such as geolocation indexes to find items.
- *Real-time operational intelligence*—Ad targeting, real-time sentiment analysis, customized customer-facing dashboards, and social media monitoring.
- *Product data management*—Store and query complex and highly variable product data.

- *User data management*—Store and query user-specific data on highly scalable web applications. Used by video games and social network applications.
- *High-volume data feeds*—Store large amounts of real-time data into a central database for analysis characterized by asynchronous writes to RAM.

4.4.7 Case study: CouchDB, a large-scale object database

In 2005, Damien Katz was looking for a better way to store a large number of complex objects using only commodity hardware. A veteran Lotus Notes user, he was familiar with its strengths and weaknesses, but he wanted to do things differently and created a system called *CouchDB* (cluster of unreliable commodity hardware), which was released as an open source document store with many of the same features of distributed computing as part of its core architecture.

CouchDB has document-oriented data synchronization built in at a low level. This allows multiple remote nodes to each have different versions of documents that are automatically synchronized if communication between the two nodes is interrupted. CouchDB uses MVCC to archive document-oriented ACID transactions, and also has support for document versioning. Written in *Erlang*, a functional programming language, CouchDB has the ability to rapidly and reliably send messages between nodes without a high overhead. This feature makes CouchDB remarkably reliable even when using a large number of processors over unreliable networks.

Like MongoDB, CouchDB stores documents in a JSON-style format and uses a JavaScript-like language to perform queries on the documents. Because of its powerful synchronization abilities, CouchDB is also used to synchronize mobile phone data.

Although CouchDB remains an active Apache project, many of the original developers of CouchDB, including Katz, are now working on another document store through the company *Couchbase*. Couchbase provides a distinct version of the product with an open source license.

The four main patterns—key-value store, graph store, Bigtable store, and document store—are the major architecture patterns associated with NoSQL. As with most things in life, there are always variations on a theme. Next, we'll take a look at a representative sample of the types of pattern variations and how they can be combined to build NoSQL solutions in organizations.

4.5 Variations of NoSQL architectural patterns

The key-value store, graph store, Bigtable store, and document store patterns can be modified by focusing on a different aspect of system implementation. We'll look at variations on the architectures that use RAM or solid state drives (SSDs), and then talk about how the patterns can be used on distributed systems or modified to create enhanced availability. Finally, we'll look at how database items can be grouped together in different ways to make navigation over many items easier.

4.5.1   *Customization for RAM or SSD stores*

In chapter 2 we reviewed how access times change based on the type of memory media used. Some NoSQL products are designed to specifically work with one type of memory; for example, Memcache, a key-value store, was specifically designed to see if items are in RAM on multiple servers. A key-value store that only uses RAM is called a RAM cache; it's flexible and has general tools that application developers can use to store global variables, configuration files, or intermediate results of document transformations. A RAM cache is fast and reliable, and can be thought of as another programming construct like an array, a map, or a lookup system. There are several things about them you should consider:

- Simple RAM resident key-value stores are generally empty when the server starts up and can only be populated with values on demand.
- You need to define the rules about how memory is partitioned between the RAM cache and the rest of your application.
- RAM resident information must be saved to another storage system if you want it to persist between server restarts.

The key is to understand that RAM caches must be re-created from scratch each time a server restarts. A RAM cache that has no data in it is called a *cold cache* and is why some systems get faster the more they're used after a reboot.

SSD systems provide permanent storage and are almost as fast as RAM for read operations. The Amazon DynamoDB key-value store service uses SSDs for all its storage, resulting in high-performance read operations. Write operations to SSDs can often be buffered in large RAM caches, resulting in fast write times until the RAM becomes full.

As you'll see, using RAM and SSDs efficiently is critical when using distributed systems that provide for higher volume and availability.

4.5.2   *Distributed stores*

Now let's see how NoSQL data architecture patterns vary as you move from a single processor to multiple processors that are distributed over data centers in different geographic regions. The ability to elegantly and transparently scale to a large number of processors is a core property of most NoSQL systems. Ideally, the process of data distribution is transparent to the user, meaning that the API doesn't require you to know how or where your data is stored. But knowing that your NoSQL software can scale and how it does this is critical in the software selection process.

If your application uses many web servers, each caching the result of a long-running query, it's most efficient to have a method that allows the servers to work together to avoid duplication. This mechanism, known as *memcache*, was introduced in the LiveJournal case study in chapter 1. Whether you're using NoSQL or traditional SQL systems, RAM continues to be the most expensive and precious resource in an application server's configuration. If you don't have enough RAM, your application won't scale.

The solution used in a distributed key-value store is to create a simple, lightweight protocol that checks whether any other server has an item in its cache. If it does, this item is quickly returned to the requester and no additional searching is required. The protocol is simple: each memcache server has a list of the other memcache servers it's working with. Whenever a memcache server receives a request that's not in its own cache, it checks with the other peer servers by sending them the key.

The memcache protocol shows that you can create simple communication protocols between distributed systems to make them work efficiently as a group. This type of information sharing can be extended to other NoSQL data architectures such as Bigtable stores and document stores. You can generalize the key-value pair to other patterns by referring to them as *cached items.*

Cached items can also be used to enhance the overall reliability of a data service by replicating the same items in multiple caches. If one server goes down, other servers quickly fill in so that the application gives the user the feeling of service without interruption.

To provide a seamless data service without interruption, the cached items need to be replicated automatically on multiple servers. If the cached items are stored on two servers and the first one becomes unavailable, the second server can quickly return the value; there's no need to wait for the first server to be rebooted or restored from backup.

In practice, almost all distributed NoSQL systems can be configured to store cached items on two or three different servers. The decision of which server stores which key can be determined by implementing a simple round-robin or random distribution system. There are many trade-offs relating to loads distributed over large clusters of key-value store systems and how the cached items in unavailable systems can be quickly replicated onto new nodes.

NoSQL systems dominate organizations that have large collections of data items, and it becomes cumbersome to deal with these items if they can only be accessed in a single linear listing. You can group items together in different ways to make them easier to manage and navigate, as you'll next see.

4.5.3   *Grouping items*

In the key-value store section, we looked at how web pages can be stored in a key-value store using a website URL as the key and the web page as the value. You can extend this construct to filesystems as well. In a filesystem, the key is the directory or folder path, and the value is the file content. But unlike web pages, filesystems have the ability to list all the files in a directory without having to open the files. If the file content is large, it would be inefficient to load all of the files into memory each time you want a listing of the files.

To make this easier and more efficient, a key-value store can be modified to include additional information in the structure of the key to indicate that the key-value pair is associated with another key-value pair, creating a *collection*, or general-purpose structures used to group resources. Though each key-value store system might call it something different (such as folders, directories, or buckets), the concept is the same.

The implementation of a collection system can also vary dramatically based on what NoSQL data pattern you use. Key-value stores have several methods to group similar items based on attributes in their keys. Graph stores associate one or more group identifiers with each triple. Big data systems use column families to group similar columns. Document stores use a concept of a document collection. Let's take a look at some examples used by key-value stores.

One approach to grouping items is to have two key-value data types, the first called *resource keys* and the second *collection keys*. You can use collection keys to store a list of keys that are in a collection. This structure allows you to store a resource in multiple collections and also to store collections within collections. Using this design poses some complex issues that require careful thought and planning about what should be done with a resource if it's in more than one collection and one of the collections is deleted. Should all resources in a collection be automatically deleted?

To simplify this process and subsequent design decisions, key-value systems can include the concept of creating collection hierarchies and require that a resource be in one and only one collection. The result is that the path to a resource is essentially a distinct key for retrieval. Also known as a *simple document hierarchy*, the familiar concept of folders and documents resonates well with end users.

Once you've established the concept of a collection hierarchy in a key, you can use it to perform many functions on groups of key-value pairs; for example:

- Associate metadata with a collection (who created the collection, when it was created, the last time it was modified, and who last modified the collection).
- Give the collection an owner and group, and associate access rights with the owner group and other users in the same way UNIX filesystems use permissions.
- Create an access control permission structure on a collection, allowing only users with specific privileges the ability to read or modify the items within the collection.
- Create tools to upload and/or download a group of items into a collection.
- Set up systems that compress and archive collections if they haven't been accessed for a specific period of time.

If you're thinking, "That sounds a lot like a filesystem," you're right. The concept of associating metadata with collections is universal, and many file and document management systems use concepts similar to key-value stores as part of their core infrastructure.

4.6   *Summary*

In this chapter, we reviewed some of the basic NoSQL data architectural patterns and data structures. We looked at how simple data structures like key-value stores can lead to a simple API, which make the structures easy to implement and highly portable across systems. We progressed from a simple interface such as key-value stores to the more complex document store, where each branch or leaf in a document can be selected to create query results.

By looking at the fundamental data structures being used by each data architecture pattern, you can understand the strengths and weaknesses of each pattern for various business problems. These patterns are useful for classifying many commercial and open source products and understanding their core strengths and weaknesses. The challenge is that many real-world systems rarely fit into a single category. They may start with a single pattern, but then so many features and plug-ins are added, they become difficult to put neatly into a single classification system. Many products that began as simple key-value stores have many features common to Bigtable stores. So it's best to treat these patterns as guidelines rather than rigid classification rules.

In our next chapter, we'll take an in-depth look at the richest data architecture pattern: the native XML database with complex content. We'll see some case studies where native XML database systems are used for enterprise integration and content publishing.

4.7   *Further reading*

- Berners-Lee, Tim. "What the Semantic Web can represent." September 1998. http://mng.bz/L9a2.
- "Cypher query language." From *The Neo4j Manual.* http://mng.bz/hC3g.
- DeCandia, Giuseppe, et al. "Dynamo: Amazon's Highly Available Key-value Store." Amazon.com. 2007. http://mng.bz/YY5A.
- MongoDB. Glossary: collection. http://mng.bz/Jl5M.
- Stardog. An RDF triple store that uses SPARQL. http://stardog.com
- "The Linking Open Data cloud diagram." September 2011. http://richard.cyganiak.de/2007/10/lod/.
- W3C. "Packaging System: EXPath Candidate Module 9." May 2012. http://expath.org/spec/pkg.

Native XML databases

5

This chapter covers

- Building native XML database applications
- Using XML standards to accelerate application development
- Design and validate documents with XML schemas
- Extending XQuery with custom modules

The value of a standard is proportional to the square of the number of systems that use it.

—rephrasing of Metcalfe's law
and the network effect as applied to standards

Have you ever wanted to perform a query on the information in a web page, a Microsoft Word document, or an Open Office presentation? Just think, if you have links in an HTML page, wouldn't it be nice to run a query to validate that all the links are working? All of these document types have a common property referred to as *mixed content* (data containing text, dates, numbers, and facts). One of the challenges of using document databases is that they don't support the use of queries on mixed content. Native XML databases, which have been around longer than other NoSQL databases, do allow queries on mixed content and as a result can support a number of security models and standardized query languages.

Native XML databases store and query a wider range of data types than any other NoSQL data store. They have an expressive data format that allows you to store structured tables as well as unstructured documents, and they provide superior search services. They tend to support web standards better than other document stores, which increases their portability between native XML systems. But the reason most organizations choose native XML databases is because they increase application development productivity and their ease of use allows nondevelopment staff to build and maintain applications.

After reading this chapter, you'll understand the basic features of native XML databases and how they're used to solve business problems in specific areas such as publishing or search. You'll become familiar with the process of building a native XML database application and transforming XML data, searching, and updating elements, and you'll see how standards are used to accelerate application development. Finally, since almost all native XML databases use the XQuery language to query documents, we'll look at how XQuery is used to transform XML documents and how it can be extended to include new functionality.

Defining a native XML database is the first step in understanding when and how they can help you solve business problems. In the next section, we'll start with a definition and then give some examples of the types of problems native XML databases can help you solve.

5.1 What is a native XML database?

Native XML databases use a document data architecture pattern. Like other document-oriented databases, they have no need for middle-tier, object-relational mapping, nor do they use join operations to store or extract complex data. Their ability to calculate hashes for each query and document makes them cache-friendly, and their ability to store data in a distributed environment allows them to scale elegantly.

Native XML databases existed before the term *NoSQL* was popular. They're more mature in some areas, and they integrate well with web standards managed by the World Wide Web consortium (W3C). Today you see native XML databases such as MarkLogic in areas of government, intelligence, integration, publishing, and content management.

Native XML databases are unique in the NoSQL world because they attempt to reuse data formats and standards to lower overall development costs. The philosophy is driven by avoiding the introduction of proprietary database-specific query languages that will lock your application into a single database. Native XML databases are forced to compete against each other in terms of ease of use, performance, and the ability to scale queries without needing to introduce new APIs. Many of the open source native XML databases share both concepts and extension functions.

Like the JSON (JavaScript Object Notation) data format (a text-based standard for human-readable data interchange), XML stores its information in a hierarchical tree structure. Unlike JSON, XML can store documents with mixed content and namespaces. Mixed-content systems allow you to mix sequences of text and data in any order. Elements in XML can contain text that has other trees of data interspersed throughout the text. For example, you can add HTML links that contain bold, italic, links, or images anywhere inside a paragraph of text. HTML files are a perfect example of the type of mixed content that can't be stored by or queried in a document database that only supports the JSON format.

Figure 5.1 shows the relationship between the features of *comma-separated value (CSV)* flat files used in many SQL systems, JSON, and XML documents.

If you use spreadsheets or load data into RDBMS tables, you know that CSV files are an ideal mechanism for storing data that's loaded into a single table. The CSV structure of commas separating fields and newline characters separating rows is frequently used to transfer data between spreadsheets and RDBMS tables.

JSON files are ideal for sending serialized objects to and from a web browser. JSON allows objects to contain other objects, and works well in hierarchical structures that don't need to store mixed content or use multiple namespaces. Due to its familiarity in the JavaScript world, JSON is the de facto standard for storing hierarchical documents within a document store. But it was never designed as a general-purpose container for mixed-content markup languages such as HTML.

As mentioned, XML files are the best choice when your document includes mixed content. XML also supports an often-controversial feature: namespaces. Namespaces allow you to mix data elements from different domains within the same document, yet retain the source meaning of each element. Documents that support multiple namespaces allow applications to add new elements in new namespaces without disrupting existing data queries.

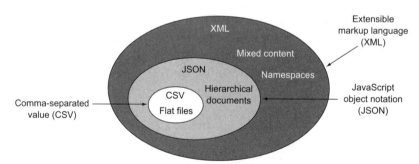

Figure 5.1   The expressiveness of three document formats. Comma-separated value (CSV) files are designed to only store flat files that don't contain hierarchy. JavaScript Object Notation (JSON) files can store flat files as well as hierarchical documents. Extensible Markup Language (XML) files can store flat files, hierarchical documents, and documents that contain mixed content and namespaces.

For example, a database of online articles may contain elements that reference an external library classification standard called the *Dublin Core* (elements like title, author, and subject from traditional book cataloguing), tags for RSS feeds (Atom), and additional presentation elements (HTML). By noting they're in the Dublin Core namespace, all cataloguing tools can be set up to automatically recognize these elements. Reusing external standards instead of inventing new tag names and constantly remapping them to external standards makes it easier for external tools to understand these documents.

Though useful, namespaces also have a cost. Tools that use multiple namespaces need to be aware of multiple namespaces, and developers need training to use these tools correctly. Namespaces are controversial in that they add an additional layer of complexity that's frequently not necessary in simple domain documents. Since single-domain documents are used in training development staff, namespaces may seem unnecessary and difficult to understand when first introduced. Without proper tools and training, developers can become frustrated with documents that contain multiple namespaces.

If you're familiar with the format of a web page that uses HTML, you'll quickly understand how XML works. Figure 5.2 shows a sales order with XML markup.

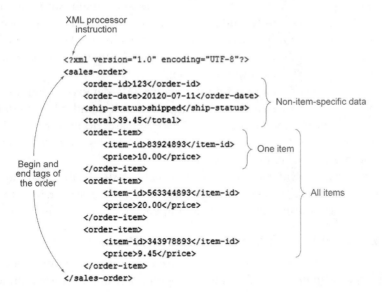

Figure 5.2   A sales order in XML markup format. The file begins with a processor instruction that indicates what version of XML the file uses, as well as what character encoding system is used (UTF-8). Each element has matching begin and end tags. The begin tags start with < and the end tags start with </. The sales order includes all of the items within the document, so no primary for foreign keys are needed. To generate a full report that includes item names or descriptions, a product lookup function can be used to convert the item ID into a full product description. This product lookup function would replace a join statement. The product lookup function extracts product information from another XML file.

The key difference between HTML and XML is that the semantics (or meaning) of each HTML element has been predefined by W3C standards. In the sales order example, the meaning of each sales order element is determined by the individual organization. Even though there may be an XML standard for sales orders, each organization can decide to create data element names specific to their organization and store those element names, and their definition, in a data dictionary.

Anyone who's familiar with XML recognizes it as a mature standard with an ecosystem of tools to support it. There are tools to extract subtrees from XML documents (*XPath*), tools to query XML documents (*XQuery*), tools to validate XML documents (XML Schema and Schematron), and tools to transform XML documents from one format to another.

RDBMS vendors like Oracle, Microsoft, and IBM have included XML management features in their products. Their approach is to add an XML column type to the RDBMS. Once added, XML documents are stored in the column in the same way a *binary large object (BLOB)* is stored. Though this strategy meets the needs of many use cases, it lacks portability since object-relational mapping tools don't generate the correct SQL to select XML elements within BLOBs.

The main disadvantage of XML, and a limitation of native XML systems, is that XML is a standard that attempts to solve many different types of problems with a single format. Without adequate tools and training, development staff may become frustrated with XML's complexity and continue to use simpler formats such as JSON or CSV. Without good GUI tools, developers are forced to view raw XML files that can be more verbose than the corresponding JSON representation.

Despite this issue, many developers find that native XML databases offer a simpler way of solving problems. Their rich query language and XML standards help to lower overall costs. It should also be noted that native XML databases don't store literal XML. They store a compact version in a compressed format. XML files are only used to put data into and retrieve data from the database.

Now that you have an understanding of what native XML databases are and the kinds of problems they solve, let's explore how native XML databases are used to build applications that can add, transform, search, and update XML documents.

5.2   *Building applications with a native XML database*

Native XML databases and their associated tools are key to increasing developer productivity. Using simple query languages allows programmers and nonprogrammers to simply create and customize reports. The combination of standards, mature query languages, robust tools, and document orientation makes the application development process faster. You'll find it difficult to convince native XML users to move to another platform once they've created applications with these systems.

Getting started with a native XML database can be simpler than you think. If you understand the concept of dragging files and folders, you're well on your way to creating your first native XML database. As you browse through the next section, you'll see how simple it can be to get started.

5.2.1 Loading data can be as simple as drag-and-drop

Most people are familiar with the concept of dragging and dropping to copy files from one location to another. Adding data to a native XML database can be that easy. Figure 5.3 shows how simple it can be to add new sales order data to an XML database.

You should note that you don't need to perform any entity-relational modeling prior to loading your data. The metadata structures of an XML file will be used to create all relevant indexes within the database. By default, every element is indexed for immediate search, and each leaf element is treated as a string unless previously associated with a data type such as a decimal or date.

Native XML databases have many options to load data. For example, you can

- Use an integrated XML IDE such as the Eclipse-based oXygen XML editor with built-in support for a native XML databases to upload a single file or a collection of XML files. The oXygen IDE can be used as a standalone program or as an Eclipse plug-in. Note: oXygen is a commercial product sold by SyncroSoft.
- Use a command-line tool or a UNIX shell script to load data from a file on your filesystem.
- Use a build script and Apache Ant task to load data. Many native XML databases come with Apache Ant extensions for all database operations.
- Use an "uploader" web page that allows you to upload a local file into a remote XML database.
- Use a backup-and-restore tool to load many XML files from an archive file.

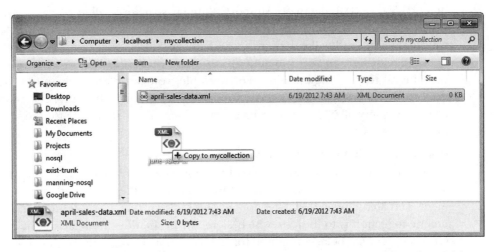

Figure 5.3 Adding new sales order data to an XML database can be as easy as doing a drag-and-drop. Many desktop operating systems such as Windows and Mac OS X support remote access using the WebDAV protocol. This allows you to add new files to your XML database by dragging an XML file into a database collection. All metadata associated with the XML file is used to index each element. As soon as the file is added, the data can be immediately searched using XQuery. Data modeling is not required before the data is added.

- Use a full desktop-based client that has been created for use with a specific native XML database. For example, a thick Java client provided with the database may provide upload or store features.
- Use a low-level Java API or an *XML-RPC* interface to load data (this requires you have a background in Java development).

There are also third-party applications like Cyberduck (for Windows and OS X) or Transmit (for OS X) that support a WebDAV protocol and will make your database look like an extension of your filesystem. These tools are preferred by many developers for managing native XML collections because they can be used by nonprogrammers. These tools can be used for uploading new documents as well as moving, copying, and renaming files in the same way you move and copy files in a filesystem.

If you wanted to perform these same move, copy, or rename operations on RDBMSs, it would require writing complex SQL statements or using a graphical user interface tool customized for database administration. With native XML systems, these operations are done with generic tools that may already be on your desktop and familiar to your users, which results in rapid learning and fewer dollars invested in training development skills.

Now that you know that native XML databases can be manipulated like folders, let's see how these structures (called *collections*) are used by native XML databases.

5.2.2 Using collections to group your XML documents

Filesystems use a folder concept where folders can contain other folders as well as documents. Native XML databases support a similar structure called *collection hierarchies*, which can contain both XML files and other collections. Using collections to store your documents will make them easier to manage.

Collections group your documents and data into subcollections in a way that's meaningful to your organization. For example, you can place daily sales orders for each month into a separate collection for that year and month. Native XML databases can easily query all XML documents in any folder or any subfolder to find the document you request.

CUSTOMIZING UPDATE BEHAVIOR WITH TRIGGERS

Collections also allow you to customize behavior for any action for all documents within a collection by using *database triggers*. These triggers are then executed when any document is created, updated, deleted, or viewed. Let's say that a typical function of a document collection is to indicate which elements in the document should be indexed. Once a trigger has been configured for the collection, changes to any document below that collection/subcollection will be automatically updated and indexed. The triggers are usually defined by placing an XML configuration file in the collection. The XML file will associate an XQuery function with each of the trigger types (insert, update, delete). Triggers are ideal places to specify document rule checks (such as validation), copy the prior version of a document into a version store, place a backup copy on a remote server, or log specific events.

WORKING WITH FLEXIBLE DATABASES

XML databases are designed to be flexible with the amount of data stored in a collection or XML file. They work equally well if you have a single file with 10,000 sales transactions or 10,000 individual transaction files. The query you write won't need to be changed if you alter how the files are grouped as long as you reference the root collection of your documents.

There are some design considerations to think about when you're performing concurrent reads and writes on a document collection. Some native XML databases only guarantee atomic operations within a single document, so placing two different data elements that must be consistent within an single document might be a good practice. For example, a sales order might have both the individual line item amounts and the sales order total within the same XML document. When the document is updated, all numbers will be updated in a consistent state.

You may also want to use a database lock on a document or a subdocument to prevent other processes from modifying it at critical times. This feature is similar to the file locks that are performed on a shared file in a filesystem. For example, if you're using a forms application to edit a document, you may not want someone else to save their version over your document. Locking a document helps you avoid conflicts when multiple people attempt to edit the same document at the same time. You can also calculate hash tags on a document as you load it into an editor to verify that it hasn't been modified by someone else while you've been editing it. This strategy and the use of HTTP ETags help you avoid the missing updates problem: when two users open the same file and changes from user 1 are overwritten by user 2.

STORING DOCUMENTS OF DIFFERENT TYPES

Native XML database collections can be used as a "primary taxonomy" to store documents of different types. This is similar to the categorization of a book in a library where the book is found according to its primary subject. But unlike a physical book, a document can contain many different category elements and thus doesn't have to be copied or moved between collections. An XML document can contain keywords and category terms that allow search tools to find documents that fit multiple subject categories.

GROUPING DOCUMENTS BY ACCESS PERMISSIONS

Collections can also be used as a way to group documents according to who can access them. You may have an internal policy that only allows users with a particular role to modify a document. Some native XML systems provide basic UNIX-style permissions on each collection to allow specific groups write access. The UNIX-style permissions result in a fast calculation of which users have access to a document.

The disadvantage of using UNIX-style permissions is that only a single group can be associated with a collection. Other native XML collection management systems add more flexible access control lists to protect each collection according to multiple groups or roles. Role-based collection management is the most robust permission system and is preferred by large organizations with many concurrent users from multiple business units. Unfortunately, only some native XML databases support role-based access control.

An example of using security-based collections to group web application functionality is shown in figure 5.4.

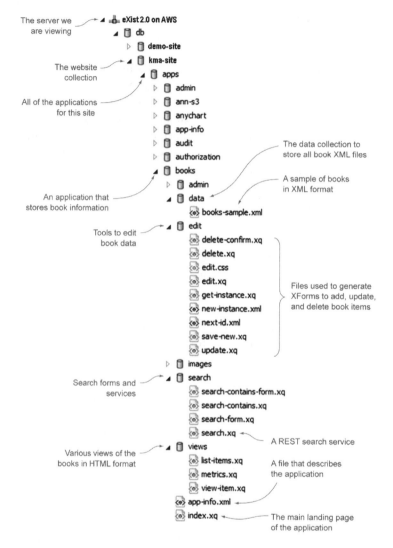

Figure 5.4 An example of using native XML collections to manage a set of web applications. The root folder in the main database and `kma-site` is a subfolder for one specific website. The `apps` folder within this contains all of the applications, one collection per application. The `books` collection contains subfolders for the application. `books/data` contains the location of the XML book data. Other collections include `books/edit` that stores tools to change the book data, and `books/views` for different report views of the book data. Each collection may have different permissions associated with it so that users who don't have modify rights may not be able to access the `books/edit` collection.

In this example, only a subset of all roles can add or update the XML files in the data collection. A larger number of roles can view and search for books using the queries in the view and search collections. The settings in the overall application information file (app-info.xml) associate each role with specific read and write permissions.

Native XML databases can store many different views of the same structure. Each view is a different transformation of the underlying XML data. In the next two sections, you'll see how XPath and XQuery are used to create these views.

5.2.3 *Applying simple queries to transform complex data with XPath*

XPath, a language that works within XQuery, allows you to easily retrieve the data you're looking for even in complex documents using short path expressions. Keeping your path expressions short allows you to quickly locate and retrieve the specific information within the document you're interested in, and not spend time writing long queries or looking at extraneous data.

XPath expressions are similar to the path commands you type into a DOS or UNIX shell to navigate to a specific directory or folder. XPath expressions consist of a series of steps that tell the system how to navigate to a specific part of the document. For example, the XPath expression `$my-sales-order/order-item[3]/price` will return the price of the third item in a sales order. The forward slash indicates that the next step in the hierarchy should be the child of the current location.

XML documents have a reputation for being complex, with good reason. When you apply all the features of XML into a single document (for example, mixed content, namespaces, and encoded elements) you can create documents that are difficult for humans to read. These documents are often complex because they try to accurately capture the structure of the real world—which is sometimes complex. Yet using complex structures doesn't imply that the queries must also be complex. This fact may not be intuitive, but it's one of the most important and sometimes overlooked qualities of native XML databases and XQuery. Let's review this concept using a concrete example.

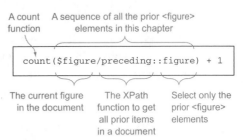

Each of the figures in this book is assigned a number. The first digit represents the chapter number (1, 2, 3), and the number following the chapter is a sequential number which represents where the figure is located in the chapter. To calculate the figure number, we only need to count the number of prior figures in each chapter. Figure 5.5 is an example of an XPath expression that does this.

Figure 5.5   How a complex document is queried using a simple XPath query expression. The expression is used to count figure numbers in each chapter of a book. It does this by counting the number of preceding <figure> elements in each chapter and adding one to calculate the current figure number. This allows sequential numbering of figures in each chapter as the book is converted from XML to HTML or PDF.

This XPath expression may be unfamiliar to many, but its structure isn't complex. You tell the system to start at the current figure, count the number of preceding figures in the chapter, and add one to get the current figure number. To make finding path expressions easy, there are also XML tools that allow you to select any element in an XML file, and the tools will show you the path expression required to select that specific element.

XPath is a key component that makes managing complexity easy. If you were using SQL, you'd need to store your complex data in many tables and use joins to extract the right data. Although an individual RDBMS table may have a simple structure, storing complex data in SQL usually requires complex queries. Native XML systems are just the opposite. Even if the data is complex, there are often simple XPath expressions that can be used to efficiently get the data you need out of the system.

Unlike other XML systems, native XML databases tend to use short, single-element XPath expressions because each individual element is indexed as it's added to the database. For example, the path expression `collection('/my-collection')//PersonBirthDate` will find all the person birth date records in a collection even if each document has a radically different structure. The downside to this is that you need more disk space to store your XML data. The upside is that queries are simple and fast.

Now that you have a feel for how XPath works, let's look at how the XQuery language is used to integrate XPath expressions to deliver a full solution that converts XML data directly into other structures.

5.2.4 *Transforming your data with XQuery*

Using the XQuery language and its advanced functional programming and parallel query execution features allows you to rapidly and effortlessly transform large datasets. In the NoSQL world, XQuery replaces both SQL and application-level functional programming languages with a single language.

One of the greatest advantages of using native XML databases over other document stores is how they use the XQuery language to transform XML data. As you'll see, XQuery is designed to query tabular as well as unstructured document data. XQuery is a mature and widely adopted standardized query language, carefully constructed by query experts using a rigorous peer review process. Although other languages can be used with native XML databases, XQuery is preferred due to its advanced functional structure and ability to run on parallel systems. A sample of XQuery is shown in figure 5.6.

As we move into our next few sections, you'll see why users that need to query large amounts of unstructured data prefer XQuery over other transformation languages.

XQUERY—A FLEXIBLE LANGUAGE

The XQuery language was developed by the World Wide Web consortium (W3C), the same organization that defined many other web and XML standards. Not long after XML standards were published, the W3C formed a standards body that included many

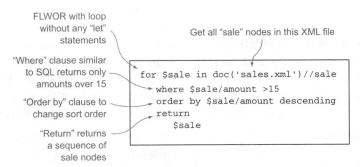

FLWOR with loop without any "let" statements

"Where" clause similar to SQL returns only amounts over 15

"Order by" clause to change sort order

"Return" returns a sequence of sale nodes

Get all "sale" nodes in this XML file

```
for $sale in doc('sales.xml')//sale
where $sale/amount >15
order by $sale/amount descending
return
    $sale
```

Figure 5.6 A sample FLWOR statement in XQuery that shows the for, where, order, and return statements. Many structures in XQuery, such as the where and order by statements, are similar to SQL, so many SQL developers quickly learn basic XQuery statements.

experts in query language design. Some of these experts assisted in developing standards for SQL, and in time found SQL inappropriate for querying nontabular data. The W3C query standards group was charged with creating a single query language that would work well for all use cases, which included business as well as text documents, books, and articles. Beginning with a list of relational and document query languages and a set of 70 use cases for structured and unstructured data sets, the W3C group embarked on an multiyear mission to define the XQuery language.

XQuery was designed to be a flexible language that allowed each of the 70 use cases to be queried and run on multiple processors, and to be easy to learn, parse, and debug. To accomplish its task, it borrowed concepts from many other query systems. This rigorous process resulted in a query language that's widely adopted and used in many products. These XQuery products include not only native XML databases, but also tools for in-memory data transformation and integration tools.

XQUERY—A FUNCTIONAL PROGRAMMING LANGUAGE

XQuery is defined as a *functional programming language* because its focus is the parallel transformation of sequences of data items using functions. Note that we'll cover the topic of functional programming in depth in chapter 11. With XQuery, functions can be passed as parameters to other functions. XQuery has many features not found in SQL that are used for the efficient transformation of hierarchical XML data. For example, XQuery allows you to call recursive functions and returns not only tables but any other tree-like data structures. XQuery can return simple XML or a sequence of items including JSON or graph structures. Due to its functional nature, XQuery can be easier to execute on multiple CPU systems.

The parallel processing power of XQuery is the *FLWOR statement*. FLWOR stands for *for, let, where, order, and return*, as shown in figure 5.6. Unlike the for loops found in procedural languages such as Java or .Net, FLWOR statements can execute in independent parallel processes and run on a large number of parallel CPUs or different processors.

XQUERY—CONSISTENT WITH WEB STANDARDS

XQuery is designed to be consistent with other W3C standards beyond XPath. For example, XQuery shares data types with other XML standards such as XML Schema, XProc, and Schematron. Because of this standardization, XQuery implementations tend to be more portable than applications that are ported between SQL databases.

XQuery can return any tree-structure data including tables, graphs, or entire web pages. This feature eliminates the need for a middle-tier, table-to-HTML translation layer. Avoiding a middle-tier translation, which includes a separate programming language and another data type translation, makes the software development process simpler and more accessible to nonprogrammers. The elimination of the middle-tier, relational-to-object-to-HTML translation is one of the core simplification patterns that makes NoSQL systems more agile and allows faster development of web applications.

ONE QUERY LANGUAGE OR MANY?

There are many trade-offs to consider when selecting a query language for your database. Small template languages are easy to create and easy to learn, but can be difficult to extend. Other languages are designed to be extensible with hundreds of extension functions. Of the many new query languages created over the last dozen years, XQuery stands out as the most ambitious. Defined by the W3C over a six-year period using query experts from many domains, its goal was to create a single language that can query a broad spectrum of data structures. Where SQL is perfect for working with tabular data, and languages like XSLT are ideal for transforming documents, XQuery alone has become the central unification language for querying diverse types of data in a single language. XQuery also attempts to combine the best features of modern functional programming languages to prevent side effects and promote caching (see chapter 10 for further details). Some of the use cases that drove the specifications of XQuery include these:

- *Queries on hierarchical data*—Generating a table of contents on a document with nested sections and subsections.
- *Queries on sequences*—Queries based on a sequence of items. For example, in a calendar what events happen between two other events?
- *Queries on relational data*—Queries similar to SQL where joins are used to merge data from multiple tables that share common keys.
- *Queries on documents*—Finding titles, paragraphs, or other markup within the chapter of a book.
- *Queries on strings*—Scanning news feeds and merging data from press releases and stock data.
- *Queries on mixed vocabularies*—XML data that merges information from auctions, product descriptions, and product reviews.
- *Recursive parts explosion*—How a recursive query can be used to construct a hierarchical document of arbitrary depth from flat structures.
- *Queries with strongly typed data*—Using type information in an XML schema to transform a document.

Now that we've discussed the steps used to import XML and how to use XPath and XQuery to transform XML data from one form into another, we'll review how to run updates on XML data and search XML documents that contain full text (structures that contain natural-language text, for example, English language).

> ### JSONiq and XSPARQL
>
> There are two proposed language extensions to XQuery: JSONiq, which adds the ability to query JSON documents as well as XML structures, and XSPARQL, which allows RDF data stores to be queried using XQuery. Some of the features can be implemented using standard XQuery functions, but there are additional benefits to extending the XQuery language definition to include these features.

5.2.5 Updating documents with XQuery updates

As you may recall from section 5.2.1, we talked about how when new XML documents are loaded into a native XML database, every element is immediately indexed. If you think about it, you'll see that this can be an expensive process, especially when you have large documents that also contain many full-text structures that must be re-indexed each time the document is saved.

To make saving documents with small changes easier, the W3C has provided a standard for updating one or more elements within an XML document without having to update the entire document and the associated indexes. The update operations are

- `insert`—Insert a new element or attribute into a document.
- `delete`—Delete an element or attribute in a document.
- `replace`—Replace an element or attribute in a document with a new value.
- `rename`—Change the name of any element or attribute to a new name.
- `transform`—Transform an element into a new format without changing the underlying structure on disk.

For example, to change the price of a specific book in your database, the code might look like figure 5.7.

XQuery update operations weren't part of the original 2006 XQuery 1.0 specification, and at this point you might see books and XML systems that haven't taken advantage of the full specification. Some systems provide a method of updating XML, but use a nonstandard method of doing so. Update operations are critical to make it easy

```
replace value of node
doc('books.xml')//book[ISBN='12345']/price with 39.95
```

The XML file of books   The book you want to update   The new price

Figure 5.7 A sample XQuery `replace` statement that changes the price of a book with a specific ISBN number to a new price. `replace value of node` is placed before the element and `with` is placed before the new price. The net effect is that you can update a specific element without the overhead of replacing and re-indexing the entire document.

and efficient to update XML documents. The larger the XML documents are, the more critical it is to use the update function.

The W3C standardized XQuery updates in 2011. The other XQuery specification that was released by the W3C in 2011 was the full-text extension, which we'll cover next.

5.2.6   *XQuery full-text search standards*

Native XML systems are used to store both business documents like sales orders and invoices, and written documents like articles or books. Because native XML databases are used to store large amounts of textual information, there's a strong demand for high-quality search of these documents. Fortunately, the W3C has also created XQuery-based standards for full-text search.

XQuery supports a search extension module that standardizes how search functions are performed on a full-text database (a database that contains a complete text of the books, journals, magazines, newspapers, or other kinds of textual material in a collection). This extension to the XQuery language specifies how search queries should be specified in terms of XQuery functions

Search standards are important because they allow your XQuery search applications to be portable to multiple native XML databases. In addition, using standards in full-text search code and processes allows staff to port their knowledge from one XML database to another, reducing training and application development time.

The specification also provides guidelines on advanced functions such as Boolean and nearness operations. The key difference is that with native XML databases, each node can be considered its own document and have its own indexing rules. This allows you to set up rules to weight matches in the title of a document above matches in the body of a document. We'll review the concepts of search and weighting in greater detail in chapter 7.

We've now reviewed how to build a web application using a native XML database. You've seen how data is loaded, transformed, updated, and searched using XQuery and XQuery extensions. Now let's take a look at other standards used in native XML databases that allow you to build portable applications.

5.3   *Using XML standards within native XML databases*

XML standards allow you to reuse your knowledge and code as you move from one native XML database to another. They also allow you to keep your NoSQL applications portable across different implementations of NoSQL databases and prevent vendor lock-in. Standards make it easier to learn a new NoSQL system, which helps you and your team get your products to market faster. If you're already familiar with an API or data standard, your application development using that standard will be faster with each subsequent project.

Let's begin with an overview of some of the XML standards we've discussed and add some new standards to the mix. Table 5.1 lists the key standards used in native XML systems, the organization associated with the standard, and a description of how the standard is used.

Table 5.1   XML standards. Application portability between native XML systems is highly sensitive to the standards each database implements. Note that not all standards are published by the W3C.

Standard name	Standards organization	Description
Extensible Markup Language (XML)	W3C	The XML standard specifies how tree-structured data is stored in a text file using elements and attributes. The standard has precise information about what character sets are used, how special characters are escaped, and any special processing instructions that might be used by an application. Unlike JSON, XML supports multiple namespaces and mixed content.
XPath	W3C	The XPath specification describes how to select a subset of an XML file using simple path expressions. Path expressions are steps into a part of the document or complex expressions with conditional statements and loops. XPath is a building block specification that's used in other XML specifications including XSLT, XQuery, Schematron, XForms, and XProc.
XML Schema	W3C	XML schemas are XML files used to quickly validate the structure of an XML document in a single pass and check the format rules of each leaf element. XML schemas are designed so that validation on large documents occurs quickly. XML Schema 1.1 has added new features that allow XPath expressions to be used to validate documents. XML Schema is a mature standard and is supported by graphical design tools.
XQuery	W3C	XQuery is a W3C standard for querying XML files and XML databases. XQuery is considered a functional programming language and is built around a parallel programming construct called a FLWOR statement that can be easily executed on multiple processors.
XQuery/XPath full-text Search	W3C	The W3C full-text search standard specifies how full-text searches should be implemented in any XQuery or XPath engine.
Schematron	ISO/IEC	Schematron is a rule-based validation language for making assertions about the presence or absence of patterns in XML trees. Unlike XML Schema, Schematron allows you to express if/then rules in XPath that can apply to any node in an XML document. A rule about the last node in a large file may reference an element in the first node of the file, so the entire file may need to be in memory to validate the rules.
XProc	W3C	XProc is a W3C XML declarative language for pipeline processing of documents. Typical steps might include expanding includes, validating, splitting documents, joining documents, transforming, and storing documents. XProc leverages other XML standards including XPath.
XForms	W3C	XForms is a W3C XML declarative language standard for building client applications that use a model-view-controller (MVC) architecture. It has the ability to create complex web applications without using JavaScript.

Table 5.1   XML standards. Application portability between native XML systems is highly sensitive to the standards each database implements. Note that not all standards are published by the W3C. *(continued)*

Standard name	Standards organization	Description
XSL-FO	W3C	XSL-FO is a document formatting standard ideal for specifying paginated layout used in printed material. Unlike HTML, XSL-FO has features that allow you to avoid placing items on page break boundaries.
EXPath	EXPath— W3C Committee	Repository of XML-related standards that aren't currently in the scope of other standards organizations. Example libraries include HTTP, cryptography, filesystems, FTP, SFTP, and packaging and compression libraries for XML applications.
NVDL	ISO/IEC	NVDL (Namespace-based Validation Dispatching Language) is an XML schema language for validating XML documents that integrate with multiple namespaces. It's used within rule-based text editing systems that provide as-you-type rule checking.

You may find each of the standards listed here applicable in different business situations. Some standards are used to define document structures, and others focus on validating or transforming XML documents. This isn't an exhaustive list, but rather a representative sample of available standards. As we move into our next section, you'll see how you can apply the XML Schema standard to validate your XML data.

5.4   *Designing and validating your data with XML Schema and Schematron*

XML schemas are used to design and validate XML documents stored in native XML databases. A schema can be used to precisely communicate the structure of your documents with others as well as validate the XML document structure. Frequently, simple graphical tools are used in the design process, which lets subject matter experts and business analysts participate and take control of this task.

The terms *schemaless* and *schema-free* occur frequently in NoSQL. In general, the terms indicate that you don't have to create a full entity-relation-driven physical schema, using a data definition language, prior to storing data into your NoSQL system. This is true for all of the NoSQL databases we've discussed (key-value stores, graph stores, Bigtable stores, and document stores). Native XML databases, though, provide the option of designing and validating documents at any time in the data loading lifecycle using a schema. In our case, the schemas aren't required to load data; they're only optionally used to design and validate documents.

5.4.1   *XML Schema*

XML Schema is a foundational W3C specification that's reused by other specifications to make XML standards consistent. A good example of this reuse is the data type system defined in the original XML Schema specification. This data type system is reused in other XML specifications. Because XPath, XQuery, XProc, and XForms all use the same data types defined in the original XML Schema specification, it's easy to verify data types and check for data types in your functions. Once you learn the data types used on one system, you'll know how to use them in all systems.

For example, if you have a data element that must be a nonzero positive integer, you can declare the data type of that element in your XML schema as xs:positive-Integer. You can then use an XML schema to validate those elements and receive notification when data varies from a valid format. If a zero, negative, or non-integer is used in that element, you can receive a notification at any stage of your data loading process. Even if you have data issues, you can choose to load the data and perform cleanup operations using a script later on. In a similar way, an XQuery function that must have a positive integer as a parameter can use the same positive integer data type and perform the same consistency checks on input or output elements.

Because XML Schema is a widely used mature standard, there are graphical tools available to create and view these structures. A example of this view is shown in figure 5.8 using the oXygen IDE.

This figure shows how simple graphical symbols are used to show both the structure and rules of a document. After learning the meaning of around a dozen symbols, nontechnical users can play an active role in the design and verification of document structures. For example, a solid black line in a schema diagram indicates that a required element must be present for the document to be valid. A gray line implies that an element is optional. One quick glance at a diagram can quickly indicate a specific rule. Using a black solid line for required elements isn't part of any W3C standards, but most XML developer tools use similar conventions.

XML schemas are designed to perform a single pass, looking at the structure of the document and the data formats in each of the leaf elements. This single-pass approach can check approximately 95% of the rules that concern business users. There are still a few types of rules that XML schemas aren't designed to check. For these rules, you use a companion format called Schematron.

5.4.2 *Using Schematron to check document rules*

Schematron is considered the "feather duster" of document validation. Schematron's focus is the hard-to-reach areas of data type checking that can't be done in a single pass with XML Schema. Let's say you want to check that the sum of all the line items in a sales order is equal to the sales total; you could do this with a Schematron rule. Schematron rules are used whenever you're comparing two or more places in an XML document.

Users like Schematron document rules because they can customize the error message associated with each rule to have a user-appropriate meaning. This customization is more difficult with XML Schema, where an error message tells you where the error occurred within the file but may not return a user-friendly message. For this reason, sometimes Schematron is preferred in situations where error messages are sent to a system user.

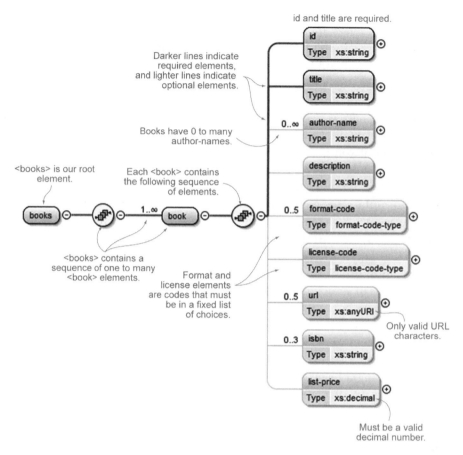

Figure 5.8   Sample XML schema diagram showing how symbols are used to display document structure. In this example, the file shows the structure of a collection of one to many books. Each book has required elements (shown with darker lines, like `id` and `title`) as well as optional elements (shown with lighter lines, like description). Some elements, such as `author-name`, can be repeated, allowing many authors to be associated with a single book. The XML schema elements that have a suffix of `code` use enumerated values to specify the possible element values. Data types such as `decimal` can also be specified with each element.

All Schematron rules are expressed using XPath expressions. This means you can use simple path statements to select two parts of a document and do a comparison. Since native XML databases index each element specified by a path, only part of the document needs to be moved into RAM when running a rules check. Schematron rules can also be configured to perform date checks and run web service validations. Schematron is both simple and powerful. Many users say it's one of the most underutilized features in the XML family of products.

Together, XML Schema and Schematron provide powerful and easy-to-use tools to design XML documents and validate their structures. Graphical tools and simple path expressions make these tools available to a wide audience. Making projects easier to use is a central theme of many XML projects.

Next you'll see how XQuery developers are creating custom modules that make it easier to take advantage of and use XQuery extensions.

5.5 Extending XQuery with custom modules

Originally, XQuery was designed to have a narrow focus: querying XML files and databases. Today, XQuery is used in a broader context that includes additional use cases. For example, XQuery is replacing middle-tier languages like PHP in many web applications. As a result, there's an increased demand for new functions and modules that go beyond the original functions that were part of the original XQuery 1.0 specification. *EXPath* is a central repository of these functions and can be used with multiple databases. Using EXPath functions will make your applications more portable between these databases.

Unlike SQL, XQuery is extensible, allowing you to use your own as well as other developers' custom functions. XQuery functions are ideal for removing repetitive code or abstracting complex code into understandable units.

The XQuery 1.0 specification contains more than 100 built-in functions for tasks like processing strings, dates, URIs, sums, and other common data structures. XQuery 3.0 has also added a handful of new functions for formatting dates and numbers. But the real strength of XQuery is the easy way new functions are added. An excellent example of this is the FunctX library.

FunctX contains almost 150 additional functions that can be added to your system by downloading the function library and adding an import statement to your program. The FunctX library extends the basic XQuery functions to allow you to perform operations on strings, numbers, dates, times, and durations, as well as work with sequences, XML elements, attributes, nodes, and namespaces.

EXPath modules pick up where the XQuery 1.0 function library leaves off. They include cryptography functions, filesystem libraries, HTTP client calls, and functions to compress and uncompress data. Many EXPath modules are wrappers to existing libraries written in Java or other languages.

5.6 Case study: using NoSQL at the Office of the Historian at the Department of State

In this case study, the ability to store, modify, and search historical documents containing mixed content was a key business requirement. You'll see how the Office of the Historian at the Department of State used an open source native XML database to build a low-cost system with advanced features typically found in enterprise content management systems.

The historical mixed content documents contain presentation annotations (bold, italics, and so on) as well as object entity annotations such as people, dates, terms, and organizations. Object entity annotations are critical for high-value documents when precision search and navigation is required.

After reading this case study, you'll understand how annotations are used to solve business problems and how native XML databases are unique in their ability to query text with rich annotations. You'll also become familiar with how open source native XML databases use XQuery and Lucene full-text search library functions to create high-quality search tools.

The Office of the Historian at the Department of State is charged by statute with publishing the official records associated with US foreign relations. A declassified analysis of specific periods of US diplomatic history is published in a series of volumes titled *Foreign Relations of the United States (FRUS)*. Through a detailed editing and peer review process, the Office of the Historian has become the "gold standard" for accuracy in the history of international diplomacy. FRUS documents are used in political science and diplomacy classes as well as for other training throughout the world.

In 2008, the Office of the Historian embarked on an initiative to convert the printed FRUS textbooks into an online format that could be easily searched and viewed using multiple formats. The Office of the Historian chose a standard XML format widely used for encoding historical documents called *Text Encoding Initiative (TEI)*. TEI was chosen because it has precise XML elements to encode a digital representation of historical documents and includes elements for indicating the people, organizations, locations, dates, and terms used in the documents.

To convert the FRUS volumes (each over 1,000 pages long) to TEI format, the documents are first sent to an outside service that enters the information into two separate XML documents using an XML editor. The two XML files are compared against each other to ensure accuracy. The TEI-encoded XML documents are then returned to the Office of the Historian ready to be indexed and transformed into HTML, PDF, or other formats. Figure 5.9 outlines this encoding process.

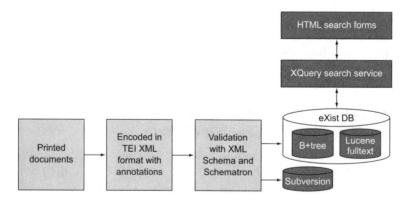

Figure 5.9   The overall document workflow for converting printed historical documents into an online system using TEI encoding. TEI-encoded documents are validated using XML schemas and Schematron rules files and saved into a Subversion revision control system. XML documents are then loaded into the eXist native XML database. Search forms are used to send keyword queries to a REST XQuery search service. This service uses the eXist document tree indexes and Lucene indexes to create search results.

The TEI-encoded FRUS documents are validated using XML validation tools (XML Schema and Schematron) and uploaded into the *eXist DB* native XML database, where each data element is automatically indexed. When XML elements contain text, they're also automatically indexed using Apache Lucene libraries, resulting in full-text indexes of each document. When pages are viewed on the website, XQuery performs a transformation and converts the TEI XML format into HTML. XQuery programs are also used to transform the TEI XML into other formats, including RSS/Atom feeds, PDF, and EPUB. No preconversion of TEI to other formats is required until a page or document is requested on the website.

A critical success factor for the Office of the Historian at the Department of State project was the need for high-quality search. A sample search result for the query "nixon in china" is shown in figure 5.10.

Figure 5.10   A sample web search result from the Office of the Historian at the Department of State. The result page uses Apache Lucene full-text indexes to quickly search and rank many documents. The bold words in the search result use the key-word-in-context (KWIC) function to show the search keywords found in the documents. The search interface allows users to utilize advanced search options to limit scope, and includes features such as Boolean, wildcard, and nearness, or proximity search.

The TEI documents contain many entities (people, dates, terms) that are annotated with TEI tags. For example, each person has a `<person>` tag wrapping the name of the individual mentioned. A sample of these tags is shown in table 5.2.

Table 5.2 Sample of TEI entity annotations for people, dates, glossary terms, and geolocations. Note that an XML attribute such as `corresp` for persons is used to reference a global dictionary of entities. Annotations are wrappers around text to describe the text. Attributes such as `corresp=""` are key-value pairs within the annotation elements that add specificity to the annotations.

Entity type	Example
Person	`<persName corresp="nixon-richard-m">the president</persName>`
Date	`<date when="1967-06-09">June 9th</date>`
Glossary term	`<gloss target="t_F41">Phantom F-4 aircraft</gloss>`
Geolocations	`<placeName key="t_ROC1">China</placeName>`

XQuery makes it easy to query any XML document for all entities within the document. For example, in figure 5.11 the XPath expression `//person` will return all person elements found in a document including those found at the beginning, in the middle, and at the end.

An important note to this project: it was done on a modest budget, by nontechnical internal staff and limited outside contractors. The internal staff had no prior

Figure 5.11   Each page of the FRUS document lists the entities found on that page. For example, the people and terms referenced in this page are also shown in the right margin of the page. Users can click on each entity for a full definition of that person or term.

experience with native XML systems nor the XQuery language. One member of the staff, a historian by training, learned XQuery over the course of several months and created a prototype website using online examples and assistance from other members of the eXist and TEI community.

There are currently hundreds of completed FRUS volumes in the system, with more being added each month. Search performance has met all the requirements for the site with page rendering and web searches all averaging well under 500ms.

5.7   Case study: managing financial derivatives with MarkLogic

In this case study, we'll look at how a financial institution implemented a commercial, native XML database (MarkLogic) to manage a high-stakes financial derivatives system.

This study is an excellent example of how organizations with highly-variable data are moving away from relational databases even if they're managing high-stakes financial transactions. High-variability data is difficult to store in relational databases, since each variation may need new columns and tables created in a RDBMS as well as new reports.

After reading this study, you'll understand how organizations with high-variability data can use document stores for transactional data. You'll also see how these organizations manage ACID transactions and use database triggers to process event streams.

5.7.1   Why financial derivatives are difficult to store in RDBMSs

This section presents an overview of financial derivatives and provides insight as to why they're not well suited for storage in tables within a RDBMS.

Let's start with a quick comparison. If you purchase items from any web retailer, the information you enter for each item you want to purchase is limited. When you purchase a dress or shirt, you choose the item name or number, size, color, and perhaps a few other details such as the material type or item length. This information fits neatly into the rows of an RDBMS.

Now consider purchasing a complex financial instrument like a derivative, where each item has thousands of parameters and the parameters for every item are different. Most derivatives contain a product ID, but they also contain conditional logic, mathematical equations, lookup tables, decision trees, and even the full text of legal contracts. In short, the information doesn't lend itself to an RDBMS table. Note that it's possible to store the item as a binary large object (BLOB) in a traditional RDBMS, but you wouldn't be able to access any property inside the BLOB for reporting.

5.7.2   An investment bank switches from 20 RDBMSs to one native XML system

A large investment bank was using 20 different RDBMSs to store complex financial instruments called *over-the-counter derivative contracts*, as shown in figure 5.12.

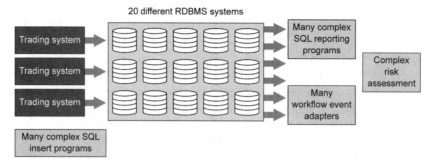

Figure 5.12   A sample data flow of an operational data store (ODS) for a complex financial derivatives system using multiple RDBMSs to store the data. The trading systems each stored data into RDBMSs using complex SQL INSERT statements. SQL SELECT statements were used to extract data. Each new derivative type required custom software to be written.

Highlights of the banks conversion process included these:

- Each system had its own method for ingesting the transactions, converting them to row structures, storing the rows in tables, and reporting on the transactions.
- Custom software was required for each new derivative type so key parameters could be stored and queried.
- In many instances, a single column stored different types of information based on other parameters in the transaction.
- After the data was stored, SQL queries were written to extract information for downstream processing when key events occurred.
- Because different data was shoehorned into the same column based on the derivative type, reporting was complex and error prone.
- Errors resulted in data quality issues and required extensive auditing of output results before the data could be used by downstream systems.

This complex conversion process made it difficult for the bank to get consistent and timely reports and to efficiently manage document workflow. What they needed was a flexible way to store the derivative documents in a standard format such as XML, and to be able to report on the details of the data. If all derivatives were stored as full XML documents, each derivative could contain its unique parameters, without changes to the database.

As a result of this analysis, the bank converted their operational data store (ODS) to a native XML database (MarkLogic) to store their derivative contracts. Figure 5.13 shows how the MarkLogic database was integrated into the financial organization's workflow.

MarkLogic is a commercial document-oriented NoSQL system that has been around since before the term *NoSQL* was popular. Like other document stores, Mark-Logic excels at storing data with high variability and is compliant with W3C standards such as XML, XPath, and XQuery.

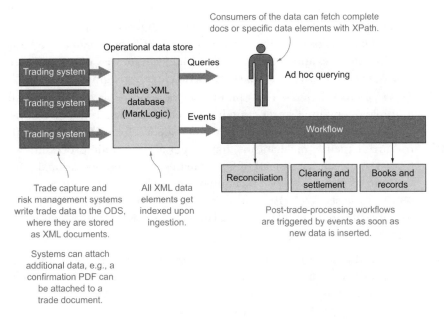

Figure 5.13 Financial derivatives are stored in a native XML database being used as an ODS. Trading systems send XML documents for each trade or contract directly to the database where each element is directly and immediately indexed. Update triggers automatically send event data to a workflow system and system users use simple XPath expressions to perform ad hoc queries.

The bank's new system was ideal as a centralized store for the highly variable derivatives contracts. Since MarkLogic supports ACID transactions and replication, the bank maintained the reliability and availability guarantees it had with its RDBMS. MarkLogic also supports *event triggers* on document collections. These are scripts that are executed each time an XML file is inserted, updated, or deleted.

Whereas RDBMSs require every record in a database to have the same structure and data types, document stores are more flexible and allow organizations to capture the variations in their data in a single database. As we move to our next section, we'll take a look at the major benefits of using a native XML document store.

5.7.3 Business benefits of moving to a native XML document store

The move to a document-centric architecture resulted in the following tangible benefits to the organization:

- *Faster development*—New instrument types added to the system by the front office traders didn't require additional software development, and therefore could be supported in a matter of hours rather than days, weeks, or even months.
- *Higher data quality*—As new derivatives were loaded into the system as XML documents, the system was able to append the document with additional XML

elements needed to more precisely describe the derivative. Downstream analysis and reporting became easier to manage and less error prone.

- *Better risk management*—New reporting capabilities aggregated the bank's position in real time, and provided an instant, accurate view of exposure to certain risk aspects such as counter-parties, currencies, or geographies.

- *Lower operational costs*—The elimination of processing errors associated with multiple operational stores containing conflicting data reduced cost per trade; the reduction of database administrators needed from 10 to 1 lowered human resource expense; mechanisms that trigger all post-trade processing workflows from a single source instead of 20 databases increased operational efficiencies; and the ability to query the content of each individual derivative lowered reporting costs. With its new infrastructure, the bank didn't need to add resources to meet regulators' escalating demands for more transparency and increased stress-testing frequency.

In addition to the more tangible benefits of the new system, the bank was able to bring new products to market faster and perform more detailed quality checks on diverse data. As a result of the new-found confidence in the data quality and accuracy, the solution was adopted by other parts of the bank.

5.7.4 *Project results*

The new MarkLogic system allowed the bank to cut the costs of building and maintaining an operational data store for complex derivatives. In addition, the bank became more responsive to the needs of the organization when new derivatives needed to be added. Derivative contracts are now kept in a semantically precise and flexible XML format while maintaining high data integrity, even as the format moves into remote reporting and workflow systems. These changes had a positive impact on the entire lifecycle of derivative contract management.

5.8 *Summary*

If you talk with people who've been using native XML databases for several years, they tell you they're happy with these systems, and express their reluctance to return to RDBMSs. Their primary reason for liking native XML systems isn't centered around performance issues, although there are commercial native XML databases such as MarkLogic that store petabtyes of information. Their primary reason is related to increased developer productivity and the ability for nonprogrammers to be able to participate in the development process.

Seasoned software developers have exposure to good training and they frequently use tools customized to the XML development process. They have large libraries of XQuery code that can quickly be customized to create new applications in a short period of time. The ability to quickly create new applications shortens development cycles and helps new products make tight time-to-market deadlines.

Although XML is frequently associated with slow processing speeds, this often has more to do with a specific implementation of an XML parser or a slow virtual machine. It has little to do with how native XML systems work. The generation of XML directly from a compressed tree storage structure is usually on par with any other format such as CSV or JSON.

All native XML databases start with the cache-friendly document store pattern and gain from the elimination of middle-tier, object-translation layers. They then leverage the power of standards to gain both portability and reuse of XQuery function libraries. The use of standard metaphors like data folders to manage document collections and simple path expressions in queries make native XML databases easy to set up and administer for nontechnical users. This combination of features has yet to appear in other NoSQL systems, since standardization is only critical as third-party software developers look for application portability.

Despite the W3C's work on extending XQuery for updates and full-text search, there are still areas that lack standardization. Although native XML databases allow you to create custom indexes for things like geolocation, RDF data, and graphs, there are still few standards in these areas, making porting applications between native XML databases more difficult than it needs to be. New work by the W3C, EXPath developers, and other researchers may mitigate these problems in the future. If these standards continue to be developed, XQuery-based document stores may become a more robust platform for NoSQL developers.

The cache-friendliness of documents and the parallel nature of the FLWOR statement make native XML databases inherently more scalable than SQL systems. In the next chapter, we'll focus on the some of the techniques NoSQL systems use when managing large datasets.

5.9 Further reading

- eXist-db. http://exist-db.org/.
- EXPath. http://expath.org.
- JSONiq. "The JSON Query Language." http://www.jsoniq.org.
- MarkLogic. http://www.marklogic.com.
- "Metcalfe's Law." Wikipedia. http://mng.bz/XqMT.
- "Network effect." Wikipedia. http://mng.bz/7dIQ.
- Oracle. "Oracle Berkeley DB XML & XQuery." http://mng.bz/6w3z.
- TEI. "TEI: Text Encoding Initiative." http://www.tei-c.org.
- W3C. "EXPath Community Group." http://mng.bz/O3j8.
- W3C. "XML Query Use Cases." http://mng.bz/h25P.
- W3C. "XML Schema Part 2: Datatypes Second Edition." http://mng.bz/F8Gx.
- W3C. "XQuery and XPath Full Text 1.0." http://mng.bz/Bd9E.
- W3C. "XQuery implementations." http://mng.bz/49rG.
- W3C. "XQuery Update Facility 1.0." http://mng.bz/SN6T.
- XSPARQL. http://xsparql.deri.org.

Part 3

NoSQL solutions

Part 3 is a tour of how NoSQL solutions solve the real-world business problems of big data, search, high availability, and agility. As you go through each chapter, you'll be presented with a business problem, and then see how one or more NoSQL technologies can be cost-effectively implemented to result in a positive return on investment for an organization.

Chapter 6 tackles the issues of big data and linear scalability. You'll see how NoSQL systems leverage large numbers of commodity CPUs to solve large dataset and big data problems. You'll also get an in-depth review of MapReduce and the need for parallel processing.

In chapter 7 we identify the key features associated with a strong search system and show you how NoSQL systems can be used to create better search applications.

Chapter 8 covers how NoSQL systems are used to address the issues of high availability and minimal downtime.

Chapter 9 looks at agility and how NoSQL systems can help organizations quickly respond to changing organizational needs. Many people who are new to the NoSQL movement underestimate how constraining RDBMSs can be when market demand or business conditions change. This chapter shows how NoSQL systems can be more adaptable to changing system and market requirements and provide a competitive edge to an organization.

Using NoSQL
to manage big data

> *By improving our ability to extract knowledge and insights from large and complex collections of digital data, the initiative promises to help solve some the Nation's most pressing challenges.*
>> —US Federal Government,
>> "Big Data Research and Development Initiative"

Have you ever wanted to analyze a large amount of data gathered from log files or files you've found on the web? The need to quickly analyze large volumes of data is the number-one reason organizations leave the world of single-processor RDBMSs and move toward NoSQL solutions. You may recall our discussion in chapter 1 on the key business drivers: volume, velocity, variability, and agility. The first two, volume and velocity, are the most relevant to big data problems.

Twenty years ago, companies managed datasets that contained approximately a million internal sales transactions, stored on a single processor in a relational database. As organizations generated more data from internal and external sources, datasets expanded to billions and trillions of items. The amount of data made it difficult for organizations to continue to use a single system to process this data. They had to learn how to distribute the tasks among many processors. This is what is known as a big data problem.

Today, using a NoSQL solution to solve your big data problems gives you some unique ways to handle and manage your big data. By moving data to queries, using hash rings to distribute the load, using replication to scale your reads, and allowing the database to distribute queries evenly to your data nodes, you can manage your data and keep your systems running fast.

What's driving the focus on solving big data problems? First, the amount of publicly available information on the web has grown exponentially since the late 1990s and is expected to continue to increase. In addition, the availability of low-cost sensors lets organizations collect data from everything; for instance, from farms, wind turbines, manufacturing plants, vehicles, and meters monitoring home energy consumption. These trends make it strategically important for organizations to efficiently and rapidly process and analyze large datasets.

Now let's look at how NoSQL systems, with their inherently horizontal scale-out architectures, are ideal for tackling big data problems. We'll look at several strategies that NoSQL systems use to scale horizontally on commodity hardware. We'll see how NoSQL systems move queries to the data, not data to the queries. We'll see how they use the hash rings to evenly distribute the data on a cluster and use replication to scale reads. All these strategies allow NoSQL systems to distribute the workload evenly and eliminate performance bottlenecks.

6.1   What is a big data NoSQL solution?

So what exactly is a big data problem? A *big data* class problem is any business problem that's so large that it can't be easily managed using a single processor. Big data problems force you to move away from a single-processor environment toward the more complex world of distributed computing. Though great for solving big data problems, distributed computing environments come with their own set of challenges (see figure 6.1).

We want to stress that big data isn't the same as NoSQL. As we've defined NoSQL in this book, it's more than dealing with large datasets. NoSQL includes concepts and use cases that can be managed by a single processor and have a positive impact on agility and data quality. But we consider big data problems a primary use case for NoSQL.

Before you assume you have a big data problem, you should consider whether you need *all* of your data or a *subset* of your data to solve your problem. Using a statistical sample allows you to use a subset of your data and look for patterns in the subset. The

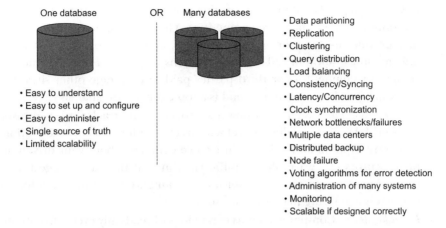

One database   OR   Many databases

• Easy to understand
• Easy to set up and configure
• Easy to administer
• Single source of truth
• Limited scalability

• Data partitioning
• Replication
• Clustering
• Query distribution
• Load balancing
• Consistency/Syncing
• Latency/Concurrency
• Clock synchronization
• Network bottlenecks/failures
• Multiple data centers
• Distributed backup
• Node failure
• Voting algorithms for error detection
• Administration of many systems
• Monitoring
• Scalable if designed correctly

Figure 6.1   One or many databases? Here are some of the challenges you face when you move from a single processor to a distributed computing system. Moving to a distributed environment is a nontrivial endeavor and should be done only if the business problem really warrants the need to handle large data volumes in a short period of time. This is why platforms like Hadoop are complex and require a complex framework to make things easier for the application developer.

trick is to come up with a process to ensure the sample you choose is a fair representation of the full dataset.

You should also consider how quickly you need your data processed. Many data analysis problems can be handled by a batch-type solution running on a single processor; you may not need an immediate answer. The key is to understand the true time-critical nature of your situation.

Now that you know that distributed databases are more complex than a single processor system and there are alternatives to using a full dataset, let's look at why organizations are moving toward these complex systems. Why is the ability to handle big data strategically important to many organizations? Answering this question involves understanding the external factors that are driving the big data marketplace.

Here are some typical big data use cases:

- *Bulk image processing*—Organizations like NASA regularly receive terabytes of incoming data from satellites or even rovers on Mars. NASA uses a large number of servers to process these images and perform functions like image enhancement and photo stitching. Medical imaging systems like CAT scans and MRIs need to convert raw image data into formats that are useful to doctors and patients. Custom imaging hardware has been found to be more expensive than renting a large number of processors on the cloud when they're needed. For example, the *New York Times* converted 3.3 million scans of old newspaper articles into web formats using tools like Amazon EC2 and Hadoop for a few hundred dollars.

- *Public web page data*—Publicly accessible pages are full of information that organizations can use to be more competitive. They contain news stories, RSS feeds, new product information, product reviews, and blog postings. Not all of the information is authentic. There are millions of pages of fake product reviews created by competitors or third parties paid to disparage other sites. Finding out which product reviews are valid is a topic for careful analysis.

- *Remote sensor data*—Small, low-power sensors can now track almost any aspect of our world. Devices installed on vehicles track location, speed, acceleration, and fuel consumption, and tell your insurance company about your driving habits. Road sensors can warn about traffic jams in real time and suggest alternate routes. You can even track the moisture in your garden, lawn, and indoor plants to suggest a watering plan for your home.

- *Event log data*—Computer systems create logs of read-only events from web page hits (also called *clickstreams*), email messages sent, or login attempts. Each of these events can help organizations understand who's using what resources and when systems may not be performing according to specification. Event log data can be fed into operational intelligence tools to send alerts to users when key indicators fall out of acceptable ranges.

- *Mobile phone data*—Every time users move to new locations, applications can track these events. You can see when your friends are around you or when customers walk through your retail store. Although there are privacy issues involved in accessing this data, it's forming a new type of event stream that can be used in innovative ways to give companies a competitive advantage.

- *Social media data*—Social networks such as Twitter, Facebook, and LinkedIn provide a continuous real-time data feed that can be used to see relationships and trends. Each site creates data feeds that you can use to look at trends in customer mood or get feedback on your own as well as competitor products.

- *Game data*—Games that run on PCs, video game consoles, and mobile devices have back-end datasets that need to scale quickly. These games store and share high scores for all users as well as game data for each player. Game site back ends must be able to scale by orders of magnitude if viral marketing campaigns catch on with their users.

- *Open linked data*—In chapter 4 we looked at how organizations can publish public datasets that can be ingested by your systems. Not only is this data large, but it may require complex tools to reconcile, remove duplication, and find invalid items.

When looking at these use cases, you see that some problems can be described as independent parallel transforms since the output from one transform isn't used as an input to another. This includes problems like image and signal processing. Their focus is on the efficient and reliable data transformation at scale. These use cases don't need the query or transactions support provided by many NoSQL systems. They read and write to key-value stores or distributed filesystems like *Amazon's Simple Storage Service (S3)* or *Hadoop Distributed File System (HDFS)* and may not need the advanced features of a document store or an RDBMS.

Other use cases are more demanding and need more features. Big data problems like event log data and game data do need to store their data directly into structures that can be queried and analyzed, so they will need different NoSQL solutions.

To be a good candidate for a general class of big data problems, NoSQL solutions should

- Be efficient with input and output and scale linearly with growing data size.
- Be operationally efficient. Organizations can't afford to hire many people to run the servers.
- Require that reports and analyses be performed by nonprogrammers using simple tools—not every business can afford a full-time Java programmer to write on-demand queries.
- Meet the challenges of distributed computing, including consideration of latency between systems and eventual node failures.
- Meet both the needs of overnight batch processing economy-of-scale and time-critical event processing.

RDBMS can, with enough time and effort, be customized to solve some big data problems. Applications can be rewritten to distribute SQL queries to many processors and merge the results of the queries. Databases can be redesigned to remove joins between tables that are physically located on different nodes. SQL systems can be configured to use replication and other data synchronization processes. Yet these steps all take considerable time and money. In the long run, it might make sense to move to a framework that has already solved many of these problems.

Original SQL systems were revolutionary with their standardized *declarative language*. By declarative, we mean that a developer can "declare" *what* data they want and yet not be concerned with *how* they get it or *where* they get the data from. SQL developers want and need to be isolated from the question of how to optimize a query, how to fetch the data, and what server the data is on. Unless your database isolates you from these questions, you lose many of the benefits of declarative systems like SQL.

NoSQL systems try to isolate the developers from the complexities of distributed computing. They provide interfaces that allow users to tell a cluster how many nodes a record must be read to or written from before a valid response is returned. The goal is to keep the benefits of both declarative systems and horizontal scalability as you move to distributed computing platforms.

If NoSQL systems really do have better horizontal scaling characteristics, you need to be able to measure these characteristics. So let's take a look at how horizontal scalability and NoSQL might be measured.

6.2   *Getting linear scaling in your data center*

One of the core concepts in big data is *linear scaling*. When a system has linear scaling, you automatically get a proportional performance gain each time you add a new processor to your cluster, as shown in figure 6.2.

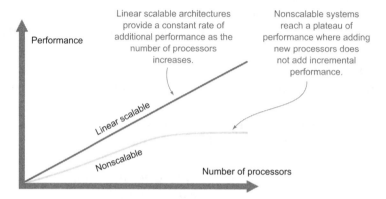

Figure 6.2   How some systems continue to add performance as more nodes are added to the system. Performance can be a measure of read operations, write operations, or transformations. Systems are considered linearly scalable if the performance curve doesn't flatten out at some threshold. Many components can cause bottlenecks in performance, so testing for linear scalability is critical in system design.

There are additional types of scaling that might be important to you based on the type of problem you're trying to solve. For example:

- *Scaling independent transformations*—Many big data problems are driven by discrete transformations on individual items without interaction among the items. These types of problems tend to be the easiest to solve: simply add a new node to your cluster. Image transformation is a good example of this.
- *Scaling reads*—In order to keep your read latency low, you must replicate your data on multiple servers and move the servers as close to the users as possible using tools like *content distribution networks (CDNs)*. CDNs keep copies of data in each geographic region so that the distance that data moves over a network can be minimized. The challenge is that the more servers you have and the farther apart they are, the more difficult it is to keep them in sync.
- *Scaling totals*—Scaling totals involves how quickly you can perform simple math functions (count, sum, average) on large quantities of data. This type of scaling is most often addressed by OLAP systems by precalculating subset totals in structures called *aggregates* so that most of the math is already done. For example, if you have the total daily hits for a website, the weekly total is the sum of each day in a particular week.
- *Scaling writes*—In order to avoid blocking writes, it's best to have multiple servers that accept writes and never block each other. To make reads of these writes

consistent, the servers should be as close to each other as possible. Users that write their own data should always be able to read it back in a consistent state.

- *Scaling availability*—Duplicate the writes onto multiple servers in data centers in distinct geographic regions. If one data center experiences an outage, the other data centers can supply the data. Scaling availability keeps replica copies in sync and automates the switchover if one system fails.

Figure 6.3 is an example of linear write scalability analysis done by Netflix using an Amazon Elastic Compute Cloud (EC2) system.

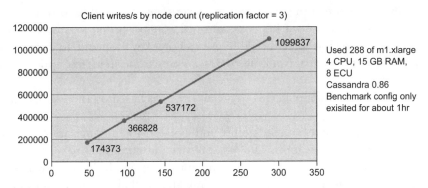

Figure 6.3 An example of a Cassandra cluster that has been used to simulate a large number of writes per second on multiple nodes. The start of the simulation shows around 50 nodes accepting 170,000 writes per second. As the cluster grows to over 300 nodes, the system can accept over a million writes per second. The simulation was done on a rented cluster of Amazon Elastic Compute Cloud (EC2). The ability to "rent" CPUs on an hourly basis has made it easy to test a NoSQL system for linear scalability. (Reference: Netflix)

The ability to scale linearly is critical to cost-effective big data processing. But the ability to read and write single records isn't the only concern of many business problems. Systems must also be able to effectively perform queries on your data, as you'll see next.

6.3   *Understanding linear scalability and expressivity*

What's the relationship between scalability and your ability to perform complex queries on your data? As we mentioned earlier, linear scalability is the ability to get a consistent amount of performance improvement as you add additional processors to your cluster. *Expressivity* is the ability to perform fine-grained queries on individual elements of your dataset.

Understanding how well each NoSQL technology performs in terms of scalability and expressivity is necessary when you're selecting a NoSQL solution. To select the right system, you'll need to identify the scalability and expressivity requirements of your system and then make sure the system that you select meets both of these criteria. Scalability and expressivity can be difficult to quantify, and vendor claims may not match actual performance for a particular business problem. If you're making critical business decisions, we recommend you create a pilot project and simulate an actual load using leased cloud systems.

Let's look at two extreme cases: a key-value store and a document store. After reviewing the vendor brochures, you feel that both of these systems have similar linear scalability rules that meet your business growth needs. Which one is right for your project?

The answer lies in how you want to retrieve the data from each of these systems. If you only need to store images and using a URL to specify an image is appropriate, then a key-value store is the right choice. If you need to be able to store items and query on a specific subset of items based on the items' properties, then a key-value store isn't a good match since the value portion of a key is opaque to queries. In contrast, a document store that can index dates, amounts, and item descriptions might be a better match.

Figure 6.4 shows a sample chart that ranks systems based on their scalability versus expressivity.

The challenge is that both scalability and expressivity rankings are dependent on your specific business situation. The scalability requirements for some systems might focus on a high number of reads per second and others might focus on writes per second. Other scalability requirements might only specify that a large amount of data be transformed overnight. In the same way, your expressivity could include the requirements for ranked full-text search or the ability to query for annotations within text.

If you're involved in the software selection process, you want to remember that there's seldom one perfect solution. The scalability and expressivity analysis is a good example of this trade-off analysis. As we look at other tools to help you make these trade-off decisions, you'll see that understanding your data will help you classify your big data problems.

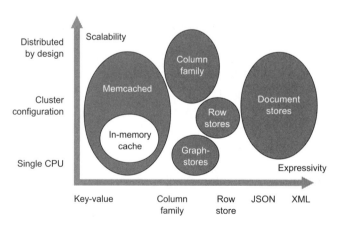

Figure 6.4 **A sample of how you might rank scalability (vertical axis) and expressivity (horizontal axis) for your requirements. Simple key-value stores are almost always the least expressive but most scalable. Document stores are usually the most expressive. How you rate scalability and expressivity may depend on your business situation.**

6.4 Understanding the types of big data problems

There are many types of big data problems, each requiring a different combination of NoSQL systems. After you've categorized your data and determined its type, you'll find there are different solutions. How you build your own big data classification system might be different from this example, but the process of differentiating data types should be similar.

Figure 6.5 is a good example of a high-level big data classification system.

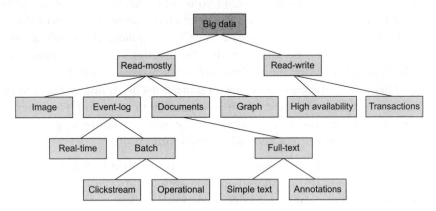

Figure 6.5 **A sample of a taxonomy of big data types. This chapter deals with read-mostly problems. Chapter 8 has a focus on read/write big data problems that need high availability.**

Let's take a look at some ways you classify big data problems and see how NoSQL systems are changing the way organizations use data.

- *Read-mostly*—Read-mostly data is the most common classification. It includes data that's created once and rarely altered. This type of data is typically found in data warehouse applications but is also identified as a set of non-RDBMS items like images or video, event-logging data, published documents, or graph data. Event data includes things like retail sales events, hits on a website, system logging data, or real-time sensor data.
- *Log events*—When operational events occur in your enterprise, you can record it in a log file and include a timestamp so you know when the event occurred. Log events may be a web page click or an out-of-memory warning on a disk drive. In the past, the cost and amount of event data produced were so large that many organizations opted not to gather or analyze it. Today, NoSQL systems are changing companies' thoughts on the value of log data as the cost to store and analyze it is more affordable.

  The ability to cost-effectively gather and store log events from all computers in your enterprise has lead to BI *operational intelligence* systems. Operational intelligence goes beyond analyzing trends in your web traffic or retail transactions. It can integrate information from network monitoring systems so you can detect problems before they impact your customers. Cost-effective NoSQL systems can be part of good operations management solutions.

- *Full-text documents*—This category of data includes any document that contains natural-language text like the English language. An important aspect of document stores is that you can query the entire contents of your office document in the same way you would query rows in your SQL system.

  This means that you can create new reports that combine traditional data in RDBMSs as well as the data within your office documents. For example, you could create a single query that extracted all the authors of titles of PowerPoint slides that contained the keywords *NoSQL* or *big data*. The result of this list of authors could then be filtered with a list of titles in the HR database to show which people had the title of *Data Architect* or *Solution Architect*.

  This is a good example of how organizations are trying to tap into the hidden skills that already exist within an organization for training and mentorship. Integrating documents into what can be queried is opening new doors in knowledge management and efficient staff utilization.

As you can see, you might encounter many different flavors of big data. As we move forward, you'll see how using a shared-nothing architecture can help you with most of your big data problems, whether they're read-mostly or read/write data.

6.5   *Analyzing big data with a shared-nothing architecture*

There are three ways that resources can be shared between computer systems: shared RAM, shared disk, and shared-nothing. Figure 6.6 shows a comparison of these three distributed computing architectures.

Of the three alternatives, a shared-nothing architecture is most cost effective in terms of cost per processor when you're using commodity hardware. As we continue,

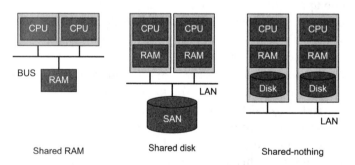

Figure 6.6   Three ways to share resources. The left panel shows a shared RAM architecture, where many CPUs access a single shared RAM over a high-speed bus. This system is ideal for large graph traversal. The middle panel shows a shared disk system, where processors have independent RAM but share disk using a storage area network (SAN). The right panel shows an architecture used in big data solutions: cache-friendly, using low-cost commodity hardware, and a shared-nothing architecture.

you'll see how each of these architectures works to solve big data problems with different types of data.

Of the architectural data patterns we've discussed so far (row store, key-value store, graph store, document store, and Bigtable store), only two (key-value store and document store) lend themselves to cache-friendliness. Bigtable stores scale well on shared-nothing architectures because their row-column identifiers are similar to key-value stores. But row stores and graph stores aren't cache-friendly since they don't allow a large BLOB to be referenced by a short key that can be stored in the cache.

For graph traversals to be fast, the entire graph should be in main memory. This is why graph stores work most efficiently when you have enough RAM to hold the graph. If you can't keep your graph in RAM, graph stores will try to swap the data to disk, which will decrease graph query performance by a factor of 1,000. The only way to combat the problem is to move to a shared-memory architecture, where multiple threads all access a large RAM structure without the graph data moving outside of the shared RAM.

The rule of thumb is if you have over a terabyte of highly connected graph data and you need real-time analysis of this graph, you should be looking for an alternative to a shared-nothing architecture. A single CPU with 64 GB of RAM won't be sufficient to hold your graph in RAM. Even if you work hard to only load the necessary data elements into RAM, your links may traverse other nodes that need to be swapped in from disk. This will make your graph queries slow. We'll look into alternatives to this in a case study later in this chapter.

Knowing the hardware options available to big data is an important first step, but distributing software in a cluster is also important. Let's take a look at how software can be distributed in a cluster.

6.6   *Choosing distribution models: master-slave versus peer-to-peer*

From a distribution perspective, there are two main models: master-slave and peer-to-peer. Distribution models determine the responsibility for processing data when a request is made.

Understanding the pros and cons of each distribution model is important when you're looking at a potential big data solution. Peer-to-peer models may be more resilient to failure than master-slave models. Some master-slave distribution models have single points of failure that might impact your system availability, so you might need to take special care when configuring these systems.

Distribution models get to the heart of the question *who's in charge here?* There are two ways to answer this question: one node or all nodes. In the master-slave model, one node is in charge (master). When there's no single node with a special role in taking charge, you have a peer-to-peer distribution model.

Figure 6.7 shows how these models each work.

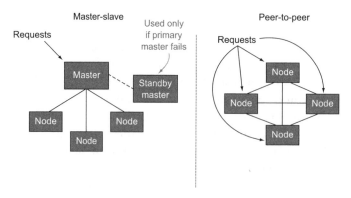

Figure 6.7   Master-slave versus peer-to-peer—the panel on the left illustrates a master-slave configuration where all incoming database requests (reads or writes) are sent to a single master node and redistributed from there. The master node is called the NameNode in Hadoop. This node keeps a database of all the other nodes in the cluster and the rules for distributing requests to each node. The panel on the right shows how the peer-to-peer model stores all the information about the cluster on each node in the cluster. If any node crashes, the other nodes can take over and processing can continue.

Let's look at the trade-offs. With a master-slave distribution model, the role of managing the cluster is done on a single master node. This node can run on specialized hardware such as RAID drives to lower the probability that it crashes. The cluster can also be configured with a standby master that's continually updated from the master node. The challenge with this option is that it's difficult to test the standby master without jeopardizing the health of the cluster. Failure of the standby master to take over from the master node is a real concern for high-availability operations.

Peer-to-peer systems distribute the responsibility of the master to each node in the cluster. In this situation, testing is much easier since you can remove any node in the cluster and the other nodes will continue to function. The disadvantage of peer-to-peer networks is that there's an increased complexity and communication overhead that must occur for all nodes to be kept up to date with the cluster status.

The initial versions of Hadoop (frequently referred to as the 1.x versions) were designed to use a master-slave architecture with the NameNode of a cluster being responsible for managing the status of the cluster. NameNodes usually don't deal with any MapReduce data themselves. Their job is to manage and distribute queries to the correct nodes on the cluster. Hadoop 2.x versions are designed to remove single points of failure from a Hadoop cluster.

Using the right distribution model will depend on your business requirements: if high availability is a concern, a peer-to-peer network might be the best solution. If you can manage your big data using batch jobs that run in off hours, then the simpler master-slave model might be best. As we move to the next section, you'll see how Map-Reduce systems can be used in multiprocessor configurations to process your big data.

6.7   *Using MapReduce to transform your data over distributed systems*

Now let's take an in-depth look to see how MapReduce systems can be used to process large datasets on multiple processors. You'll see how MapReduce clusters work in conjunction with distributed filesystems such as the Apache Hadoop Distributed File System (HDFS) and review how NoSQL systems such as Hadoop use both the map and reduce functions to transform data that's stored in NoSQL databases.

If you've been moving data between SQL systems, you're familiar with the extract, load, and transform (ETL) process. The ETL process is typically used when extracting data from an operational RDBMS to transfer it into the staging area of a data warehouse. We reviewed this process and ETL in chapter 3 when we covered OLAP systems.

ETL systems are typically written in SQL. They use the SELECT statement on a source system and INSERT, UPDATE, or DELETE functions on the destination system. SQL-based ETL systems usually don't have the inherent ability to use a large number of processors to do their work. This single-processor bottleneck is common in data warehouse systems as well as areas of big data.

To solve this type of problem, organizations have moved to a distributed transformation model built around the map and reduce functions. To effectively distribute work evenly over a cluster of processors, the output of a map phase must be a set of key-value pairs where part of the key structure is used to correlate results into the reduce phase. These functions are designed to be inherently linearly scalable using a large number of shared-nothing processors.

Yet, at its core, the fundamental process of MapReduce is the parallel transformation of data from one form to another. MapReduce processes don't require the use of databases in the middle of the transformation. To work effectively on big data problems, MapReduce operations do require a large amount of input and output. In an ideal situation, data transformed by a MapReduce server will have all the input on the local disk of a shared-nothing cluster and write the results to the same local disk. Moving large datasets in and out of a MapReduce cluster can be inefficient.

The MapReduce way of processing data is to specify a series of stepwise functions on uniform input data. This process is similar to the functional programming constructs that became popular in the 1950s with the LISP systems at MIT. Functional programming is about taking a function and a list, and returning a list where the function has been applied to each member of the list. What's different about modern MapReduce is all the infrastructure that goes with the reliable and efficient execution of transforms on lists of billions of items. The most popular implementation of the MapReduce algorithm is the Apache Hadoop system.

The Hadoop system doesn't fundamentally change the concepts of mapping and reducing functions. What it does is provide an entire ecosystem of tools to allow map and reduce functions to have linear scalability. It does this by requiring that the output of all map functions return a key-value pair. This is how work can then be distributed evenly over the nodes of a Hadoop cluster. Hadoop addresses all of the hard parts of distributed computing for large datasets for you so that you can concentrate on writing the map and reduce operations.

It's also useful to contrast the MapReduce way with RDBMSs. MapReduce is a way of explicitly specifying the steps in a transformation, with the key being to use key-value pairs as a method of distribution to different nodes in a cluster. SQL, on the other hand, attempts to shield you from the process steps it uses to get data from different tables to perform optimal queries.

If you're using Hadoop, MapReduce is a disk-based, batch-oriented process. All input comes from disk, and all output writes to disk. Unlike MapReduce, the results of SQL queries can be loaded directly into RAM. As a result, you'd rarely use the result of a MapReduce operation to populate a web page while users are waiting for a web page to render.

The Hadoop MapReduce process is most similar to the data warehouse process of precalculating sums and totals in an OLAP data warehouse. This process is traditionally done by extracting new transactions each night from an operational data store and converting them to facts and aggregates in an OLAP cube. These aggregates allow sums and totals to be quickly calculated when users are looking for trends in purchasing decisions.

NoSQL systems each vary in how they implement map and reduce functions and how they integrate with existing Hadoop clusters. Some NoSQL systems such as *HBase* are designed to run directly within a Hadoop system. Their default behavior is to read from HDFS and write the results of their transforms to HDFS. By taking this approach, HBase can leverage existing Hadoop infrastructure and optimize input and output processing steps.

Most other NoSQL systems that target big data problems provide their own ways to perform map and reduce functions or to integrate with a Hadoop cluster. For example, MongoDB provides their own map and reduce operations that work directly on MongoDB documents for both input and output. Figure 6.8 shows an example comparing MongoDB map reduce functions with SQL.

Now that you have an understanding of how MapReduce leverages many processors, let's see how it interacts with the underlying filesystems.

6.7.1 *MapReduce and distributed filesystems*

One of the strengths of a Hadoop system is that it's designed to work directly with a filesystem that supports big data problems. As you'll see, Hadoop makes big data processing easier by using a filesystem structure that's different from a traditional system.

The Hadoop Distributed File System (HDFS) provides many of the supporting features that MapReduce transforms need to be efficient and reliable. Unlike an ordinary filesystem, it's customized for transparent, reliable, write-once, read-many operations. You can think of HDFS as a fault-tolerant, distributed, key-value store tuned to work with large files.

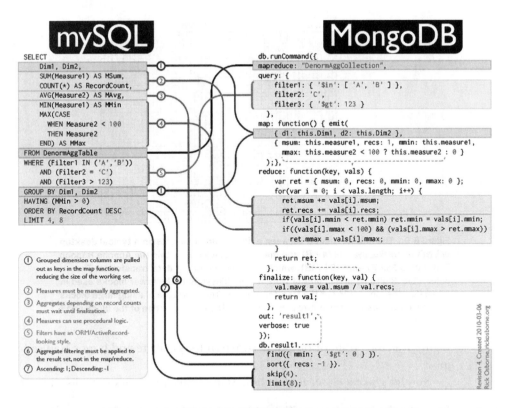

Figure 6.8   A comparison of a mySQL SQL query with MongoDB's map and reduce functions. The queries perform similar functions, but the MongoDB query can easily be distributed over hundreds of processors. (Attribution to Rick Osborne)

Traditional filesystems store data in a single location; if a drive fails, data is restored from a backup drive. By default, files in HDFS are stored in three locations; if a drive fails, the data is automatically replicated to another drive. It's possible to get the same functionality using a fault-tolerant system like RAID drives. But RAID drives are more expensive and difficult to configure on commodity hardware.

HDFSs are different: they use a large (64 megabytes by default) block size to handle data. Figure 6.9 shows how large HDFS blocks are compared to a typical operating system.

HDFS also has other properties that make it different from an ordinary filesystem. You can't update the value of a few bytes in an existing block without deleting the old block and adding an entirely new block. HDFS is designed for large blocks of immutable data that are created once and read many times. Efficient updates aren't a primary consideration for HDFS.

Although HDFS is considered a filesystem, and can be mounted like other filesystems, you don't usually work with HDFS as you would an additional disk drive on your Windows or UNIX system. An HDFS system wouldn't be a good choice for storing typical Microsoft office documents that are updated frequently. HDFS is designed to be a

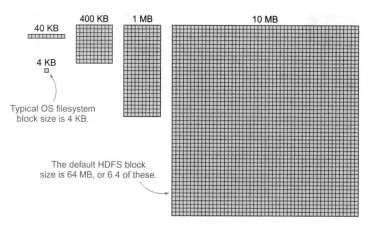

Figure 6.9   The size difference between a filesystem block size on a typical desktop or UNIX operating system (4 KB) and the logical block size within the Apache Hadoop Distributed File System (64 MB), which is optimized for big data transforms. The default block size defines a unit of work for the filesystem. The fewer blocks used in a transfer, the more efficient the transfer process. The downside of using large blocks is that if data doesn't fill an entire physical block, the empty section of the block can't be used.

highly available input or output destination for gigabyte and larger MapReduce batch jobs.

Now let's take a closer look at how MapReduce jobs work over distributed clusters.

6.7.2   *How MapReduce allows efficient transformation of big data problems*

In previous chapters, we looked at MapReduce and its exceptional horizontal scale-out properties. MapReduce is a core component in many big data solutions. Figure 6.10 provides a detailed look at the internal components of a MapReduce job.

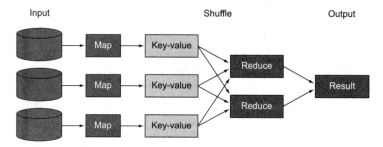

Figure 6.10   The basics of how the map and reduce functions work together to gain linear scalability over big data transforms. The map operation takes input data and creates a uniform set of key-value pairs. In the shuffle phase, which is done automatically by the MapReduce framework, key-value pairs are automatically distributed to the correct reduce node based on the value of the key. The reduce operation takes the key-value pairs and returns consolidated values for each key. It's the job of the MapReduce framework to get the right keys to the right reduce nodes.

The first part of a MapReduce job is the map operation. Map operations retrieve data from your source database and convert it into a series of independent transform operations that can be executed on different processors. The output of all map operations is a key-value structure where the keys are uniform across all input documents. The second phase is the reduce operation. The reduce operation uses the key-value pairs created in the map as input, performs the requested operation, and returns the values you need.

When creating a MapReduce program, you must ensure that the map function is only dependent on the inputs to the map function and that the output of the map operation doesn't change the state of data; it only returns a key-value pair. In MapReduce operations, no other intermediate information can be passed between map functions.

At first glance, it may seem like creating a MapReduce framework would be simple. Realistically, it's not. First, what if your source data is replicated on three or more nodes? Do you move the data between nodes? Not if you want your job to be efficient. Then you must consider which node the map function should run on. How do you assign the right key to the right reduce processor? What happens if one of the map or reduce jobs fails in mid-operation? Do you need to restart the entire batch or can you reassign the work to another node? As you can see, there are many factors to consider and in the end it's not as simple as it appears.

The good news is that if you stick to these rules, a MapReduce framework like Hadoop can do most of the hard work finding the right processor to do the map, making sure the right reduce node gets the input based on the keys, and making sure that the job finishes even if there's hardware failure during the job.

Now that we've covered the types of big data problems and some of the architecture patterns, let's look into the strategies that NoSQL systems use to attack these problems.

6.8 Four ways that NoSQL systems handle big data problems

As you've seen, understanding your big data is important in determining the best solution. Now let's take a look at four of the most popular ways NoSQL systems handle big data challenges.

Understanding these techniques is important when you're evaluating any NoSQL system. Knowing that a product will give you linear scaling with these techniques will help you not only to select the right NoSQL system, but also to set up and configure your NoSQL system correctly.

6.8.1 Moving queries to the data, not data to the queries

With the exception of large graph databases, most NoSQL systems use commodity processors that each hold a subset of the data on their local shared-nothing drives. When a client wants to send a general query to all nodes that hold data, it's more efficient to send the query to each node than it is to transfer large datasets to a central processor. This may seem obvious, but it's amazing how many traditional databases still can't distribute queries and aggregate query results.

This simple rule helps you understand how NoSQL databases can have dramatic performance advantages over systems that weren't designed to distribute queries to the data nodes. Consider an RDBMS that has tables distributed over two different nodes. In order for the SQL query to work, information about rows on one table must all be moved across the network to the other node. Larger tables result in more data movement, which results in slower queries. Think of all the steps involved. The tables can be extracted, serialized, sent through the network interface, transmitted over networks, reassembled, and then compared on the server with the SQL query.

Keeping all the data within each data node in the form of logical documents means that only the query itself and the final result need to be moved over a network. This keeps your big data queries fast.

6.8.2   *Using hash rings to evenly distribute data on a cluster*

One of the most challenging problems with distributed databases is figuring out a consistent way of assigning a document to a processing node. Using a *hash ring* technique to evenly distribute big data loads over many servers with a randomly generated 40-character key is a good way to evenly distribute a network load.

Hash rings are common in big data solutions because they consistently determine how to assign a piece of data to a specific processor. Hash rings take the leading bits of a document's hash value and use this to determine which node the document should be assigned. This allows any node in a cluster to know what node the data lives on and how to adapt to new assignment methods as your data grows. Partitioning keys into ranges and assigning different key ranges to specific nodes is known as *keyspace management*. Most NoSQL systems, including MapReduce, use keyspace concepts to manage distributed computing problems.

In chapters 3 and 4 we reviewed the concept of hashing, consistent hashing, and key-value stores. A hash ring uses these same concepts to assign an item of data to a specific node in a NoSQL database cluster. Figure 6.11 is a diagram of a sample hash ring with four nodes.

As you can see from the figure, each input will be assigned to a node based on the 40-character random key. One or more nodes in your cluster will be responsible for storing this key-to-node mapping algorithm. As your database grows, you'll update the algorithm so that each new node will also be assigned some range of key values. The algorithm also needs to replicate items with these ranges from the old nodes to the new nodes.

The concept of a hash ring can also be extended to include the requirement that an item must be stored on multiple nodes. When a new item is created, the hash ring rules might indicate both a primary and a secondary copy of where an item is stored. If the node that contains the primary fails, the system can look up the node where the secondary item is stored.

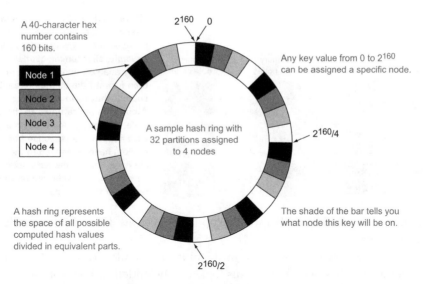

Figure 6.11　Using a hash ring to assign a node to a key that uses a 40-character hex number. This number can be expressed in 2^{160} bits. The first bits in the hash can be used to map a document directly to a node. This allows documents to be randomly assigned to nodes and new assignment rules to be updated as you add nodes to your cluster.

6.8.3　*Using replication to scale reads*

In chapter 3 we showed how databases use replication to make backup copies of data in real time. We also showed how load balancers can work with the application layer to distribute queries to the correct database server. Now let's look at how using replication allows you to horizontally scale read requests. Figure 6.12 shows this structure.

This replication strategy works well in most cases. There are only a few times when you must be concerned about the lag time between a write to the read/write node and a client reading that same record from a replica. One of the most common operations after a write is a read of that same record. If a client does a write and then an immediate read from that same node, there's no problem. The problem occurs if a read

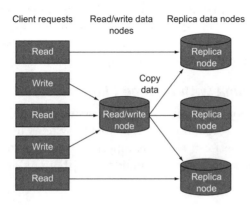

Figure 6.12　How you can replicate data to speed read performance in NoSQL systems. All incoming client requests enter from the left. All reads can be directed to any node, either a primary read/write node or a replica node. All write transactions can be sent to a central read/write node that will update the data and then automatically send the updates to replica nodes. The time between the write to the primary and the time the update arrives on the replica nodes determines how long it takes for reads to return consistent results.

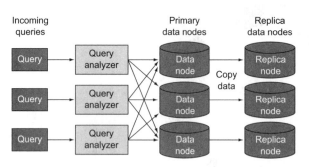

Figure 6.13 NoSQL systems move the query to a data node, but don't move data to a query node. In this example, all incoming queries arrive at query analyzer nodes. These nodes then forward the queries to each data node. If they have matches, the documents are returned to the query node. The query won't return until all data nodes (or a response from a replica) have responded to the original query request. If the data node is down, a query can be redirected to a replica of the data node.

occurs from a replica node before the update happens. This is an example of an inconsistent read.

The best way to avoid this type of problem is to only allow reads to the same write node after a write has been done. This logic can be added to a session or state management system at the application layer. Almost all distributed databases relax database consistency rules when a large number of nodes permit writes. If your application needs fast read/write consistency, you must deal with it at the application layer.

6.8.4   *Letting the database distribute queries evenly to data nodes*

In order to get high performance from queries that span multiple nodes, it's important to separate the concerns of query evaluation from query execution. Figure 6.13 shows this structure.

The approach shown in figure 6.13 is one of moving the query to the data rather than moving the data to the query. This is an important part of NoSQL big data strategies. In this instance, moving the query is handled by the database server, and distribution of the query and waiting for all nodes to respond is the sole responsibility of the database, not the application layer.

This approach is somewhat similar to the concept of *federated search*. Federated search takes a single query and distributes it to distinct servers and then combines the results together to give the user the impression they're searching a single system. In some cases, these servers may be in different geographic regions. In this case, you're sending your query to a single cluster that's not only performing search queries on a single local cluster but also performing update and delete operations.

6.9   *Case study: event log processing with Apache Flume*

In this case study, you'll see how organizations use NoSQL systems to gather and report on distributed *event logs*. Many organizations use NoSQL systems to process their event log data because the datasets can be large, especially in distributed environments. As you can imagine, each server generates hundreds of thousands of event records every day. If you multiply that by the number of servers to monitor, well, you get the picture: it's big data.

Few organizations store their raw event log data in RDBMSs, because they don't need the update and transactional processing features. Because NoSQL systems scale and integrate with tools like MapReduce, they're cost effective when you're looking to analyze event log data.

Though we'll use the term *event log data* to describe this data, a more precise term is timestamped *immutable data* streams. Timestamped immutable data is created once but never updated, so you don't have to worry about update operations. You only need to focus on the reliable storage of the records and the efficient analysis of the data, which is the case with many big data problems.

Distributed log file analysis is critical to allow an organization to quickly find errors in systems and take corrective action before services are disrupted. It's also a good example of the need for both real-time analysis and batch analysis of large datasets.

6.9.1 Challenges of event log data analysis

If you've ever been responsible for monitoring web or database servers, you know that you can see what's happening on a server by looking at its detailed log file. Log events add a record to the log file when your system starts up, when a job runs, and when warnings or errors occur.

Events are classified according to their *severity level* using a standardized set of severity codes. An example of these codes (from lowest to highest severity level) might be TRACE, DEBUG, INFO, WARNING, ERROR, or FATAL. These codes have been standardized in the Java Log4j system.

Most events found in log files are informational (INFO level) events. They tell you how fast a web page is served or how quickly a query is executed. Informational events are generally used for looking at system averages and monitoring performance. Other event types such as WARNING, ERROR, or FATAL events are critical and should notify an operator to take action or intervene.

Filtering and reporting on log events on a single system is straightforward and can be done by writing a script that searches for keywords in the log file. In contrast, big data problems occur when you have hundreds or thousands of systems all generating events on servers around the world. The challenge is to create a mechanism to get immediate notification of critical events and allow the noncritical events to be ignored.

A common solution to this problem is to create two channels of communication between a server and the operations center. Figure 6.14 shows how these channels work. At the top of the diagram, you see where all events are pulled from the sever, transformed, and then the aggregates updated in a reliable filesystem such as HDFS. In the lower part of the diagram, you see the second channel, where critical events are retrieved from the server and sent directly to the operations dashboard for immediate action.

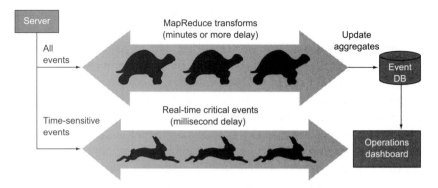

Figure 6.14   Critical time-sensitive events must be quickly extracted from log event streams and routed directly to an operators console. Other events are processed in bulk using MapReduce transforms after they've been stored in a reliable filesystem such as HDFS.

To meet these requirements, your system must meet the following objectives:

- It must filter out time-sensitive events based on a set of rules.
- It must efficiently and reliably transmit all events in large batch files to a centralized event store.
- It must reliably route all time-sensitive events using a fast channel.

Let's see how you can meet these objectives with Apache Flume.

6.9.2   How Apache Flume works to gather distributed event data

Apache Flume is an open source Java framework specifically designed to process event log data. The word *flume* refers to a water-filled trough used to transport logs in the lumber industry. Flume is designed to provide a distributed, reliable, and available system for efficiently collecting, aggregating, and moving large amounts of log data from different sources to a centralized data store. Because Flume was created by members of the Hadoop community, HDFS and HBase are the most common storage targets.

Flume is built around the concept of a flow pipeline, as depicted in figure 6.15.

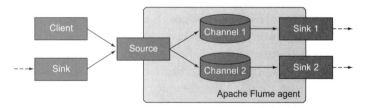

Figure 6.15   The key components of an Apache Flume flow pipeline. Data arrives at a Flume agent through a source component that's driven by a client Java component. The agent contains multiple data channels that are made available to one or more sink objects.

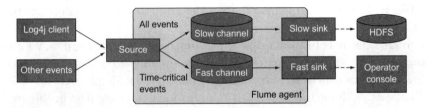

Figure 6.16   How Log4j agents might be configured to write log data to a Flume agent with a slow and a fast channel. All data will be written directly to HDFS. All time-critical data will be written directly to an operator console.

Here's a narrative of how a flow pipeline works:

1   A *client* program such as a Log4jAppender writes log data into a log file. The client program typically is part of the application being monitored.

2   A *source* within a Flume agent program receives all events and writes it to one or more durable *channels*. Channel events persist even if a server goes down and must be restarted.

3   Once an event arrives in a channel, it'll stay there until a *sink* service removes it. The channel is responsible for making sure that all events are reliably delivered to a sink.

4   A sink is responsible for pulling events off of the channel and delivering them to the next stage. This can be another source of another Flume agent, or a terminal destination such as HDFS. Terminal sinks will typically store the event in three or more separate servers to provide redundancy in case of a node failure.

Now let's look at how you can configure Apache Flume to meet the specific slow and fast processing requirements we just described. Figure 6.16 is an example of this configuration.

Once log events are stored in HDFS, a regularly scheduled batch tool can be periodically run to summarize totals and averages for various events. For example, a report might generate average response times of web services or web page rendering times.

6.9.3   *Further thoughts*

This case study showed how Apache Flume supplies an infrastructure for allowing programs to subscribe to key events and route them to different services with different latency requirements.

Apache Flume is a custom-built framework specifically created with the intent of reliably transferring event log data into a central data store such as HDFS. HDFS, in turn, is ideally suited to storing large blocks of read-mostly data. HDFS has no extra overhead for transaction control or update operations; its focus is large and reliable storage. HDFS is designed as an efficient source for all your analytical reports written in MapReduce. Since data can be evenly distributed over hundreds of nodes in a Hadoop cluster, the MapReduce reports can quickly build whatever summary data you need. This is ideal for creating materialized views and storing them in your RDBMSs or NoSQL database.

Although Apache Flume was originally written for processing log files, it's a general-purpose tool and can be used on other types of immutable big data problems such as data loggers or raw data from web crawling systems. As data loggers get lower in price, tools like Apache Flume will be needed to preprocess more big data problems.

6.10   *Case study: computer-aided discovery of health care fraud*

In this case study, we'll take a look at a problem that can't be easily solved using a shared-nothing architecture. This is the problem of looking for patterns of fraud using large graphs. Highly connected graphs aren't partition tolerant—meaning that you can't divide the queries on a graph on two or more shared-nothing processors. If your graph is too large to fit in the RAM of a commodity processor, you may need to look at an alternative to a shared-nothing system.

This case study is important because it explores the limits of what a cluster of shared-nothing systems can do. We include this case study because we want to avoid a tendency for architects to recommend large shared-nothing clusters for all problems. Although shared-nothing architectures work for many big data problems, they don't provide for linear scaling of highly connected data such as graphs or RDBMSs containing joins. Looking for hidden patterns in large graphs is one area that's best solved with a custom hardware approach.

6.10.1   *What is health care fraud detection?*

The US Congressional Office of Management and Budget estimates that improper payments in Medicare and Medicaid came to $50.7 billion in 2010, nearly 8.5% of the annual Medicare budget. A portion of this staggering figure is the result of improper documentation, but it's certain that Medicare fraud costs taxpayers tens of billions of dollars annually.

Existing efforts to detect fraud have focused on searching for suspicious submissions from individual beneficiaries and health care providers. These efforts yielded $4.1 billion in fraud recovery in 2011, around 10% of the total estimated fraud.

Unfortunately, fraud is becoming more sophisticated, and detection must move beyond the search for individuals to the discovery of patterns of collusion among multiple beneficiaries and/or health care providers. Identifying these patterns is challenging, as fraudulent behaviors continuously change, requiring the analyst to hypothesize that a pattern of relationships could indicate fraud, visualize and evaluate the results, and iteratively refine their hypothesis.

6.10.2 Using graphs and custom shared-memory hardware to detect health care fraud

Graphs are valuable in situations where data discovery is required. Graphs can show relationships between health care beneficiaries, their claims, associated care providers, tests performed, and other relevant data. Graph analytics search through the data to find patterns of relationships between all of these entities that might indicate collusion to commit fraud.

The graph representing Medicare data is large: it represents six million providers, a hundred million patients, and billions of claim records. The graph data is interconnected between health care providers, diagnostic tests, and common treatments associated with each patient and their claim records. This amount of data can't be held in the memory of a single server, and partitioning the data across multiple nodes in a computing cluster isn't feasible. Attempts to do so may result in incomplete queries due to all the links crossing partition boundaries, the need to page data in and out of memory, and the delays added by slower network and storage speeds. Meanwhile, fraud continues to occur at an alarming rate.

Medicare fraud analytics requires an in-memory graph solution that can merge heterogeneous data from a variety of sources, use queries to find patterns, and discover similarities as well as exact matches. With every item of data loaded into memory, there's no need to contend with the issue of graph partitioning. The graph can be dynamically updated with new data easily, and existing queries can integrate the new data into the analytics being performed, making the discovery of hidden relationships in the data feasible.

Figure 6.17 shows the high-level architecture of how shared-memory systems are used to look for patterns in large graphs.

With these requirements in mind, a US federally funded lab with a mandate to identify Medicare and Medicaid fraud deployed YarcData's Urika appliance. The appliance is capable of scaling from 1–512 terabytes of memory, shared by up to 8,192

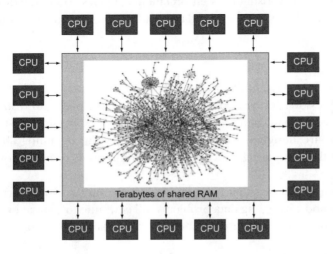

Figure 6.17 How large graphs are loaded into a central shared-memory structure. This example shows a graph in a central multi-terabyte RAM store with potentially hundreds or thousands of simultaneous threads in CPUs performing queries on the graph. Note that, like other NoSQL systems, the data stays in RAM while the analysis is processing. Each CPU can perform an independent query on the graph without interfering with each other.

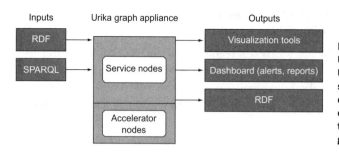

Inputs   Urika graph appliance   Outputs

RDF

SPARQL

Service nodes

Accelerator nodes

Visualization tools

Dashboard (alerts, reports)

RDF

Figure 6.18   Interacting with the Urika graph analytics appliance. Users load RDF data into the system and then send graph queries using SPARQL. The results of these queries are then sent to tools that allow an analyst to view graphs or generate reports.

graph accelerator CPUs. It's worth noting that these graph accelerator CPUs were purposely built for the challenges of graph analytics, and are instrumental in enabling Urika to deliver two to four orders of magnitude better performance than conventional clusters.

The impact of this performance is impressive. Interactive responses to queries become the norm, with responses in seconds instead of days. That's important because when queries reveal unexpected relationships, analysts can, within minutes, modify their searches to leverage the findings and uncover additional evidence. Discovery is about finding unknown relationships, and this requires the ability to quickly test new hypotheses.

Now let's see how users can interact with a typical graph appliance. Figure 6.18 shows how data is moved into a graph appliance like Urika and how outputs can be visualized by a user.

The software stack of the appliance leverages the RDF and SPARQL W3C standards for graphs, which facilitates the import and integration of data from multiple sources. The visualization and dashboard tools required for fraud analysis have their own unique requirements, so the appliance's ability to quickly and easily integrate custom visualization and dashboards is key to rapid deployment.

Medicare fraud analytics is similar to financial fraud analysis, or the search for persons of interest in counter-terrorism or law enforcement agencies, where the discovery of unknown or hidden relationships in the data can lead to substantial financial or safety benefits.

6.11   *Summary*

In this chapter, we reviewed the ability of NoSQL systems to handle big data problems using many processors. It's clear that moving from a single CPU to distributed database systems adds new management challenges that must be considered. Luckily, most NoSQL systems are designed with distributed processing in mind. They use techniques to spread the computing load evenly among hundreds or even thousands of nodes.

The problems of large datasets that need rapid analysis won't go away. Barring an event like the zombie apocalypse, big data problems will continue to grow at exponential rates. As long as people continue to create and share data, the need to quickly analyze it and discover patterns will continue to be part of most business plans. To be players in the future, almost all organizations will need to move away from single processor systems to distributed computing to handle the ever-increasing demands of big data analysis.

Having large numbers of records and documents in your NoSQL database can complicate the process of finding one or more specific items. In our next chapter, we'll tackle the problems of search and findability.

6.12 *Further reading*

- Apache Flume. http://flume.apache.org/.
- Barney, Blaise. "Introduction to Parallel Computing." https://mng.bz/s59m.
- Doshi, Paras. "Who on earth is creating Big data?" Paras Doshi—Blog. http://mng.bz/wHtd.
- "Expressive Power in Database Theory." Wikipedia. http://mng.bz/511S.
- "Federated search." Wikipedia. http://mng.bz/oj3i.
- Gottfrid, Derek. "The New York Times Archives + Amazon Web Services = Times-Machine." *New York Times*, August 2, 2013. http://mng.bz/77N6.
- Hadoop Wiki. "Mounting HDFS." http://mng.bz/b0vj.
- Haslhofer, Bernhard, et al. "European RDF Store Report." March 8, 2011. http://mng.bz/q2HP.
- "Java logging framework" Wikipedia. http://mng.bz/286z.
- Koubachi. http://www.koubachi.com/features/system.
- McColl, Bill. "Beyond Hadoop: Next-Generation Big Data Architectures." GigaOM, October 23, 2010. http://mng.bz/2FCr.
- whitehouse.gov. "Obama Administration Unveils 'Big Data' Initiative: Announces $200 Million in New R&D Investments." March 29, 2012. http://mng.bz/nEZM.
- YarcData. http://www.yarcdata.com.

Finding information
with NoSQL search

This chapter covers

- Types of search
- Strategies and methods for NoSQL search
- Measuring search quality
- NoSQL index architectures

What we find changes who we become.

—Peter Morville

We're all familiar with web search sites such as Google and Bing where we enter our search criteria and quickly get high-quality search results. Unfortunately, many of us are frustrated by the lack of high-quality search tools on our company intranets or within our database applications. NoSQL databases make it easier to integrate high-quality search directly into a database application by integrating the database with search frameworks and tools such as Apache Lucene, Apache Solr, and ElasticSearch.

NoSQL systems combine document store concepts with full-text indexing solutions, which results in high-quality search solutions and produces results with better search quality. Understanding why NoSQL search results are superior will help you evaluate the merits of these systems.

In this chapter, we'll show you how NoSQL databases can be used to build high-quality and cost-effective search solutions, and help you understand how findability impacts NoSQL system selection. We'll start this chapter with definitions of search terms, and then introduce some more complex concepts used in search technologies. Later, we'll look at three case studies that show how reverse indexes are created and how search is applied in technical documentation and reporting.

7.1 What is NoSQL search?

For our purposes, we'll define search as finding an item of interest in your NoSQL database when you have partial information about an item. For example, you may know some of the keywords in a document, but not know the document title, author, or date of creation.

Search technologies apply to highly structured records similar to those in an RDBMS as well as "unstructured" plain-text documents that contain words, sentences, and paragraphs. There are also a large number of documents that fall somewhere in the middle called *semi-structured data.*

Search is one of the most important tools to help increase the productivity of knowledge workers. Studies show that finding the right document quickly can save hours of time each day. Companies such as Google and Yahoo!, pioneers in the use of NoSQL systems, were driven by the problems involved in document search and retrieval. Before we begin looking at how NoSQL systems can be used to create search solutions, let's define some terms used when building search applications.

7.2 Types of search

As you're building applications, you'll come to the point where building and providing search will be important to your users. So let's look at the types of search that you could provide: Boolean search used in RDBMSs, full-text keyword search used in frameworks such as Apache Lucene, and structured search popular in NoSQL systems that use XML or JSON type documents.

7.2.1 Comparing Boolean, full-text keyword, and structured search models

If you've used RDBMSs, you might be familiar with creating search programs that look for specific records in a database. You might also have used tools such as Apache Lucene and Apache Solr to find specific documents using full-text keyword search. In this section, we'll introduce a new type of search: structured search. Structured search combines features from both Boolean and full-text keyword search. To get us started, table 7.1 compares the three main search types.

Table 7.1   A comparison of Boolean, full-text keyword, and structured search. Most users are already familiar with the benefits of Boolean and full-text keyword search. NoSQL databases that use document stores offer a third type, structured search, that retains the best features of Boolean and full-text keyword search. Only structured search gives you the ability to combine AND/OR statements with ranked search results.

Search type	Structures used	Ranked search results	Combine full-text and conditional logic	Best for
Boolean search— used in RDBMSs. Ideal for searches where AND/OR logic can be applied to highly structured data.	Rows of tables that conditionally match a WHERE clause.	No	No	Highly structured data
Full-text keyword search— used for unstructured document search of natural language text.	Documents, keywords, and vector distance results.	Yes	No	Unstructured text files
Structured search— combination of full-text and Boolean search tools.	XML or JSON documents. XML document may include entity markup.	Yes	Yes	Semi-structured documents

The challenge with Boolean search systems is that they don't provide any "fuzzy match" functions. They either find the information you're looking for or they don't. To find a record, you must use trial and error by adding and deleting parameters to expand and contract the search results. RDBMS search results can't be sorted by how closely the search results match the request. They must be sorted by database properties such as the date last modified or the author.

In contrast, the challenge with full-text keyword search is that it's sometimes difficult to narrow your search by document properties. For example, many document search interfaces don't allow you to restrict your searches to include documents created over a specific period of time or by a specific group of authors.

If you use structured search, you get the best of both worlds in a single search function. NoSQL document stores can combine the complex logic functions of Boolean AND/OR queries and use the ranked matches of full-text keywords to return the right documents in the right order.

7.2.2   *Examining the most common types of search*

If you're selecting a NoSQL system, you'll want to make sure to look at the findability of the system. These are the characteristics of a database that help users find the records they need. NoSQL systems excel at combining both structure and fuzzy search logic that may not be found in RDBMSs. Here are a few types of searches you may want to include in your system:

- *Full-text search*—Full-text search is the process of finding documents that contain natural language text such as English. Full-text search is appropriate when your data has free-form text like you'd see in an article or a book. Full-text search techniques include processes for removing unimportant short *stop words* (and, or, the) and removing suffixes from words (stemming).

- *Semi-structured search*—Semi-structured searches are searches of data that has both the rigid structure of an RDBMS and full-text sentences like you'd see in a Microsoft Word document. For example, an invoice for hours worked on a consulting project might have long sentences describing the tasks that were performed on a project. A sales order might contain a full-text description of products in the order. A business requirements document might have structured fields for who requested a feature, what release it will be in, and a full-text description of what the feature will do.

- *Geographic search*—Geographic search is the process of changing search result ranking based on geographic distance calculations. For example, you might want to search for all sushi restaurants within a five-minute drive of your current location. Search frameworks such as Apache Lucene now include tools for integrating location information in search ranking.

- *Network search*—Network search is the process of changing search result rankings based on information you find in graphs such as social networks. You might want your search to only include restaurants that your friends gave a four- or five-star rating. Integrating network search results can require use of social network APIs to include factors such as "average rating by my Facebook friends."

- *Faceted search*—Faceted search is the process of including other document properties within your search criteria, such as "all documents written by a specific author before a specific date." You can think of facets as subject categories to narrow your search space, but facets can also be used to change search ranking.

  Setting up faceted search on an ordinary collection of Microsoft Word documents can be done by manually adding multiple subject keywords to each document. But the costs of adding keywords can be greater than the benefits gained. Faceted search is used when there's high-quality metadata (information about the document) associated with each document. For example, most libraries purchase book metadata from centralized databases to allow you to narrow searches based on subject, author, publication date, and other standardized fields. These fields are sometimes referred to as the *Dublin Core* properties of a document.

- *Vector search*—Vector search is the process of ranking document results based on how close they are to search keywords using multidimensional vector distance models. Each keyword can be thought of as its own dimension in space and the distance between a query and each document can be calculated as a geographical distance calculation. This is illustrated in figure 7.1.

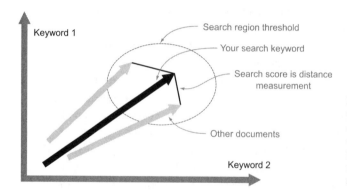

Figure 7.1   Vector search is a way to find documents that are closest to a keyword. By counting the number of keywords per page, you can rank all documents by a keyword space dimension.

As you might guess, calculating search vectors is complex. Luckily, vector distance calculations are included in most full-text search systems. Once your full-text indexes have been created, the job of building a search engine can be as easy as combining your query with a search system query function.

Vector search is one of the key technologies that allow users to perform fuzzy searches. They help you find inexact matches to documents that are "in the neighborhood" of your query keywords. Vector search tools also allow you to treat entire documents as a keyword collection for additional searches. This feature allows search systems to add functions such as "find similar documents" to an individual document.

- *N-gram search*—N-gram search is the process of breaking long strings into short, fixed-length strings (typically three characters long) and indexing these strings for exact match searches that may include whitespace characters. N-gram indexes can take up a large amount of disk space, but are the only way to quickly search some types of text such as software source code (where all characters including spaces may be important). N-gram indexes are also used for finding patterns in long strings of text such as DNA sequences.

Although there are clearly many types of searches, there are also many tools that make these searches fast. As we move to our next section, you'll see how NoSQL systems are able to find and retrieve your requested information rapidly.

7.3   Strategies and methods that make NoSQL search effective

So how are NoSQL systems able to take your requested search information and return the results so fast? Let's take a look at the strategies and methods that make NoSQL search systems so effective:

- *Range index*—A range index is a way of indexing all database element values in increasing order. Range indexes are ideal for alphabetical keywords, dates, timestamps, or amounts where you might want to find all items equal to a specific value or between two values. Range indexes can be created on any data type as long as that data type has a logically distinct way of sorting items. It wouldn't make sense to create a range index on images or full-text paragraphs.

- *Reverse index*—A reverse index is a structure similar to the index you'll find in the back of a book. In a book, each of the entries is listed in alphabetical order at the end of the book with the page numbers where the entry occurs. You can go to any entry in the index and quickly see where that term is used in the book. Without an index, you'd be forced to scan through the entire book. Search software uses reverse indexes in the same way. For each word in a document collection there's a list of all the documents that contain that word.

   Figure 7.2 contains a screen image of a Lucene index of the works of Shakespeare.

   Search frameworks such as Apache Lucene are designed to create and maintain reverse indexes for large document collections. These reverse indexes are used to speed the lookup of documents that contain keywords.

- *Search ranking*—Search ranking is the process of sorting search results based on the likelihood that the found item is what the user is looking for. So, if a document has a higher keyword density of the requested word, then there is a higher chance that document is about this keyword. The term *keyword density*

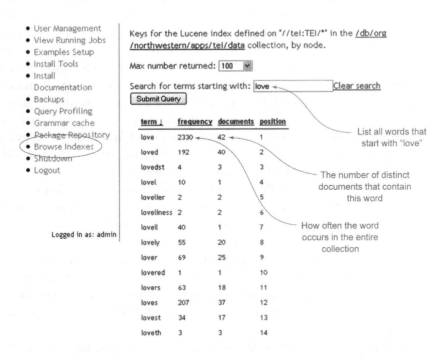

Figure 7.2   Browsing a reverse index of Shakespeare plays for the keywords that start with the string "love." In this example, the plays were encoded in the TEI XML format and then indexed by Apache Lucene.

refers to how often the word occurs in a document weighted by the size of the document. If you only counted the total number of words in a document, then longer documents with more keywords would always get a higher ranking. Search ranking should take into account the number of times a keyword appears in a document and the total number of words in the document so that longer documents don't always appear first in search results. Ranking algorithms might consider other factors such as document type, recommendations from your social networks, and relevance to a specific task.

- *Stemming*—Stemming is the process of allowing a user to include variations of a root word in a search but still match different forms of a word. For example, if a person types in the keyword `walk` then documents with the words *walks, walked,* and *walking* might all be included in search results.

- *Synonym expansion*—Synonym expansion is the process of including synonyms of specific keywords in search results. For example, if a user typed in `aspirin` for a keyword, the chemical names for the drugs *salicylic acid* and *acetylsalicylic acid* might be added to the keywords used in a search. The WordNet database is a good example of using a thesaurus to include synonyms in search results.

- *Entity extraction*—Entity extraction is the process of finding and tagging named entities within your text. Objects such as dates, person names, organizations, geolocations, and product names might be types of entities that should be tagged by an entity extraction program. The most common way of tagging text is by using XML wrapper elements. Native XML databases, such as MarkLogic, provide functions for automatically finding and tagging entities within your text.

- *Wildcard search*—Wildcard search is the process of adding special characters to indicate you want multiple characters to match a query. Most search frameworks support *suffix wildcards* where the user specifies a query such as `dog*`, which will match words such as *dog, dogs,* or *dogged.* You can use * to match zero or more characters and ? to match a single character. Apache Lucene allows you to add a wildcard in the middle of a string.

  Most search engines don't support *leading wildcards*, or wildcards before a string. For example `*ing` would match all words that end with the suffix *ing*. This type of search isn't frequently requested, and adding support for leading wildcards doubles the sizes of indexes stored.

- *Proximity search*—Proximity search allows you to search for words that are near other words in a document. Here you can indicate that you're interested in all documents that have *dog* and *love* within 20 words of each other. Documents that have these words closer together will get a higher ranking in the returned results.

- *Key word in context (KWIC)*—Key-word-in-context libraries are tools that help you add keyword highlighting to each search result. This is usually done by adding an element wrapper around the keywords within the resulting document fragments in the search results page.

- *Misspelled words*—If a user misspells a keyword in a search form and the word the user entered is a nondictionary word, the search engine might return a "Did you mean" panel with spelling alternatives for the keyword. This feature requires that the search engine be able to find words similar to the misspelled word.

Not all NoSQL databases support all of these features. But this list is a good starting point if you're comparing two distinct NoSQL systems. Next we look at one type of NoSQL database, the document store, that lends itself to high-quality search.

7.4   *Using document structure to improve search quality*

In chapter 4 we introduced the concept of document stores. You may recall that document stores keep data elements together in a single object. Document stores don't "shred" elements into rows within tables; they keep all information together in a single hierarchical tree.

Document stores are popular for search because this retained structure can be used to pinpoint exactly where in the document a keyword match is found. Using this keyword match position information can make a big difference in finding a single document in a large collection of documents.

If you retain the structure of the document, you can in effect treat each part of a large document as though it were another document. You can then assign different search result scores based on where in the document each keyword was found. Figure 7.3 shows how document stores leverage a retained structure model to create better search results.

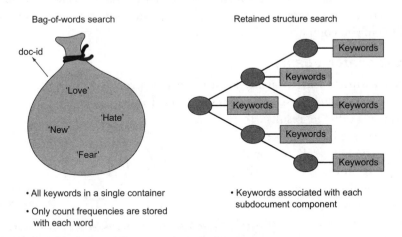

Figure 7.3   Comparison of two types of document structures used in search. The left panel is the bag-of-words search based on an extraction of all words in a document without consideration of where words occur in the document structure. The right panel shows a retained structure search that treats each node in the document tree as a separate document. This allows keyword matches in the title to have a higher rank than keywords in the body of a document.

Let's assume you're searching for books on the topic of NoSQL. When you go to a publisher's website and type `NoSQL` into a keyword search form, you'll get many matches. The search system finds the keyword *NoSQL* in multiple places in each book:

- In the title of a book or title of a chapter
- In a glossary term or back-of-book index term
- In the body of the text of a book
- In a bibliographic reference

As you can guess, if a book has the keyword *NoSQL* in the title, there's a good chance that the entire book is about NoSQL. On the other hand, there may be related books that have a chapter on the topic of NoSQL and a larger set of books that reference the term NoSQL in the text or in a bibliographic reference. When the search system returns the results to the user, it would make sense to give the matches to a book title the highest score and the matches to a chapter title the second-highest score. A match in a glossary term or indexed word term might be next, followed by a match in body text. The last results might be in a bibliographic reference.

The business rules for raising the search score based on where in a document the word is found are called *boosting*. If you have no way to specify and find book and chapter titles within your documents, it'll be difficult to boost their ranking. Using a larger font or a different font color won't help search tools find the right documents. This is why using structured document formats such as DocBook can create higher-precision search rankings than using the bag-of-words patterns.

You can see how easy it is to improve your search results by using a document's original structure. As we move to our next section, you'll see how measuring search quality will help you compare NoSQL options.

7.5   *Measuring search quality*

Accurately measuring search quality is an important process in selecting a NoSQL database. From a quality perspective, you want your results to contain the search key and accurately rank the results. To measure search quality, you use two metrics: *precision* and *recall*. As you'll see, combining these metrics will help you objectively measure the quality of your search results.

An illustration of search quality is shown in figure 7.4.

Your goal is to maximize *both* precision and recall. A metric called the *F-measure* is roughly the mean of these values and a larger F-measure indicates higher search quality.

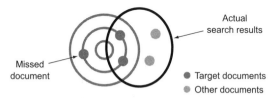

Figure 7.4   Search precision and recall. Search precision shows you the percent of target documents that are returned in actual search results. Two of the four documents in the actual search result are in the target area for a precision of .5. Recall is the fraction of all target documents (darker dots) found in your actual search results. In this example, only two of the three darker dots are in the actual search results, for a recall of .66.

Organizations that sell search services have dedicated quality teams that continually monitor and modify search ranking algorithms to get higher F-measures. They develop processes that detect which search results users click on and look for ways to automatically increase the ranking score of relevant items while lowering the ranking score of items that users deem to be unrelated to their query.

Each search system has a way of changing the balance of precision and recall by including a broader set of documents in search results. A search engine can look up synonyms for a keyword and return all documents that contain both the keyword and the synonyms. Adding more documents to the search results will lower precision numbers and increase recall numbers. It's important to strike a balance between precision and recall percentages to fit into your system requirements.

Not all database selection projects will take the time to carefully measure precision and recall of competing systems. Setting up a large collection of documents and measuring relevancy of ranked search results can be time consuming and difficult to automate. But by retaining document structure, document stores have shown dramatic gains in both precision and recall.

Now that we've covered the types of searches and how NoSQL systems speed up these searches, we can compare how distributed systems use different strategies to store indexes used in search optimization.

7.6 *In-node indexes versus remote search services*

There are two different ways that NoSQL systems store search indexes: in-node indexes and using a remote search service. Most NoSQL systems keep their data and indexes on the same node. But some NoSQL systems use external search services for full-text search. These systems keep the full-text indexes on a remote cluster and use a search API to generate search results. Since most NoSQL systems use one method or another, understanding the trade-offs of each method will help you evaluate NoSQL options. Figure 7.5 illustrates these two options.

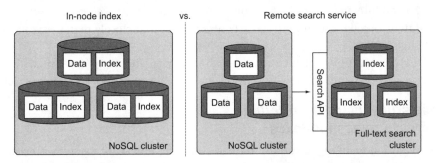

Figure 7.5 Integrated search vs. search services. The panel on the left shows how NoSQL systems store the indexes on the same node as the indexed data. The panel on the right shows a remote search service where indexes are stored on a remote cluster that executes a search service through an API.

When you use an in-node search system, the reverse indexes are located on the same node as the data. This allows you to send a query to each node and have it respond with the search results without having to do any additional input/output to include search information. If you retain document structure, you can also use structural match rules to change the query results based on where in a document a match occurs.

In contrast, a search service sends documents to an external search cluster when they need to be indexed. This is usually done by a collection trigger that's fired when any document is added or updated in the database. Even if a single word within a document is altered, the entire document is sent to the remote service and re-indexed. When a search is performed, the keywords in the search are sent to the remote system and all document IDs that match the search are returned. Note that the actual documents aren't returned. Only a list of the document IDs and their ranking score are returned. Apache Solr and ElasticSearch are both examples of software that can be configured as a remote search service.

Let's look at the various trade-offs of these two approaches.

Advantages of in-node index architecture:

- Lower network usage; documents aren't sent between clusters, resulting in higher performance
- Ideal for large documents that have many small and frequent changes
- Better fine-grained control search results on structured documents

Advantages of remote service architecture:

- Ability to take advantage of prebuilt and pretested components for standard functions such as creating and maintaining full-text search indexes
- Easier to upgrade to new features of remote search services
- Ideal for documents that are added once without frequent updates

These are high-level guidelines, and each NoSQL system or version might have exceptions to these rules. You can see that how often you update documents has an impact on what architecture is right for you. Whatever architecture you select, we recommend that you take the time to test a configuration that closely matches your business challenge.

Our next section will take a look at one way to speed up the initial document indexing process, and the creation of reverse indexes to support full-text search.

7.7   *Case study: using MapReduce to create reverse indexes*

One of the most time-consuming parts of building any search system is creating the reverse indexes for new full-text documents as they're imported into your NoSQL database. A typical 20-page document with 5,000 words can result in 5,000 additions to your reverse index. Indexing 1,000 documents into your collection would require approximately five million index updates. Spreading the load of this process over multiple servers is the best way to index large document collections.

MapReduce is an ideal tool to use when creating reverse indexes due to its ability to scale horizontally. Creating reverse indexes was the primary driver behind the Google MapReduce project, and the reason the Hadoop framework was created. Let's take a step-by-step look at how you can use MapReduce to create reverse indexes.

To design a MapReduce job, you must break the problem into multiple steps. The first step is to write a map function that takes your inputs (the source documents) and returns a set of key-value pairs. The second step is to write a reduce function that will return your results. In this case, the results will be the reverse index files. For each key-word, the reverse index lists what documents contain that word.

You may recall that the interface between the map and reduce phases must be a set of key-value pairs. The next question to answer is what to return for the key. The most logical key would be the word itself. The "value" of the key-value pair would be a list of all the document identifiers that contain that word.

Figure 7.6 shows the detailed steps in this process. You can see from this figure that before you process the inputs, you remove uppercase letters and small stop words such as *the, and, or,* and *to,* since it's unlikely they'll be used as keywords. You then create a list of key-value pairs for each word where the document ID is the "value" part of the key-value pair. The MapReduce infrastructure then performs the "shuffle and sort" steps and pass the output to the final reduce phase that collapses each of the word-document pairs into a word-document list item, which is the format of the reverse indexes.

In our next two sections we'll look at case studies to see how search can be used to solve specific business problems.

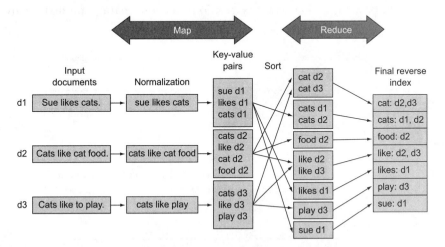

Figure 7.6 Using the MapReduce algorithm to create a reverse index. The normalization step removes punctuation and stop words and converts all words to lowercase. The output of the map phase must be a set of key-value pairs. The reduce function groups the keyword documents to form the final reverse index.

7.8   *Case study: searching technical documentation*

This case study will look at the problem of searching technical documents. Having a high-quality search for technical documentation can save you time when you're looking for information. For example. if you're using a complex software package and need help with a specific function, a high-quality, accurate search can quickly get you to the right feature.

As you'll see, retaining document structure creates search systems with higher precision and recall. In the following example, we'll use a specific XML file format called DocBook, which is ideal for search and retrieval of technical information. You'll see how Apache Lucene can be integrated directly into a NoSQL database to create high-quality search. Note that the concepts used in this section are general and can be applied to formats other than DocBook.

7.8.1   *What is technical document search?*

Technical document search focuses on helping you quickly find a specific area of interest in technical documents. For example, you might be looking for a how-to tip in a software users' guide, a diagram in a car repair manual, an online help system, or a college textbook. Technical publications use a process called *single-source publishing* where all the output formats, such as web, online help, printed, or EPUB, are all derived from the same document source format. Figure 7.7 shows an example of how the DocBook XML format stores technical documentation.

DocBook is an XML standard specifically targeting technical publishing. DocBook defines over 600 elements that are used to store the content of a technical publication including information about authors, revisions, sections, paragraph text, figures, captions, tables, glossary tags, and bibliographic information.

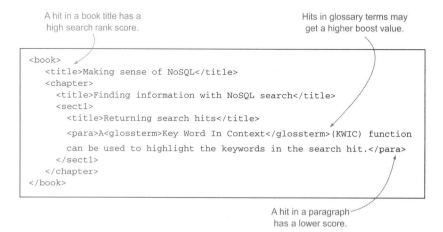

Figure 7.7   A sample of a DocBook XML file. The `<title>` directly under the `<book>` element is the title of the book. A keyword hit within a book title has a higher score than a hit within the body text of the book.

DocBook is frequently customized for different types of publishing. Each organization that's publishing a document will select a subset of DocBook elements and then add their own elements to meet their specific application. For example, a math textbook might include XML markup for equations (MathML), a chemistry textbook might include markup for chemical symbols (ChemML), and an economics textbook might add charts in XML format. These new XML vocabularies can be placed in different namespaces added to DocBook XML without disrupting the publishing processes.

7.8.2 Retaining document structure in a NoSQL document store

There are several ways to perform search on large collections of DocBook files. The most straightforward is to strip out all the markup information and send each document to Apache Lucene to create a reverse index. Each word would then be associated with a single document ID. The problem with this approach is that all the information about the word location within the document is lost. If a word occurs in a book or chapter title, it can't be ranked higher than if the word occurs in a bibliographic note.

Ideally, you want to retain the entire document structure and store the XML file in a native XML database. Then any match within a title can have a higher rank than if the match occurs within the body of the text.

The first step in creating a search function is to load all the XML documents into a collection structure. This structure logically groups similar documents and makes it easy to navigate the documents, similar to a file browser. After the documents have been loaded, you can run a script to find all unique elements in the document collection. This is known as an *element inventory.*

The element inventory is then used as a basis for deciding what elements might contain information that you want to index for quick searches, and what index types you'll use. Elements that contain dates might use a range index and elements such as `<title>` and `<para>` that contain full text might use a full-text index.

In addition to the index type, you can also rank the probability that any element might be a good summary of the concepts in a section. We call this ranking process setting the *boost values* for a document collection. For example, a match on the title of a chapter will rank higher than a section title or a glossary keyword. After semantic weights have been created, a configuration file is created and the indexing process begins. Table 7.2 shows an example of these boost values.

We should note that the boost values are also stored with the search result indexes so that they can be used to create precise

Table 7.2 Example of boost values for a technical book search site

Element	Boost value
Book title	5.0
Chapter title	4.0
Glossary term	3.0
Indexed term	2.0
Paragraph text	1.0
Bibliographic reference	0.5

search rankings. This means that if you change the boost values, the documents must be re-indexed. Although this example is somewhat simplified, it shows that accurate markup of book elements is critical to the search ranking process.

Once you've determined the elements and boost values, you'll create a configuration file that identifies the fields you're interested in indexing. From there you can run a process that takes each document and creates a reverse full-text index using the element and boost values from your configuration file. Apache Lucene is an example of a framework that creates and maintains these type of indexes. All the keywords found in that element can then be associated with that element using a node identifier for that element. By storing the element node as well as the document, you know exactly in what element of the document the keyword was found.

After indexing, you're now ready to create search functions that can work with both range and full-text indexes. The most common way to integrate text searches is by using an XQuery full-text library that returns the ranked results of a keyword query. The query is similar to a WHERE clause in SQL, but it also returns a score used to order all search results. Your XQuery can return any type of node within DocBook, such as a book, article, chapter, section, figure, or bibliographic entry.

The final step is to return a fragment of HTML for each hit in the search. At the top of the page, you'll see the hits with the highest score. Most search tools return a block of text that shows the keyword highlighted within the text. This is known as a *key-word-in-context (KWIC)* function.

7.9   *Case study: searching domain-specific languages— findability and reuse*

Although we frequently think of search quality as a characteristic associated with a large number of text documents, there are also benefits to finding items such as software subroutines or specific types of programs created with *domain-specific languages (DSLs)*. This case study shows how a search tool saved an organization time and money by allowing employees to find and reuse financial chart objects.

A large financial institution had thousands of charts used to create graphical financial dashboards. Most charts were generated by an XML specification file that described the features of each chart such as the chart type (line chart, bar chart, scatter-plot), title, axis, scaling, and labels. One of the challenges that the dashboard authors faced was how to lower the cost of creating a new chart by using an existing chart as a starting template.

All charts were stored on a standard filesystem. Each organization that requested charts had a folder that contained their charts. Because of the structure, there was no way to find charts sorted by their characteristics. Experienced chart authors knew where to look in the filesystem for an example of a template, but new chart authors often spent hours digging through old charts to find an old template that matched up with the new requirement.

One day a new staff member spent most of his day re-creating a chart when a similar chart already existed, but couldn't be found. In a staff meeting a manager asked if there was some way that the charts could be loaded into a database and searched.

Storing charts in a relational database would've been a multimonth-long task. There were hundreds of chart properties and multiple chart variations. Even the process of adding keywords to each chart and placing them in a word document would've been time consuming. This is an excellent example showing that high-variability data is best stored in a NoSQL system.

Instead of loading the charts into an RDBMS, the charts were loaded into an open source native XML document store (eXist-db) and a series of path expressions were created to search for various chart types. For example, all charts that had time across the horizontal x-axis could be found using an XPath expression on the x-axis descriptor. After finding specific charts with queries, chart keywords could be added to the charts using XQuery update statements.

You might find it ironic that the XML-based charting system was the preferred solution of an organization that had hundreds of person-years experience with RDBMSs in the department. But the cost estimates to develop a full RDBMS seriously outweighed the benefits. Since the data was in XML format, there was no need for data modeling; they simply loaded and queried the information.

A search form was then added to find all charts with specific properties. The chart titles, descriptions, and developer note elements were indexed using the Apache Lucene full-text indexing tools. The search form allowed users to restrict searches by various chart properties, organization, and dates. After entering search criteria, the user performed a search, and preview icons of the charts were returned directly in the search results page.

As a result of creating the chart search service, the time for finding a chart in the chart library dropped from hours to a matter of seconds. A close match to the new target chart was usually returned within the first 10 results in the search screen.

The company achieved additional benefits from being able to perform queries over all the prior charts. Quality and consistency reports were created to show which charts were consistent with the bank's approved style guide. New charts could also be validated for quality and consistency guidelines before they were used by a business unit.

An unexpected result of the new system was other groups within the organization began to use the financial dashboard system. Instead of building custom charts with low-level C programs, statistical programs, or Microsoft Excel, there was increased use of the XML chart standard, because non-experts could quickly find a chart that was similar to their needs. Users also knew that if they created a high-quality chart and added it to the database, there was a greater chance that others could reuse their work.

This case study shows that as software systems increase in complexity, finding the right chunk of code becomes increasingly important. Software reuse starts with findability. The phrase "you can't reuse what you can't find" is a good summary of this approach.

7.10   Apply your knowledge

Sally works in an information technology department with many people involved in the software development lifecycle (SDLC). SDLC documents include requirements, use cases, test plans, business rules, business terminology, report definitions, bug reports, and documentation, as well as the actual source code being developed.

Although Sally's department built high-quality search solutions for their business units, the proverb "The shoemaker's children go barefoot" seemed to apply to their group. SDLC documents were stored in many formats such as MS Word, wikis, spreadsheets, and source code repositories, in many locations. There were always multiple versions and it wasn't clear which versions were approved by a business unit or who should approve documents.

The source code repositories the department used had strong keyword search, yet there was no way users could perform faceted queries such as "show all new features in the 3.0 release of an internal product approved by Sue Johnson after June 1."

Sally realized that putting SDLC documents in a single NoSQL database that had integrated search features could help alleviate these problems. All SDLC documents from requirements, source code, and bugs could be treated as documents and searched with the tools provided by the NoSQL database vendor. Documents that had structure could also be queried using faceted search interfaces. Since almost all documents had timestamps, the database could create timeline views that allowed users to see when code was checked in and by what developers and relate these to bugs and problem reports.

The department also started to add more metadata into the searchable database. This included information about database elements and their definitions, list of tables, columns, business rules, and process flows. This became a flexible metadata registry for an official reviewed and approved "single version of the truth."

Using a NoSQL database as a integrated document store and metadata registry allowed the team to quickly increase the productivity of the department. In time, new web forms and easy-to-modify wiki-like structures were created to make it easier for developers to add and update SDLC data.

7.11   Summary

In the chapter on big data, you saw that the amount of available data generated by the web and internal systems continues to grow exponentially. As organizations continue to put this information to use, the ability to locate the right information at the right time is of growing concern. In this chapter, we've focused attention on showing you how to find the right item in your big data collection. We've talked about the types of searches that can be done by your NoSQL database and the ways in which NoSQL systems make searching fast.

You've seen how retaining a document's structure in a document store can increase the quality of search results. This process is enabled by associating a keyword, not with a document, but with the element that contains the keyword within a document.

Although we focused on topics you'll need to fairly evaluate search components of a NoSQL system, we also demonstrated that highly scalable processes such as Map-Reduce can be used to create reverse indexes that enable fast search. Finally, our case studies showed how search solutions can be created using open source native XML databases and Apache Lucene frameworks.

Both the previous chapter on big data and this chapter on search emphasize the need for multiple processors working together to solve problems. Most NoSQL systems are a great fit for these tasks. NoSQL databases integrate the complex concepts of information retrieval to increase the findability of items in your database. In our next chapter, we'll focus on high availability: how to keep all these systems running reliably.

7.12 *Further reading*

- AnyChart. "Building a Large Chart Ecosystem with AnyChart and Native XML Databases." http://mng.bz/Pknr.
- DocBook. http://docbook.org/.
- "Faceted search." Wikipedia. http://mng.bz/YgQq.
- Feldman, Susan, and Chris Sherman. "The High Cost of Not Finding Information." 2001. http://mng.bz/IX01.
- Manning, Christopher, et al. *Introduction to Information Retrieval*. 2008, Cambridge University Press.
- McCreary, Dan. "Entity Extraction and the Semantic Web." http://mng.bz/20A7.
- Morville, Peter. *Ambient Findability*. October 2005, O'Reilly Media.
- NLP. "XML retrieval." http://mng.bz/1Q9i.

Building high-availability solutions with NoSQL

This chapter covers

- What is high availability?
- Measuring availability
- NoSQL strategies for high availability

> *Anything that can go wrong will go wrong.*
>
> —Murphy's law

Have you ever been using a computer application when it suddenly stops responding? Intermittent database failures can be merely an annoyance in some situations, but high database availability can also mean the success or failure of a business. NoSQL systems have a reputation for being able to scale out and handle big data problems. These same features can also be used to increase the availability of database servers.

There are several reasons databases fail: human error, network failure, hardware failure, and unanticipated load, to name a few. In this chapter, we won't dwell on human error or network failure. We'll focus on how NoSQL architectures use parallelism and replication to handle hardware failure and scaling issues.

You'll see how NoSQL databases can be configured to handle lots of data and keep data services running without downtime. We'll begin by defining high-availability database systems and then look at ways to measure and predict system availability. We'll review techniques that NoSQL systems use to create high-availability systems even when subcomponents fail. Finally, we'll look at three real-world NoSQL products that are associated with high-availability service.

8.1 What is a high-availability NoSQL database?

High-availability NoSQL databases are systems designed to run without interruption of service. Many web-based businesses require data services that are available without interruption. For example, databases that support online purchasing need to be available 24 hours a day, 7 days a week, 365 days a year. Some requirements take this a step further, specifying that the database service must be "always on." This means you can't take the database down for scheduled maintenance or to perform software upgrades.

Why must they be always on? Companies demanding an always-on environment can document a measurable loss in income for every minute their service isn't available. Let's say your database supports a global e-commerce site; being down for even a few minutes could wipe out a customer's shopping cart. Or what if your system stops responding during prime-time shopping hours in Germany? Interruptions like these can drive shoppers to your competitor's site and lower customer confidence.

From a software development perspective, always-on databases are a new requirement. Before the web, databases were designed to support "bankers' hours" such as 9 a.m. to 5 p.m., Monday through Friday in a single time zone. During off hours, these systems might be scheduled for downtime to perform backups, run software updates, run reports, or export daily transactions to data warehouse systems. But bankers' hours are no longer appropriate for web-based businesses with customers around the world.

A web storefront is a good example of a situation that needs a high-availability database that supports both reads and writes. Read-mostly systems optimized for big data analysis are relatively simple to configure for high availability using data replication. Our focus here is on high availability for large-volume read/write applications that run on distributed systems.

Always-on database systems aren't new. Companies like Tandem Computers' Non-Stop system have provided commercial high-availability database systems for ATM networks, telephone switches, and stock exchanges since the 1970s. These systems use symmetrical, peer-to-peer, shared-nothing processors that send messages between processors about overall system health. They use redundant storage and high-speed failover software to provide continuous database services. The biggest drawbacks to these systems are that they're proprietary, difficult to set up and configure, and expensive on a cost-per-transaction basis.

Distributed NoSQL systems can lower the per-transaction cost of systems that need to be both scalable and always-on. Although most NoSQL systems use nonstandard query languages, their design and the ability to be deployed on low-cost cloud computing platforms make it possible for startups, with minimal cash, to provide always-on databases for their worldwide customers.

Understanding the concept of system availability is critical when you're gathering high-level system requirements. Since NoSQL systems use distributed computing, they can be configured to achieve high availability of a specific service at a minimum cost.

To understand the concepts in this chapter, we'll draw on the CAP theorem from chapter 2. We said that when communication channels between partitions are broken, system designers need to choose the level of availability they'll provide to their customers. Organizations often place a higher priority on availability than on consistency. The phase "A trumps C" implies that keeping orders flowing through a system is more important than consistent reporting during a temporary network failure to a replica server. Recall that these decisions are only relevant when there are network failures. During normal operations, the CAP theorem doesn't come into play.

Now that you have a good understanding of what high-availability NoSQL systems are and why they're good choices, let's find out how to measure availability.

8.2   *Measuring availability of NoSQL databases*

System availability can be measured in different ways and with different levels of precision. If you're writing availability requirements or comparing the SLAs of multiple systems, you may need to be specific about these measurements. We'll start with some broad measures of overall system availability and then dig deeper into more subtle measurements of system availability.

The most common notation for describing overall system availability is to state availability in terms of "nines," which is a count of how many times the number 9 appears in the designed availability. So *three nines* means that a system is predicted to be up 99.9% of the time, and *five nines* means the system should be up 99.999% of the time.

Table 8.1 shows some sample calculations of downtime per year based on typical availability targets.

Stating your uptime requirements isn't an exact science. Some businesses can associate a revenue-lost-per-minute to total data service unavailability. There are also gray areas where a system is so slow that a few customers abandon their shopping carts and

Table 8.1   Sample availability targets and annual downtime

Availability %	Annual downtime
99% (two nines)	3.65 days
99.9% (three nines)	8.76 hours
99.99% (four nines)	52.56 minutes
99.999% (five nines)	5.26 minutes

move on to another site. There are other factors, not as easily measured, which can lead to losses as well, such as poor reputation and lack of confidence.

Measuring overall system availability is more than generating a single number. To fairly evaluate NoSQL systems, you need an understanding of the subtleties of availability measurements.

If a business unit indicates they can't afford to be down more than eight hours in a calendar year, then you want to build an infrastructure that would provide three-nines availability. Most land-line telephone switches are designed for five-nines availability, or no more than five minutes of downtime per year. Today five nines is considered the gold standard for data services, with few situations warranting greater availability.

Although the use of counted nines is a common way to express system availability, it's usually not detailed enough to understand business impact. An outage for 30 seconds may seem to users like a slow day on the web. Some systems may show partial outage but have other functions that can step in to take their place, making the system only appear to work slowly. The end result is that no simple metric can be used to measure overall system availability. In practice, most systems look at the percentage of service requests that go beyond a specific threshold.

As a result, the term *service level agreement* or *SLA* is used to describe the detailed availability targets for any data service. An SLA is a written agreement between a service provider and a customer who uses the service. The SLA doesn't concern itself with how the data service is provided. It defines what services will be provided and the availability and response time goals for the service. Some items to consider when creating an SLA are

- What are the general service availability goals of the service in terms of percentage uptime over a one-year period?
- What are the typical average response times for the service under normal operations? Typically these are specified in milliseconds between service request and response.
- What is the peak volume of requests that the service is designed to handle? This is typically specified in requests per second.
- Are there any cyclical variations in request volumes? For example, do you expect to see peaks at specific times of day, days of the week or month, or times of the year like holiday shopping or sporting events?
- How will the system be monitored and service availability reported?
- What is the shape of the service-call response distribution curve? Keeping track of the average response time may not be useful. Organizations focus on the slowest 5% of service calls.
- What procedures should be followed during a service interruption?

NoSQL system configuration may be dependent on some of the exceptions to the general rules. The key focus should not be a single availability metric.

8.2.1 *Case study: the Amazon's S3 SLA*

Now let's look at Amazon's SLA for their S3 key-value store service. Amazon's S3 is known as the most reliable cloud-based, key-value store service available. S3 consistently performs well, even when the number of reads or writes on a bucket spikes. The system is rumored to be the largest, containing more than 1 trillion stored objects as of the summer of 2012. That's about 150 objects for every person on the planet.

Amazon discusses several availability numbers on their website:

- *Annual durability design*—This is the designed probability that a single key-value item will be lost over a one-year period. Amazon claims their design durability is 99.999999999%, or 11 nines. This number is based on the probability that your data object, which is typically stored on three hard drives, has all three drives fail before the data can be backed up. This means that if you store 10,000 items each year in S3 and continue to do so for 10 million years, there's about a 50% probability you'll lose one file. Not something that you should lose much sleep over. Note that a design is different from a service guarantee.

- *Annual availability design*—This is a worst-case measure of how much time, over a one-year period, you'll be unable to write new data or read your data back. Amazon claims a worst-case availability of 99.99%, or four-nines availability for S3. In other words, in the worse case, Amazon thinks your key-value data store may not work for about 53 minutes per year. In reality, most users get much better results.

- *Monthly SLA commitment*—In the S3 SLA, Amazon will give you a 10% service credit if your system is not up 99.9% of the time in any given month. If your data is unavailable for 1% of the time in a month, you'll get a 25% service credit. In practice, we haven't heard of any Amazon customer getting SLA credits.

It's also useful to read the wording of the Amazon SLA carefully. For example, it defines an error rate as the number of S3 requests that return an internal status error code. There's nothing in the SLA about slow response times.

In practice, most users will get S3 availability that far exceeds the minimum numbers in the SLA. One independent testing service found essentially 100% availability for S3, even under high loads over extended periods of time.

8.2.2 *Predicting system availability*

If you're building a NoSQL database, you need to be able predict how reliable your database will be. You need tools to analyze the response times of database services.

Availability prediction methods calculate the overall availability of a system by looking at the predicted availability of each of the dependent (single-point-of-failure) subcomponents. If each subsystem is expressed as a simple availability prediction such as 99.9, then multiplying each number together will give you an overall availability prediction. For example, if you have three single points of failure—99.9% for network,

99% for master node, and 99.9% for power—then the total system availability is the product of these three numbers: 98.8% (99.9 x 99 x 99.9).

If there are single points of failure such as a master or name node, then NoSQL systems have the ability to gracefully switch over to use a backup node without a major service interruption. If a system can quickly recover from a failing component, it's said to have a property of *automatic failover*. Automatic failover is the general property of any service to detect a failure and switch to a redundant component. *Failback* is the process of restoring a system component to its normal operation. Generally, this process requires some data synchronization. If your systems are configured with a single failover, you must use the probability that the failover process doesn't work in combination with the odds that the failover system fails before failback.

There are other metrics you can use besides the failure metric. If your system has client request timeout of 30 seconds, you'll want to measure the total percentage of client requests that fail. In such a case, a better metric might be a factor called *client yield*, which is the probability of any request returning within a specified time interval.

Other metrics, such as a *harvest* metric, apply when you want to include partial API results. Some services, such as federated search engines, may also return partial results. For example, if you search 10 separate remote systems and one of the sites is down for your call window of 30 seconds, you'd have a 90% harvest for that specific call. Harvest is the data available divided by the total data sources.

Finding the best NoSQL service for your application may require comparing the architecture of two different systems. The actual architecture may be hidden from you behind a web service interface. In these cases, it might make the most sense to set up a small pilot project to test the services under a simulated load.

When you set up a pilot project that includes stress testing, a key measurement will be a frequency distribution chart of read and write response times. These distributions can give you hints about whether a database service will scale. A key point of this analysis is that instead of focusing on average or mean response times, you should look at how long the slowest 5% of your services take to return. In general, a service with consistent response times will have higher availability than systems that sometimes have a high percentage of slow responses. Let's take a look at an example of this.

8.2.3 *Apply your knowledge*

Sally is evaluating two NoSQL options for a business unit that's concerned about web page response times. Web pages are rendered with data from a key-value store. Sally has narrowed down the field to two key-value store options; we'll call them Service A and Service B. Sally uses *JMeter*, a popular performance monitoring tool, to create a chart that has read service response distributions, as shown in figure 8.1.

When Sally looks at the data, she sees that service A has faster mean response times. But at the 95th percentile level, they're longer than service B. Service B may have slower average response times, but they're still within the web page load time

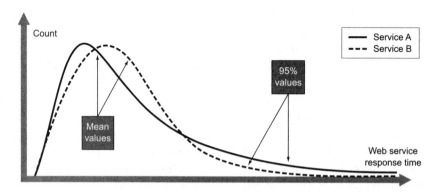

Figure 8.1 Frequency distribution chart showing mean vs. 95th percentile response times. Notice two web service response distributions for two NoSQL key-value data stores under load. Service A has a faster mean value response time but much longer response times at the 95th percentile. Service B has longer mean value response times but shorter 95% value responses.

goals. After discussing the results with the business unit, the team selects service B, since they feel it'll have more consistent response time under load.

Now that we've looked at how you predict and measure system availability, let's take a look at strategies that NoSQL clusters use to increase system availability.

8.3 NoSQL strategies for high availability

In this section, we'll review several strategies NoSQL systems use to create high-availability services backed by clusters of two or more systems. This discussion will include the concepts of load balancing, clusters, replication, load and stress testing, and monitoring.

As we look at each of these components, you'll see how NoSQL systems can be configured to provide maximum availability of the data service. One of the first questions you might ask is, "What if the NoSQL database crashes?" To get around this problem, a replica of the database can be created.

8.3.1 Using a load balancer to direct traffic to the least busy node

Websites that aim for high availability use a front-end service called a *load balancer.* A diagram of a load balancer is shown in figure 8.2.

In this figure, service requests enter on the left and are sent to a pool of resources called the *load balancer pool.* The service requests are sent to a master load balancer and then forwarded to one of the application servers. Ideally, each application server has some type of load indication that tells the load balancer how busy it is. The least-busy application server will then receive the request. Application servers are responsible for servicing the request and returning the results. Each application server may request data services from one or many NoSQL servers. The result of these query requests are returned and the service is fulfilled.

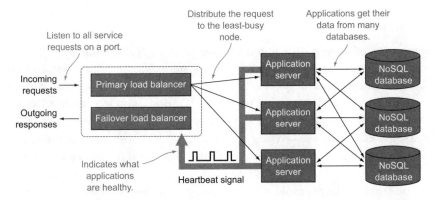

Figure 8.2   A load balancer is ideal when you have a large number of processors that can each fulfill a service request. To gain performance advantages, all service requests arrive at a load balancer service that distributes the request to the least-busy processor. A heartbeat signal from each application server provides a list of which application servers are working. An application server may request data from one or more NoSQL databases.

8.3.2   Using high-availability distributed filesystems with NoSQL databases

Most NoSQL systems are designed to work on a high-availability filesystem such as the Hadoop Distributed File System (HDFS). If you're using a NoSQL system such as Cassandra, you'll see that it has its own HDFS compatible filesystem. Building a NoSQL system around a specific filesystem has advantages and disadvantages.

Advantages of using a distributed filesystem with a NoSQL database:

- *Reuse of reliable components*—Reusing prebuilt and pretested system components makes sense with respect to time and money. Your NoSQL system doesn't need to duplicate the functions in a distributed filesystem. Additionally, your organization may already have an infrastructure and trained staff who know how to set up and configure these systems.

- *Customizable per-folder availability*—Most distributed filesystems can be configured on a folder-by-folder basis for high availability. This gets around using a local filesystem with single points of failure to store input or output datasets. These systems can be configured to store your data in multiple locations; the default is generally three. This means that a client request would only fail if all three systems crashed at the same time. The odds of this occurring are low enough that three are sufficient for most service levels.

- *Rack and site awareness*—Distributed filesystem software is designed to factor in how computer clusters are organized in your data center. When you set up your filesystem, you indicate which nodes are placed in which racks with the assumption that nodes within a rack have higher bandwidth than nodes in different racks. Racks can also be placed in different data centers, and filesystems can immediately duplicate data on racks in remote data centers if one data center goes down.

Disadvantages of using a distributed filesystem with a NoSQL database:

- *Lower portability*—Some distributed filesystems work best on UNIX or Linux servers. Porting these filesystems to other operating systems, such as Windows, may not be possible. If you need to run on Windows, you may need to add an additional virtual machine layer, which may impose a performance penalty.

- *Design and setup time*—When you're setting up a well-designed distributed filesystem, it may take some time to figure out the right folder structure. All the files within a folder share the same properties, such as replication factor. If you use creation dates as folder names, you may be able to lower replication for files that are over a specific period of time such as two years.

- *Administrative learning curve*—Someone on your staff will need to learn how to set up and manage a distributed filesystem. These systems need to be monitored and sensitive data must be backed up.

8.3.3 *Case study: using HDFS as a high-availability filesystem to store master data*

In chapter 6 on managing big data, we introduced the Hadoop Distributed File System (HDFS). As you recall, HDFS can reliably store large files, typically from a gigabyte to a terabyte. HDFS can also tune replication on a file-by-file basis. By default most files in HDFS have a replication factor of 3, meaning that the data blocks that make up these files are located on three distinct nodes. A simple HDFS shell command can change the replication factor for any HDFS file or folder. There are two reasons you should raise the replication factor of a file in HDFS:

- *To lower the chance that the data will become unavailable*—For example, if you have a data service that depends on this data with a five-nines guarantee, you might want to increase the replication factor from 3 to 4 or 5.

- *To increase the read-access times*—If files have a large number of concurrent reads, you can increase the replication factor to allow more nodes to respond to those read requests.

The primary reasons you lower replication is if you're running out of disk space or you no longer require the same service levels required by high replication counts. If you're concerned about running out of disk space, the replication factor can be lowered again when the lack of data availability costs are lower and the read requirements aren't as demanding. It's not unusual for replication counts to go down as data gets older. For example, data that's over a year old might only have a replication factor of 2, and data that's over five years only may have a replication factor of 1.

One of the nice features of HDFS is its *rack awareness*. This is the ability for you to logically group HDFS nodes together in structures that reflect the way processors are stored in physical racks and connected together by an in-rack network. Nodes that are

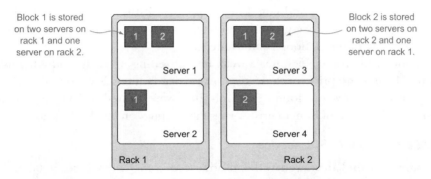

Block 1 is stored on two servers on rack 1 and one server on rack 2.

Block 2 is stored on two servers on rack 2 and one server on rack 1.

Figure 8.3 HDFS is designed to have rack awareness so that you can instruct data blocks to be spread onto multiple racks, which could be located in multiple data centers. In this example, all blocks are stored on three separate servers (replication factor of 3) and HDFS spreads the blocks over two racks. If either rack becomes unavailable, there will always be a replica of both block 1 and block 2.

physically stored in the same rack usually have higher bandwidth connectivity between the nodes and using this network keeps data off of other shared networks. This is shown in figure 8.3.

One of the advantages of rack awareness is that you can increase your availability by carefully distributing HDFS blocks on different racks.

We've also discussed how NoSQL systems move the queries to the data, not the data to the query. Since the data is stored on three nodes, which node should run the query? The answer is usually the least-busy node. How does the query distribution system know what nodes hold the data? This is where there must be a tight coupling of the filesystem and the query distribution system. The information about what node the data is on must be communicated to the client program.

The primary disadvantage of using an external filesystem is that your database may not be as portable on operating systems that don't support these filesystems. For example, HDFS is usually run on UNIX or Linux operating systems. If you want to deploy HBase—which is designed to run on HDFS—you may have more hoops to jump through to get HDFS to run on a Windows system. Using a virtual machine is one way to do this, but there can be a performance penalty with using virtual machines.

We should note that you can get the same replication factor by using an off-the-shelf storage area network (SAN). What you won't get with this configuration is an easy way to keep the query and the data on the same server. Using a SAN for high-availability databases can work for small datasets, but larger datasets will result in excessive network traffic. In the long run, the Hadoop architecture of shared-nothing processors all working on their own copy of a large dataset is the most scalable solution.

Setting up a Hadoop cluster can be a great way to make sure your NoSQL database has both high availability and scale-out performance. Early versions of Hadoop (usually referred to as version 1.x) had a single point of failure on the NameNode service. For high availability, Hadoop used a secondary failover node that was automatically replicated with the data and could be swapped in if the master NameNode failed. Since 2010, there have been specialized releases of Hadoop that removed the single point of failure of the Hadoop NameNode.

Although the NameNode was a weak link in setting up early Hadoop clusters, it was usually not the primary cause of most service failures. Facebook did a study of their service failures and found that only 10% were related to NameNode failures. Most were the result of human error or systematic bugs on all Hadoop nodes.

8.3.4   Using a managed NoSQL service

Organizations find that even with an advanced NoSQL database, it takes a huge amount of engineering to create and maintain predictable high-availability data services that scale. Unless you have a large IT budget and specialized staff, you'll find it more cost effective to let companies experienced in database setup and configuration handle the job and let your own staff focus on application development. Today the costs for using cloud-based NoSQL applications are a fraction of what internal IT departments charge to set up and configure systems.

Let's take a look at how an Amazon DynamoDB key-value store can be configured to give you high-availability.

8.3.5   Case study: using Amazon DynamoDB
for a high-availability data store

The original Amazon DynamoDB paper, introduced in chapter 1, was one of the most influential papers in the NoSQL movement. This paper detailed how Amazon rejected RDBMS designs and used its own custom distributed computing system to support the requirements of horizontal scalability and high availability for their web shopping cart.

Originally, Amazon didn't make the DynamoDB software open source. Yet despite the lack of source code, the DynamoDB paper heavily influenced other NoSQL systems such as Cassandra, Redis, and Riak. In February 2012, Amazon made DynamoDB available as a database service for other developers to use. This case study reviews the Amazon DynamoDB service and how it can be used as a fully managed, highly available, scalable database service.

Let's start by looking at DynamoDB's high-level features. Dynamo's key innovation is its ability to quickly and precisely tune throughput. The service can reliably handle a large volume of read and write transactions, which can be tuned on a minute-by-minute basis by modifying values on a web page. Figure 8.4 shows an example of this user interface.

DynamoDB handles how many servers are used and how the loads are balanced between the servers. Amazon provides an API so you can change the provisioned throughput programmatically based on the results of your load monitoring system. No operator intervention is required. Your monthly Amazon bill will be automatically adjusted as these parameters change.

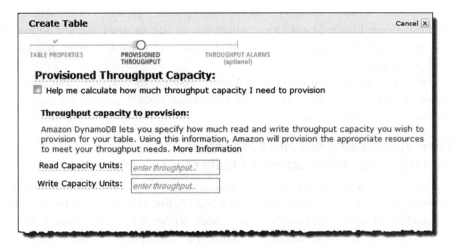

Figure 8.4 Amazon DynamoDB table throughput provisioning. By changing the number of read capacity units or write capacity units, you can tune each table in your database to use the correct number of servers based on your capacity needs. Amazon also provides tools to help you calculate the number of units your application will need.

Amazon implements the DynamoDB service using complex algorithms to evenly distribute reliable read and write transactions over tens of thousands of servers. DynamoDB is also unique in that it was one of the first systems to be deployed exclusively on solid state disks (SSDs). Using SSDs allows DynamoDB to have a predictable service level.

One of the goals of DynamoDB is to provide consistent single-digit millisecond read times. The exclusive use of SSDs means that DynamoDB never has to take disk-access latency into consideration. The net result is your users get consistent responses to all GET and PUT operations, and web pages built with data on DynamoDB will seem faster than most disk-based databases.

The DynamoDB API gives you fine-grained control of read consistency. A developer can choose if they want an immediate read of a value from the local node (called an *eventually consistent* read) or a slower but *guaranteed consistent* read of an item. The guaranteed consistent read will take a bit longer to make sure that the node you're reading from has the latest copy of your item. If your application knows that the values haven't changed, the immediate read will be faster.

This fine-grained control of how you read data is an excellent example of how you can use your knowledge of consistency (covered in chapter 2) to fine-tune your application. It's important to note that you can always force your reads to be consistent, but it would be challenging to configure SQL-backed data services to integrate this feature. SQL has no option to "make consistent before select" when working with distributed systems.

DynamoDB is ideal for organizations that have elastic demand. The notion of paying for what you use is a primary way to save on hosting expenses. Yet when you do need to scale, DynamoDB has the headroom for quick growth. DynamoDB offers scalable transform Elastic MapReduce, which allows you to move large amounts of data into and out of DynamoDB if you need efficient and scalable extract, transform, and load (ETL) processes.

Now that we've shown you how NoSQL systems use various strategies to create high-availability database services, let's look at two NoSQL products with strong reputations for high availability.

8.4   Case study: using Apache Cassandra as a high-availability column family store

This case study will look at Apache Cassandra, a NoSQL column-family store with a strong reputation for scalability and high availability, even under intense write loads. Cassandra was an early adopter of a pure peer-to-peer distribution model. All nodes in a Cassandra cluster have identical functionality, and clients can write to any node in the cluster at any time. Because Cassandra doesn't have any single master node, there's no single point of failure and you don't have to set up and test a failover node. Apache Cassandra is an interesting combination of NoSQL technologies. It's sometimes described as a Bigtable data model with a Dynamo-inspired implementation.

In addition to its robust peer-to-peer model, Cassandra has a strong focus on making it easy to set up and configure both write and read consistency levels. Table 8.2 shows the various write consistency-level settings that you can use once you've configured your replication level.

Table 8.2 **The codes used to specify consistency levels in Cassandra tables on writes. Each table in Cassandra is configured to meet the consistency levels you need when the table is created. You can change the consistency level at any time and Cassandra will automatically reconfigure to the new settings. There are similar codes for read levels**

Level	Write guarantee
ZERO (weak consistency)	No write confirmation is done. No consistency guarantees. If the server crashes, the write may never actually happen.
ANY (weak consistency)	A write confirmation from any single node, including a special "hinted hand-off" node, will be sufficient for the write to be acknowledged.
ONE (weak consistency)	A write confirmation from any single node will be sufficient for the write to be acknowledged.
TWO	Ensure that the write has been written to at least two replicas before responding to the client.
THREE	Ensure that the write has been written to at least three replicas before responding to the client.
QUORUM (strong consistency)	$N/2 + 1$ replicas where N is the replication factor.
LOCAL_QUORUM	Ensure that the write has been written to <ReplicationFactor> / 2 + 1 nodes, within the local data center (requires `NetworkTopologyStrategy`).

Table 8.2   (continued)

Level	Write guarantee
EACH_QUORUM	Ensure that the write has been written to <ReplicationFactor> / 2 + 1 nodes in each data center (requires `NetworkTopologyStrategy`).
ALL (strong consistency)	All replicas must confirm that the data was written to disk.

Next, you consider what to do if one of the nodes is unavailable during a read transaction. How can you specify the number of nodes to check before you return a new value? Checking only one node will return a value quickly, but it may be out of date. Checking multiple nodes may take a few milliseconds longer, but will guarantee you get the latest version in the cluster. The answer is to allow the client reader to specify a consistency level code similar to the write codes discussed here. Cassandra clients can select from codes of ONE, TWO, THREE, QUORUM, LOCAL_QUORUM, EACH _QUORUM, and ALL when doing reads. You can even use the EACH_QUORUM code to check multiple data centers around the world before the client returns a value.

As you'll see next, Cassandra uses specific configuration terms that you should understand before you set up and configure your cluster.

8.4.1   Configuring data to node mappings with Cassandra

In our discussion of consistent hashing, we introduced the concept of using a hash to evenly distribute data around a cluster. Cassandra uses this same concept of creating a hash to evenly distribute their data. Before we dive into how Cassandra does this, let's take a look at some key terms and definitions found in the Cassandra system.

ROWKEY

A *rowkey* is a row identifier that's hashed and used to place the data item on one or more nodes. The rowkey is the only structure used to place data onto a node. No column values are used to place data on nodes. Designing your rowkey structure is a critical step to making sure similar items are clustered together for fast access.

PARTITIONER

A *partitioner* is the strategy that determines how to assign a row to a node based on its key. The default setting is to select a random node. Cassandra uses an MD5 hash of the key to generate a consistent hash. This has the effect of randomly distributing rows evenly over all the nodes. The other option is to use the actual bytes in a rowkey (not a hash of the key) to place the row on a specific node.

KEYSPACE

A *keyspace* is the data structure that determines how a key is replicated over multiple nodes. By default, replication might be set to 3 for any data that needs a high degree of availability.

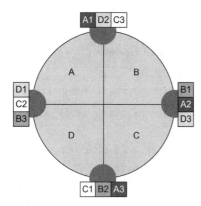

Figure 8.5   **A sample of how replication works on a Cassandra keyspace using the `SimpleStrategy` configuration. Items A1, B1, C1, and D1 are written to a four-node cluster with a replication factor of 3. Each item is stored on three distinct nodes. After writing to an initial node, Cassandra "walks around the ring" in a clockwise direction until it stores the item on two additional nodes.**

An example of a Cassandra keyspace is usually drawn as a ring, as illustrated in figure 8.5.

Cassandra allows you to fine-tune replication based on the properties of keyspace. When you add any row to a Cassandra system, you must associate a keyspace with that row. Each keyspace allows you to set and change the replication factor of that row. An example of a keyspace declaration is shown in figure 8.6.

Using this strategy will allow you to evenly distribute the rows over all the nodes in the cluster, eliminating bottlenecks. Although you can use specific bits in your key, this practice is strongly discouraged, as it leads to hotspots in your cluster and can be administratively complex. The main disadvantage with this approach is that if you change your partitioning algorithm, you have to save and restore your entire dataset.

When you have multiple racks or multiple data centers, the algorithm might need to be modified to ensure data is written to multiple racks or even to multiple data centers before the write acknowledgement is returned. If you change the placement-strategy value from `SimpleStrategy` to `NetworkTopologyStrategy`, Cassandra will walk around the ring until it finds a node that's on a different rack or a different data center.

Because Cassandra has a full peer-to-peer deployment model, it's seen as a good fit for organizations that want both scalability and availability in a column family system. In our next case study, you'll see how Couchbase 2.0 uses a peer-to-peer model with a JSON document store.

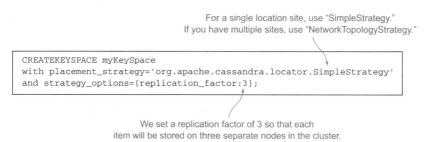

For a single location site, use "SimpleStrategy."
If you have multiple sites, use "NetworkTopologyStrategy."

```
CREATEKEYSPACE myKeySpace
with placement_strategy='org.apache.cassandra.locator.SimpleStrategy'
and strategy_options={replication_factor:3};
```

We set a replication factor of 3 so that each
item will be stored on three separate nodes in the cluster.

Figure 8.6   **A sample of how replication is configured within Cassandra. Replication is a property of keys that indicates the type of network you're on and the replication for each key.**

8.5   Case study: using Couchbase as a high-availability document store

Couchbase 2.0 is a JSON document store that uses many of the same replication patterns found in other NoSQL databases.

Couchbase vs. CouchDB

Couchbase technology shouldn't be confused with Apache CouchDB. Though both are open source technologies, they're separate open source projects that have significantly different capabilities, and they support different application developer needs and use cases. Under the covers, Couchbase has more in common with the original Memcached project than the original CouchDB project. Couchbase and CouchDB share the same way of generating views of JSON documents, but their implementations are different.

Like Cassandra, Couchbase uses a peer-to-peer distribution model, where all nodes provide the same services, thus eliminating the possibility of a single point of failure. Unlike Cassandra, Couchbase uses a document store rather than a column family store, which allows you to query based on a document's content. Additionally, Couchbase uses the keyspace concept that associates key ranges with individual nodes.

Figure 8.7 shows the components in a multidata-center Couchbase server. Couchbase stores document collections in containers called *buckets*, which are configured and administered much like folders in a filesystem. There are two types of buckets: a memcached bucket (which is volatile and resides in RAM), and a Couchbase bucket,

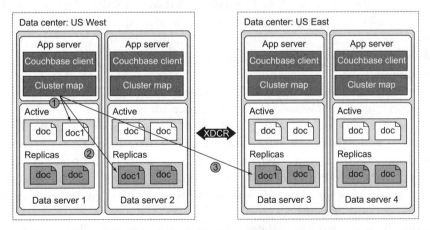

Figure 8.7   High-availability documents in Couchbase. Couchbase buckets are logical collections of documents that are configured for high availability. Couchbase clients use cluster maps to find the physical node where the active version of a document is stored. The cluster map directs the client to a file on the active node (1). If Data server 1 is unavailable, the cluster map will make a replica of doc1 on Data server 2 the active version (2). If the entire US West data center goes down, the client will use cross data center replication (XDCR) and make a copy on Data server 3 active (3) from the US East region.

which is backed up by disk and configured with replication. A Couchbase JSON document is written to one or more disks. For our discussions on high-availability systems, we'll focus on Couchbase buckets.

Internally, Couchbase uses a concept called a *vBucket* (virtual bucket) that's associated with one or more portions of a hash-partitioned keyspace. Couchbase keyspaces are similar to those found in Cassandra, but Couchbase keyspace management is done transparently when items are stored. Note that a vBucket isn't a single range in a keyspace; it may contain many noncontiguous ranges in keyspaces. Thankfully, users don't need to worry about managing keyspaces or how vBuckets work. Couchbase clients simply work with buckets and let Couchbase worry about what node will be used to find the data in a bucket. Separating buckets from vBuckets is one of the primary ways that Couchbase achieves horizontal scalability.

Using information in the cluster map, Couchbase stores data on a primary node as well as a replica node. If any node in a Couchbase cluster fails, the node will be marked with a failover status and the cluster maps will all be updated. All data requests to the node will automatically be redirected to replica nodes.

After a node fails and replicas have been promoted, users will typically initiate a rebalance operation to add new nodes to the cluster to restore the full capacity of the cluster. Rebalancing effectively changes the mapping of vBuckets to nodes. During a rebalance operation, vBuckets are evenly redistributed between nodes in the cluster to minimize data movement. Once a vBucket has been re-created on the new node, it'll be automatically disabled on the original node and enabled on the new node. These functions all happen without any interruption of services.

Couchbase has features to allow a Couchbase cluster to run without interruption even if an entire data center fails. For systems that span multiple data centers, Couchbase uses *cross data center replication (XDCR)*, which allows data to automatically be replicated between remote data centers and still be active in both data centers. If one data center becomes unavailable, the other data center can pick up the load to provide continuous service.

One of the greatest strengths of Couchbase is the built-in, high-precision monitoring tools. Figure 8.8 shows a sample of these monitoring tools.

These fine-grained monitoring tools allow you to quickly locate bottlenecks in Couchbase and rebalance memory and server resources based on your loads. These tools eliminate the need to purchase third-party memory monitoring tools or configure external monitoring frameworks. Although it takes some training to understand how to use these monitoring tools, they're the first line of defense when keeping your Couchbase clusters healthy.

Couchbase also has features that allow software to be upgraded without an interruption in service. This process involves replication of data to a new node that has a new version of software and then cutting over to that new node. These features allow you to provide a 24/365 service level to your users without downtime.

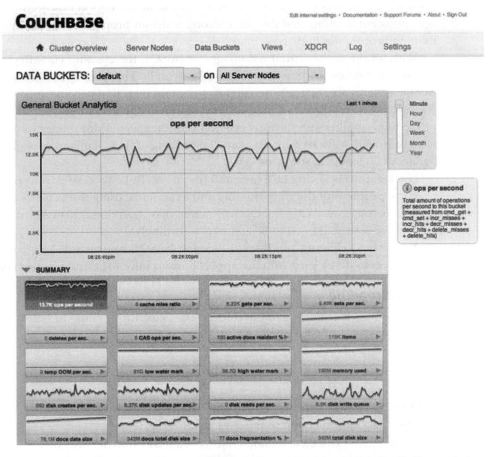

Figure 8.8   Couchbase comes with a set of customizable web-based operations monitoring reports to allow you to see the impact of loads on Couchbase resources. The figure shows a minute-by-minute, operations-per-second display on the default bucket. You can select from any one of 20 views to see additional information.

8.6   Summary

In this chapter, you learned how NoSQL systems can be configured to create highly available data services for key-value stores, column family stores, and document stores. Not only can NoSQL data services be highly available, they can also be tuned to meet precise service levels at reasonable costs. We've looked at how NoSQL databases leverage distributed filesystems like Hadoop with fine-grained control over file replication. Finally, we've reviewed some examples of how turnkey data services have been created to take advantage of NoSQL architectures.

Organizations have found that high-availability NoSQL systems that run on multiple processors can be more cost-effective than RDBMSs, even if the RDBMSs are configured for high availability. The principal reason has to do with the use of simple distributed data stores like key-value stores. Key-value stores don't use joins; they leverage consistent hashing; and they have strong scale-out properties. Simplicity of design frequently promotes high availability.

With all the architectural advantages of NoSQL for creating cost-effective, high-availability databases, there are drawbacks as well. The principal drawback is that NoSQL systems are relatively new and may contain bugs that become apparent in rare circumstances or unusual configurations. The NoSQL community is full of stories where high-visibility web startups experienced unexpected downtimes using new versions of NoSQL software without adequate training of their staff and enough time and budget to do load and stress testing.

Load and stress testing take time and resources. To be successful, your project may need the people with the right training and experience using the same tools and configuration you have. With NoSQL still newer than traditional RDBMSs, the training budgets for your staff need to be adjusted accordingly.

In our next chapter, you'll see how using NoSQL systems will help you be agile with respect to developing software applications to solve your business problems.

8.7   *Further reading*

- "About Data Partitioning in Cassandra." DataStax. http://mng.bz/TI33.
- "Amazon DynamoDB." Amazon Web Services. http://aws.amazon.com/dynamodb.
- "Amazon DynamoDB: Provisioned Throughput." Amazon Web Services. http://mng.bz/492J.
- "Amazon S3 Service Level Agreement." Amazon Web Services. http://aws.amazon.com/s3-sla/.
- "Amazon S3—The First Trillion Objects." Amazon Web Services Blog. http://mng.bz/r1Ae.
- Apache Cassandra. http://cassandra.apache.org.
- Apache JMeter. http://jmeter.apache.org/.
- Brodkin, Jon. "Amazon bests Microsoft, all other contenders in cloud storage test." Ars Technica. December 2011. http://mng.bz/ItNZ.
- "Data Protection." Amazon Web Services. http://mng.bz/15yb.
- DeCandia, Giuseppe, et al. "Dynamo: Amazon's Highly Available Key-Value Store." Amazon.com. 2007. http://mng.bz/YY5A.
- Hale, Coda. "You Can't Sacrifice Partition Tolerance." October 2010. http://mng.bz/9i3I.
- "High Availability." Neo4j. http://mng.bz/9661.
- "High-availability cluster." Wikipedia. http://mng.bz/SHs5.
- "In Search of Five 9s: Calculating Availability of Complex Systems." edgeblog. October 2007. http://mng.bz/3P2e.

- Luciani, Jake. "Cassandra File System Design." DataStax. February 2012. http://mng.bz/TfuN.
- Ryan, Andrew. "Hadoop Distributed Filesystem reliability and durability at Facebook." Lanyrd. June 2012. http://mng.bz/UAX9.
- "Tandem Computers." Wikipedia. http://mng.bz/yljh.
- Vogels, Werner. "Amazon DynamoDB—A Fast and Scalable NoSQL Database Service Designed for Internet Scale Applications." January 2012. http://mng.bz/HpN9.

Increasing agility with NoSQL

This chapter covers

- Measuring agility
- How NoSQL increases agility
- Using document stores to avoid object-relational mapping

> *Change is no longer just incremental. Radical "nonlinear change" which brings about a different order is becoming more frequent.*
>
> —Cheshire Henbury,
> "The Problem"

Can your organization quickly adapt to changing business conditions? Can your computer systems rapidly respond to increased workloads? Can your developers quickly add features to your applications to take advantage of new business opportunities? Can nonprogrammers maintain business rules without needing help from software developers? Have you ever wanted to build a web application that works with complex data, but you didn't have the budget for teams of database modelers, SQL developers, database administrators, and Java developers?

If you answered yes to any of these questions, you should consider evaluating a NoSQL solution. We've found that NoSQL solutions can reduce the time it takes to build, scale, and modify applications. Whereas scalability is the primary reason companies move away from RDBMSs, agility is the reason NoSQL solutions "stick." Once you've experienced the simplicity and flexibility of NoSQL, the old ways seem like a chore.

As we move through this chapter, we'll talk about agility. You'll learn about the challenges one encounters when attempting to objectively measure it. We'll quickly review the problems encountered when trying to store documents in a relational database and the problems associated with object-relational mapping. We'll close out the chapter with a case study that uses a NoSQL solution to manage complex business forms.

9.1 What is software agility?

Let's begin by defining software agility and talk about why businesses use NoSQL technologies to quickly build new applications and respond to changes in business requirements.

We define software *agility* as the ability to quickly adapt software systems to changing business requirements. Agility is strongly coupled with both operational robustness and developer productivity. Agility is more than rapidly creating new applications; it means being able to respond to changing business rules without rewriting code.

To expand, agility is the ability to rapidly

- Build new applications
- Scale applications to quickly match new levels of demand
- Change existing applications without rewriting code
- Allow nonprogrammers to create and maintain business logic

From the developer productivity perspective, agility includes all stages of the software development lifecycle (SDLC) from creating requirements, documenting use cases, and creating test data to maintaining business rules in existing applications. As you may know, some of these activities are handled by staff who aren't traditionally thought of as developers or programmers. From a NoSQL perspective, agility can help to increase the productivity of programmers and nonprogrammers alike.

Traditionally, we think of "programmers" as staff who have a four-year degree in computer science or software engineering. They understand the details of how

> ### Agility vs. agile development
> Our discussion of agility shouldn't be confused with *agile development*, which is a set of guidelines for managing the software development process. Our focus is the impact of database architecture on agility.

computers work and are knowledgeable about issues related to memory allocation, pointers, and multiple languages like Java, .Net, Perl, Python, and PHP.

Nonprogrammers are people who have exposure to their data and may have some experience with SQL or writing spreadsheet macros. Nonprogrammers focus on getting work done for the business; they generally don't write code. Typical nonprogrammer roles might include business analyst, rules analyst, data quality analyst, or quality assurance.

There's a large body of anecdotal evidence that NoSQL solutions have a positive impact on agility, but there are few scientific studies to support the claim. One study, funded by 10gen, the company behind MongoDB, found that more than 40% of the organizations using MongoDB had a greater than 50% improvement in developer productivity. These results are shown in figure 9.1.

When you ask people why they think NoSQL solutions increase agility, many reasons are cited. Some say NoSQL allows programmers to stay focused on their data and build data-centric solutions; others say the lack of object-relational mapping opens up opportunities for nonprogrammers to participate in the development process and shorten development timelines, resulting in greater agility.

By removing object-relational mapping, someone with a bit of background in SQL, HTML, or XML can build and maintain their own web applications with some training. After this training, most people are equipped to perform all of the key operations such as create, read, update, delete, and search (CRUDS) on their records.

Programmers also benefit from no object-relational mapping, as they can move their focus from mapping issues to creating automated tools for others to use. But the impact of all these time- and money-saving NoSQL trends puts more pressure on an enterprise solution architect to determine whether NoSQL solutions are right for the team.

If you've spent time working with multilayered software architectures, you're likely familiar with the challenges of keeping these layers in sync. User interfaces, middle tier objects, and databases must all be updated together to maintain consistency. If any layer is out of sync, the systems fail. It takes a great deal of time to keep the layers in sync. The time to sync and retest each of the layers slows down a team and hampers agility. NoSQL architectures promote agility because there are fewer layers of software,

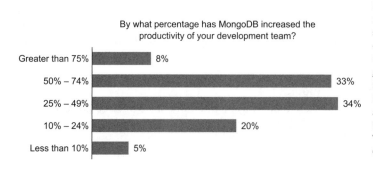

Figure 9.1 Results of 10gen survey of their users show that more than 40% of development teams using MongoDB had a greater than 50% increase in productivity. This study included 61 organizations and the data was validated in May of 2012. (Source: TechValidate. TVID: F1D-0F5-7B8)

and changes in one layer don't cause problems with other layers. This means your team can add new features without the need to sync all the layers.

NoSQL *schema-less datasets* usually refers to datasets that don't require predefined tables, columns (with types), and primary-foreign key relationships. Datasets that don't require these predefined structures are more adaptable to change. When you first begin to design your system, you may not know what data elements you need. NoSQL systems allow you to use new elements and associate the data types, indexes, and rules to new elements when you need them, not before you get the data. As new data elements are loaded into some NoSQL databases, indexes are automatically created to identify this data. If you add a new element for `PersonBirthDate` anywhere in a JSON or XML input file, it'll be added to an index of other `PersonBirthDate` elements in your database. Note that a range index on dates for fast sorting many still need to be configured. To take this a step further, let's look at how specific NoSQL data services can be more agile than an entire RDBMS.

NoSQL systems frequently deliver data services for specific portions of a large website or application. They may use dozens of CPUs working together to deliver these services in configurations that are designed to duplicate data for faster guaranteed response times and reliability. The NoSQL data service CPUs are often dedicated to these services and no other functions. As the requirements for performance and reliability change, more CPUs can be automatically added to share the load, increase response time, and lower the probability of downtime.

This architecture of using dedicated NoSQL servers to create highly tunable data services is in sharp contrast to traditional RDBMSs that typically have hundreds or thousands of tables all stored on a single CPU. Trying to create precise data service levels for one service can be difficult if not impossible if you consider that some data services will be negatively impacted by large query loads on other unrelated database tables. NoSQL data architectures, when combined with distributed processing, allow organizations to be more agile and resilient to the changing needs of businesses.

Our focus in this chapter is the impact of NoSQL database architecture on overall software agility. But before we wrap up our discussion of defining agility as it relates to NoSQL architecture, let's take a look at how deployment strategies also impact agility.

9.1.1 *Apply your knowledge: local or cloud-based deployment?*

Sally is working on a project that has a tight budget and a short timeline. The organization she works for prefers to use database servers in their own data center, but in the right situation they allow cloud-based deployments. Since the project is a new service, the business unit is unable to accurately predict either the demand for the service or the throughput requirements.

Sally wants to consider the impact of a cloud-based deployment on the project's scalability and agility. She asks a friend in operations how long it typically takes for the internal information technology department to order and configure a new database server. She gets an email message with a link to a spreadsheet shown in figure 9.2. This

Average Time to Provision Database Server

Step	Avg. Business Days
Write justification	1
Justification reviewed and approved	3
Order hardware	1
Order OS software (windows/linux)	1
Order database software	1
Order backup software	1
Review rack, power, network and cooling plan	1
Install hardware	2
Install operting systems	2
Install database software	2
Install backup software	1
Configuration and testing	3
Total Business Days	19

Figure 9.2 **Average time required to provision a new database server in a typical large organization. Because NoSQL servers can be deployed as a managed service, a month-long period of time can be dropped to a few minutes if not seconds to change the number of nodes in a cluster.**

figure shows a typical estimate of the steps Sally's information technology department uses to provision a new database server.

As you can see by the Total Business Days calculation, it'll take 19 business days or about a month to complete the project. This stands in sharp contrast to a cloud-based NoSQL deployment that can add capacity in minutes or even seconds. The company does have some virtual machine–based options, but there are no clear guarantees of average response times for the virtual machine options.

Sally opts to use a cloud-based deployment for her NoSQL database for the first year of the project. After the first year, the business unit will reevaluate the costs and compare these with internal costs. This allows the team to quickly move forward with their scale-out testing without incurring up-front capital expenditures associated with ordering and configuring up to a dozen database servers.

Our goal in this chapter is not to compare local versus cloud-based deployment methods. It's to understand how NoSQL architecture impacts a project's development speed. But the choice to use a local or cloud-based deployment should be a consideration in any project.

In chapter 1 we talked about how the business drives of volume, velocity, variability, and agility were the drivers associated with the NoSQL movement. Now that you're familiar with these drivers, you can look at your organization to see how NoSQL solutions might positively impact these drivers to help your business meet the changing demands of today's competitive marketplace.

9.2   *Measuring agility*

Understanding the overall agility of a project/team is the first step in determining the agility associated with one or more database architectures. We'll now look at developer agility to see how it can be objectively measured.

Measuring pure agility in the NoSQL selection process is difficult since it's intertwined with developer training and tools. A person who's an expert with Java and SQL might create a new web application faster than someone who's a novice with a NoSQL system. The key is to remove the tools and staff-dependent components from the measurement process.

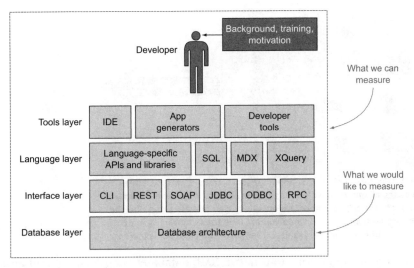

Figure 9.3   The factors that make it challenging to measure the impact of database architecture on overall software agility. Database architecture is only a single component of the entire SDLC ecosystem. Developer agility is strongly influenced by an individual's background, training, and motivation. The tools layer includes items such as the integrated development environment (IDE), app generators, and developer tools. The interface layer includes items such as the command-line interface (CLI) as well as interface protocols.

An application development architecture's overall software agility can be precisely measured. You can track the total number of hours it takes to complete a project using both an RDBMS and a NoSQL solution. But measuring the relationship between the database architecture and agility is more complex, as seen in figure 9.3.

Figure 9.3 shows how the database architecture is a small part of an overall software ecosystem. The diagram identifies all the components of your software architecture and the tools that support it. The architecture has a deep connection with the complexity of the software you use. Simple software can be created and maintained by a smaller team with fewer specialized skills. Simplicity also requires less training and allows team members to assist each other during development.

To determine the relationship between the database architecture and agility, you need a way to subtract the nondatabase architecture components that aren't relevant. One way to do this is to develop a normalization process that tries to separate the unimportant processes from agility measurements. This process is shown in figure 9.4.

This model is driven by selecting key use cases from your requirements and analyzing the amount of effort required to achieve your business goals. Although this sounds complicated, once you've done this a few times, the process seems straightforward.

Let's use the following example. Your team has a new project that involves importing XML data and creating RESTful web services that return only portions of this data using a search service. Your team meets and talks about the requirements, and the development staff creates a high-level outline of the steps and effort required. You've

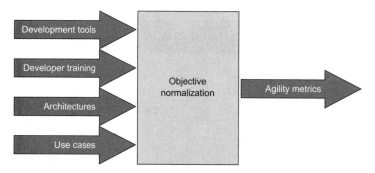

Figure 9.4   Factors such as development tools, training, architectures, and use cases all impact developer agility. In order to do a fair comparison of the impact of NoSQL architecture on agility, you need to normalize the non-architecture components. Once you balance these factors, you can compare how different NoSQL architectures drive the agility of a project.

narrowed down the options to a native XML database using XQuery and an RDBMS using a Java middle tier. For the sake of simplicity, effort is categorized using a scale of 1 to 5, where 1 is the least effort and 5 is the most effort. A sample of this analysis is shown in table 9.1.

Table 9.1   High-level effort analysis to build a RESTful search service from an XML dataset. The steps to build the service are counted and a rough effort level (1-5) is used to measure the difficulty of each step.

NoSQL document store	SQL/Java method
1. Drag and drop XML file into database collection (1) 2. Write XQuery (2) 3. Publish API document (1) Total effort: 4 units	1. Inventory all XML elements (2) 2. Design data model (5) 3. Write create table statements (5) 4. Execute create table (1) 5. Convert XML into SQL insert statements (4) 6. Run load-data scripts (1) 7. Write SQL scripts to query data (3) 8. Create Java JDBC program to query data and Java REST programs to convert SQL results into XML (5) 9. Compile Java program and install on middle-tier server (2) 10. Publish API document (1) Total effort: 29 units

Performing this type of analysis can show you how suitable an architecture is for a particular use case. Large projects may have many use cases, and you'll likely get conflicting results. The key is to involve a diverse group of people to create a fair and objective estimate of the total effort that's decoupled from background and training issues.

The amount of time you spend looking at the effort involved in each use case is up to you and your team. Informal "thought experiments" work well if the team has people with adequate experience in each alternative database and a high level of trust exists in the group's ability to fairly compare effort. If there are disputes on the relative effort, you may need to write sample code for some use cases. Although this takes time and slows a selection process, it's sometimes necessary to fairly evaluate alternatives and validate objective effort comparisons.

Many organizations that are comparing RDBMSs and document stores find a significant reduction in effort in use cases that focus on data import and export. In our next section, we'll focus on a detailed analysis of the translations RDBMSs need to convert data to and from natural business objects.

9.3 Using document stores to avoid object-relational mapping

You may be familiar with the saying *"A clever person solves a problem. A wise person avoids it."* Organizations that adopt document stores to avoid an object-relational layer are wise indeed. The conversion of object hierarchies to and from rigid tabular structures can be one of most vexing problems in building applications. Avoiding the object-relational layer mapping is a primary reason developer productivity increases when using NoSQL systems.

Early computer systems used in business focused on the management of financial and accounting data. This tabular data was represented in a flat file of consistent rows and columns. For example, financial systems stored general ledger data in a series of columns and rows that represented debits and credits. These systems were easy to model, the data was extremely consistent, and the variability between how customers stored financial information was minimal.

Later, other departments began to see how storing and analyzing data could help them manage inventory and make better business decisions. For many departments, the types of data captured and stored needed to change. A simple tabular structure could no longer meet the organization's needs. Engineers did what they do best: they attempted to work within their existing structure to accommodate the new requirements. After all, they had a sizeable investment in people and systems, so they wanted to use the same RDBMS used in accounting.

As things evolved, business components were represented in a middle tier using object models. Object models were more flexible than the original punch card models, as they naturally represented the way business entities were stored. Objects could contain other objects, which could in turn contain additional objects. To save the state of an object, many SQL statements would need to be generated to save and reassemble objects. In the late 1990s these objects also needed to be viewed and edited using a web browser, sometimes requiring additional translations.

The most common design was to create a four-step translation process, as shown in figure 9.5.

If you think this four-step translation process is complex, it can be. Let's see how you might compare the four-translation pain to putting away your clothing.

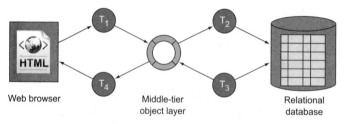

Web browser   Middle-tier   Relational
                     object layer   database

Figure 9.5   The four-translation web-object-RDBMS model. This model is used when objects are used as a middle layer between a web page and a relational database. The first translation (T1) is the conversion from HTML web pages to middle-tier objects. The second translation (T2) is a conversion from middle tier objects to relational database statements such as SQL. RDBMSs return only tables so the third translation (T3) is the transformation of tables back into objects. The fourth translation (T4) is converting objects into HTML for display in web pages.

Imagine using this process on a daily basis as you return home from a long day at the office. You'd take off your clothes and start by removing all of the thread, dismantling your clothes bit by bit, and then putting them away in uniform bolts of cloth. When you get up in the morning to go to work, you'd then retrieve your needle and thread and re-sew all your clothes back together again. If you're thinking, "This seems like a lot of unnecessary work," that's the point of the example. Today, NoSQL document stores allow you to avoid the complexities that were caused by the original requirements to store flat tabular data. They really allow development teams to avoid a lot of unnecessary work.

There have been multiple efforts to mitigate the complexities of four-step translation. Tools like Apache Hibernate and Ruby on Rails are examples of frameworks of tools that try to manage the complexity of object-relational mapping. These were the only options available until developers realized that using a NoSQL solution to store the document structure directly in the database without converting it to another format or shredding it into tables and rows is a better solution.

This lack of translation makes NoSQL systems simpler to use and, in turn, allows subject matter experts (SMEs) and other nonprogramming staff to participate directly in the application development process. By encouraging SMEs to have a direct involvement in building applications, course corrections can be made early in the software development process, saving time and money associated with rework.

NoSQL technologies show how moving from storing data in tables to storing data in documents opens up possibilities for new ways of using and presenting data. As you move your systems out of the back room to the World Wide Web, you'll see how NoSQL solutions can make implementation less painful.

Next we'll look at combining a no-translation architecture with web standards to create a development platform that's easy to use and portable across multiple NoSQL platforms.

9.4 Case study: using XRX to manage complex forms

This case study will look at how zero translation can be used to store complex form data. We'll look at the characteristics of complex forms, how XForms works, and how the XRX web application architecture uses a document store to allow nonprogrammers to build and maintain these form applications.

XRX stands for the three standards that are used to build web form–based applications. The first X stands for *XForms*; the R stands for *REST*, and the final X stands for *XQuery*, the W3C server-side functional programming language we introduced you to in chapter 5.

9.4.1 What are complex business forms?

If you've built HTML form applications, you know that building simple forms like a login page or registration form is simple and straightforward. Generally, simple forms have a few fields, a selection list, and a Save button, all of which can be built using a handful of HTML tags.

This case study looks at a complex class of forms that need more than simple HTML elements. These complex forms are similar to those you'll find in a large company or perhaps a shopping cart form on a retail website.

If you can store your form data in a single row within an RDBMS table, then you might not have a complex business application as defined here. Using simple HTML and a SQL INSERT statement may be the best solution for your problem. But our experience is that there's a large class of business forms that go beyond what HTML forms can do.

Complex business forms have complex data and also have complex user interfaces. They share some of the following characteristics:

- *Repeating elements*—Conditionally adding two or more items to a form. For example, when you enter a person they may have multiple phone numbers, interests, or skills.
- *Conditional views*—Conditionally enabling a region of a form based on how the user fills out various fields. For example, the question "Are you pregnant?" should be disabled if a patient's gender is male.
- *Cascading selection*—Changing one selection list based on the value of another list. For example, if you select a country code, a list of state or province codes will appear for that country.
- *Field-by-field validation*—Business rules check the values of each field and give the user immediate feedback.
- *Context help*—Fields have help and hint text to guide users through the selection process.
- *Role-based contextualization*—Each role in an organization might see a slightly different version of the form. For example, only users with a role of Publisher might see an Approve for Publishing button.

- *Type-specific controls*—If you know an element is a specific data type, XForms can automatically change the user interface control. Boolean true/false values appear as true/false check boxes and date fields have calendars that allow you to pick the date.
- *Autocomplete*—As users enter characters in a field, you want to be able to suggest the remainder of the text in a field. This is also known as *autosuggest*.

Although these aren't the only features that XForms supports, they give you some idea of the complexity involved in creating forms. Now let's see how these features can be added to forms without the need for complex JavaScript.

9.4.2   Using XRX to replace client JavaScript and object-relational mapping

All of the features listed in the prior section *could* be implemented by writing JavaScript within the web browser. Your custom JavaScript code would send your objects to an object-relational mapping layer for storage within an RDBMS, which is how many enterprise forms are created today. If you and your team are experienced JavaScript developers and know your way around object-relational frameworks, this is one option for you to consider. But NoSQL document stores provide a much simpler option. With XRX, you can develop these complex forms without using JavaScript or an object-relation layer. First let's review some terminology and then see how XRX can make this process simpler.

Figure 9.6 shows the three main components of a form: model, binding, and view. When a user fills out a form, the data that's stored when they click Save is called the *model*. The components that are on the screen and visible to the user, including items in a selection list, are referred to as the *view* components of a form. The process of associating the model elements with the view is called *binding*. We call this a *model-view forms architecture*.

To use a form in a web browser, you must first move the default or existing form data from the database to the model. After the model data is in place, the form takes over and manages movement of data from the model to and from the views using the bindings. As a user enters information into a field, the model data is updated. When

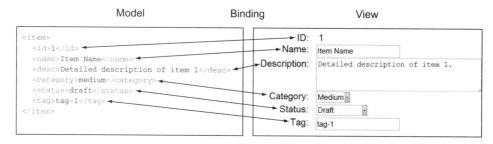

Figure 9.6   The main components in a form. The model holds the business data to be saved to the server. The view displays the individual fields, including selection list options. The binding associates the user interface fields with model elements.

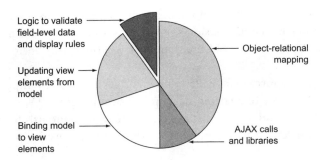

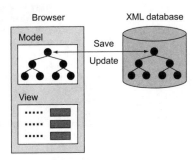

Figure 9.7 The breakdown of code used in a typical forms applications when an RDBMS, middle-tier objects, and JavaScript are used. Middle-tier objects are moved to and from a model within the client. XRX attempts to automate all but the critical business logic components of forms processing (top-left wedge).

the user selects Save, the updated model data is stored on the server. Figure 9.7 shows a typical breakdown of code needed to implement business forms using a standard model and view architecture.

From the figure, you can see that close to 90% of this code is similar for most business forms and involves moving data between layers. This code does all the work of getting data in and out of the database and moving the data around the forms as users fill in the fields. These steps include transferring the data to a middle tier, then moving the code into the model of the browser, and finally, when the user clicks Save, the path is reversed.

XRX attempts to automate all generic code that moves the data. In turn, the software developer focuses on selecting and validating field-level controls as the user enters the data and the logic to conditionally display the form. This architecture has a positive impact on agility, and it empowers nonprogrammers to build robust applications without ever learning JavaScript or object-relational mapping systems.

Figure 9.8 shows how this works within the XRX web application architecture.

With XForms, the entire structure that you're editing is stored as an XML document within the model of the browser. On the server side, document stores, such as a native XML database, are used to store these structures. The beauty of this architecture is there's no conversion or need for object-relational mapping; everything fits together like a hand in a glove.

Most native XML databases come with a built-in REST interface. This is where the *R* in XRX comes in. XForms allows you to add a single XML element called `<submission>` to specify how the Save button on your form will call a REST function on your server. These functions are usually written in XQuery, the final *X* in XRX.

Figure 9.8 How XML files from a native XML database are loaded into the model of an XForms application. This is an example of a zero-translation architecture. Once the XML data is loaded into the XForms model, views will allow the user to edit model content in a web form. When the user selects Save, the instance data in the model is saved directly to the database without the need for translation into objects or tables. No object-relational mapping layer is needed.

XForms is an example of a declarative domain-specific language customized for data entry forms. Like other declarative systems, XForms allows you to specify *what* you want the forms to do but tries to avoid the details of *how* the forms perform the work.

XForms is a collection of approximately 25 elements that are used to implement complex business forms. A sample of XForms markup is shown in figure 9.9.

Because XForms is a W3C standard, it reuses many of the same standards found in XQuery such as XPath and XML Schema datatypes. XForms works well with native XML databases.

There are several ways to implement an XForms solution. You can use a number of open source XForms frameworks (Orbeon, BetterForm, XSLTForms, OpenOffice 3) or a commercial XForms framework (IBM Workplace, EMC XForms). These tools work with web browsers to interpret the XForms elements and convert them into the appropriate behavior. Some XForms tools from Orbeon, OpenOffice, and IBM also have form-builder tools that use XForms to lay out and connect the form elements to your model.

After you've created your form, you need to be able to save your form data to the database. This is where using a native XML database shines. XForms stores the data

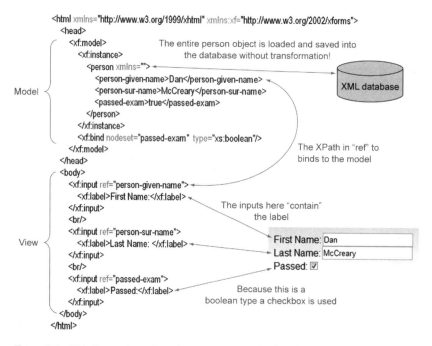

Figure 9.9   This figure shows how data from a native XML database is loaded into the model of XForms. Once the XML data is loaded into the model, XForms views will allow the user to edit the model content in a web form. When the user selects Save, the model is saved without change directly into the database. No object-relational mapping is needed.

you've entered in the form into a single XML document. Most save operations into a native XML database can be done with a single line of code, even if your form is complex.

The real strength of XRX emerges when you need to modify your application. Adding a new field can be done by adding a new element to the model and a few lines of code to the view elements. That's it! No need to change the database, no recompilation of middle-tier objects, and no need to write additional JavaScript code within the browser. XRX keeps things simple.

9.4.3 *Understanding the impact of XRX on agility*

Today, we live in a world where many information technology departments aren't focused on making it easy for business users to build and maintain their own applications. Yet this is exactly what XRX does. Form developers are no longer constrained by IT development schedules of overworked staff who don't have time to learn the complex business rules of each department. With some training, many users can maintain and update their own forms applications.

XRX is a great example of how simplicity and standards drive agility. The fewer components, the easier it is to build new and change existing forms. Because standards are reused, your team doesn't have to learn a new JavaScript library or a new data format. XRX and NoSQL can have a transformative impact on the way work is divided in a project. It means that information technology staff can focus on other tasks rather than updating business rules in Java and JavaScript every time there's a change request.

The lessons you've learned with XRX can be applied to other areas as well. If you have a JSON document store like MongoDB, Couchbase, or CouchDB, you can build JSON services to populate XForms models. There are even versions of XForms that load and save JSON documents. The important architecture element is the elimination of the object-relational layer and the ability to avoid JavaScript programs on the client. If you do this, then your SMEs can take a more active role in your projects and increase organizational agility.

9.5 *Summary*

The primary business driver behind the NoSQL movement was the need for graceful horizontal scalability. This forced a break from the past, and opened new doors to innovative ways of storing data. It allowed innovators to build mature systems that facilitate agile software development. The phrase "*We came for the scalability—we stayed for the agility*" is an excellent summary of this process.

In this chapter, we stressed that comparing agility of two database architecture alternatives is difficult, because overall agility is buried in the software developer's stack. Despite the challenges, we feel it's worthwhile to create use-case-driven thought experiments to help guide objective evaluations.

Almost all NoSQL systems demonstrate excellent scale-out architecture for operational agility. Simple architectures that drive complexity out of the process enable agility in many areas. Our evidence shows that both key-value stores and document stores can provide huge gains in developer agility if applied to the right use cases. Native XML systems that work with web standards also work well with other agility-enhancing systems and empower nonprogrammers.

This is the last of our four chapters on building NoSQL solutions for specific types of business problems. We've focused on big data, search, high availability, and agility. Our next chapter takes a different track. It'll challenge you to think about how you approach problem solving, and introduce new thinking styles that lend themselves to parallel processing. We'll then wrap up with a discussion on security before we look at the formal methods of system selection.

9.6   *Further reading*

- Henbury, Cheshire. "The Problem." http://mng.bz/9I9e.
- "Hibernate (Java)." Wikipedia. http://mng.bz/tEr6.
- Hodges, Nick. "Developer Productivity." November 2012. http://mng.bz/6c3q.
- Hugos, Michael. *Business Agility.* Wiley, 2009. http://mng.bz/6z3I.
- ———— "IT Agility Means Simple Things Done Well, Not Complex Things Done Fast." CIO, International Data Group, February 2008. http://mng.bz/dlzN.
- "JSON Processing Using XQuery." Progress Software. http://mng.bz/aMkn.
- TechValidate. 10gen, MongoDB, productivity chart. March 2012. http://mng.bz/gH0M.
- "JSON Processing Using XQuery." Progress Software. http://mng.bz/aMkn.
- Robie, Jonathan. "JSONiq: XQuery for JSON, JSON for XQuery." 2012 NoSQL Now! Conference. http://mng.bz/uBSe.
- "Ruby on Rails." Wikipedia. http://mng.bz/7q73.

Part 4

Advanced topics

In part 4 we look at two advanced topics associated with NoSQL: functional programming and system security. In our capstone chapter we combine all of the information we've covered so far and walk you through the process of selecting the right SQL, NoSQL, or some combination of systems solution for your project.

At this point the relationship between NoSQL and horizontally scalable systems should be clear. Chapter 10 covers how functional programming, REST, and actor-based frameworks can be used to make your software more scalable.

In chapter 11 we compare the fine-grained control of RDBMS systems to document-related access control systems. We also look at how you might control access to NoSQL data using views, groups, and role-based access controls (RBAC) mechanisms to get the level of security your organization requires.

In our final chapter we take all of the concepts we've explored so far and show you how to match the right database to your business problem. We cover the architectural trade-off process from gathering high-level requirements to communicating results using quality trees. This chapter provides you with a roadmap for selecting the right NoSQL system for your next project.

NoSQL and functional programming

This chapter covers

- Functional programming basics
- Examples of functional programming
- Moving from imperative to functional programming

> The world is concurrent. Things in the world don't share data. Things communicate
> with messages. Things fail.
>
> —Joe Armstrong, cocreator of Erlang

In this chapter, we'll look at functional programming, the benefits of using a functional programming language, and how functional programming forces you to think differently when creating and writing systems.

The transition to functional programming requires a paradigm shift away from software designed to control state and toward software that has a focus on independent data transformation. Most popular programming languages used today, such as C, C++, Java, Ruby, and Python, were written with the needs of a single node as a target platform in mind. Although the compilers and libraries for these languages do support multiple threads on multicore CPUs, the languages and their libraries were created before NoSQL and horizontal scalability on multiple node clusters became a business requirement. In this chapter, we'll look at how organizations are using languages that focus on isolated data transformations to make working with distributed systems easier.

In order to meet the needs of modern distributed systems, you must ask yourself how well a programming language will allow you to write applications that can exponentially scale to serve millions of users connected on the web. It's no longer sufficient to design a system that will scale to 2, 4, or 8 core processors. You need to ask if your architecture will scale to 100, 1,000, or even 10,000 processors.

As we've discussed throughout this book, most NoSQL solutions have been specifically designed to work on many computers. It's the hallmark of horizontal scalability to keep all processors in your cluster working together and adapting to changes in the cluster automatically. Adding these features after the fact is usually not possible. It must be part of the initial design, in the lowest levels of your application stack. The inability of SQL joins to scale out is an excellent example of how retrofits don't work.

Some software architects feel that to make the shift to true horizontal scale-out, you need to make a paradigm shift at the language and runtime library level. This is the shift from a traditional world of object and procedural programming to functional programming. Today most NoSQL systems are embracing the concepts of functional programming, even if they're using some traditional languages to implement the lower-level algorithms. In this chapter, we'll look into the benefits of the functional programming paradigm and show how it's a significant departure from the way things are taught in most colleges and universities today.

10.1 *What is functional programming?*

To understand what functional programming is and how it's different from other programming methods, let's look at how software paradigms are classified. A high-level taxonomy of software paradigms is shown in figure 10.1.

We'll first look at how most popular languages today are based on managing program state and memory values. We'll contrast this with functional programming, which has a focus on data transformation. We'll also look at how functional programming systems are closely matched with the requirements of distributed systems.

After reading this chapter, you'll be able to visualize functional programming as isolated transformations of data flowing through a series of pipes. If you can keep this model in mind, you'll understand how these transforms can be distributed over multiple processors and promote horizontal scalability. You'll also see how side effects prevent systems from achieving these goals.

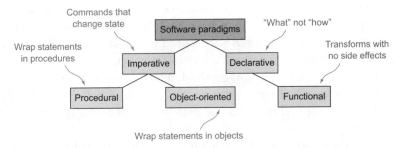

Figure 10.1 **A high-level taxonomy of software paradigms. In the English language, an imperative sentence is a sentence that expresses a command. "Change that variable now!" is an example of an imperative sentence. In computer science, an imperative programming paradigm contains sequences of commands that focus on updating memory. Procedural paradigms wrap groups of imperative statements in procedures and functions. Declarative paradigms focus on what should be done, but not how. Functional paradigms are considered a subtype of declarative programming because they focus on what data should be transformed, but not how the transforms will occur.**

10.1.1 *Imperative programming is managing program state*

The programming paradigm of most computer systems created in the past 40 years centers around state management, or what's called *imperative programming systems.* Procedural and object languages are both examples of imperative programming systems.

Figure 10.2 is an illustration of this state-management-focused system.

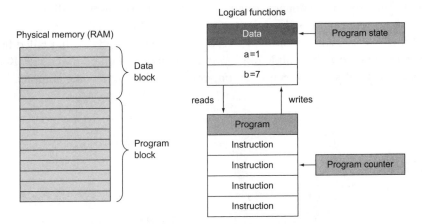

Figure 10.2 **Imperative programs divide physical memory (RAM) into two functional regions. One region holds the data block and the other the program block. The state of the program is managed by a program counter that steps through the program block, reading instructions that read and write variables in computer memory. The programs must carefully coordinate the reading and writing of data and ensure that the data is valid and consistent.**

Using program counters and memory to manage state was the goal of John von Neumann and others in the 1940s when they developed the first computer architecture. It specified that both data and programs were stored in the same type of core memory and a program counter stepped through a series of instructions and updated memory values. High-level programming languages divided memory into two regions: data and program memory. After a computer program was compiled, a *loader* loaded the program code into program memory and the data region of memory was allocated to store programming variables.

This architecture worked well for single-processor systems as long as it was clear which programs were updating specific memory locations. But as programs became more complex, there was a need to control which programs could update various regions of memory. In the late 1950s, a new trend emerged that required the ability to protect data by allowing specific access methods to update regions of data memory. The data and the methods, when used together, formed new programming constructs called *objects*.

An example of the object state is shown in figure 10.3.

Objects are ideal for simulating real-world objects on a single processor. You model the real world in a series of programming objects that represent the state of the objects you're simulating. For example, a bank account might have an account ID, an account holder name, and a current balance. A single bank location might be simulated as an object that contains all the accounts at that bank, and an entire financial institution might be simulated by many bank objects.

But the initial object model using methods to guard object state didn't have any inherent functions to manage concurrency. Objects themselves didn't take into account that there might be hundreds of concurrent threads all trying to update the state of the objects. When it came to "undoing" a series of updates that failed halfway through a transaction, the simple object model became complex to manage. Keeping track of the state of many objects in an imperative world can become complex.

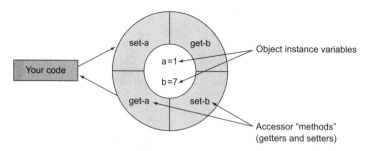

Figure 10.3 Object architecture uses encapsulation to protect the state of any object with accessor functions or methods. In this example, there are two internal states, a and b. In order to get the state of a, you must use the `get-a` method. To set the state of a, you must use the `set-a` method. These methods are the gatekeepers that guard all access to the internal state variables of an object.

Let's take a look at a single operation on an object. In this example, the objective is to increment a single variable. The code might read x = x + 1, meaning "x is assigned a new value of itself plus one." What if one computer or part of a network crashes right around this line of code? Does that code get executed? Does the current state represent the correct value or do you need to rerun that line of code?

Keeping track of the state of an ever-changing world is easy on a single system, but becomes more complex when you move to distributed computing. Functional programming offers a different way of approaching computation by recasting computation as a series of independent data transformations. After you make this transition, you don't need to worry about the details of state management. You move into a new paradigm where all variables are immutable and you can restart transforms again without worrying about what external variables you've changed in the process.

10.1.2 *Functional programming is parallel transformation without side effects*

In contrast with keeping track of the state of objects, functional programming focuses on the controlled transformation of data from one form to another with a function. Functions take the input data and generate output data in the same way that you create mathematical functions in algebra. Figure 10.4 is an example of how functional programs work in the same way mathematical functions work.

It's important to note that when using functional programming there's a new constraint. You can't update the state of the external world at any time during your transform. Additionally, you can't read from the state of the external world when you're executing a transform. The output of your transform can *only* depend on the inputs to the function. If you adhere to these rules, you'll be granted great flexibility! You can execute your transform on clusters that have thousands of processors waiting to run your code. If any processor fails, the process can be restarted using the same input data without issue. You've entered the world of side-effect-free concurrent programming, and functional programming has opened this door for you.

The concepts of serial processing are rooted in imperative systems. As an example, let's look at how a *for loop* or iteration is processed in a serial versus a parallel processing environment. Whereas imperative languages perform transformations of data

Recall functions in your algebra class.   The output y is the result of
    An example using the cosine. $y = f(x)$ applying a function f on x.

```
        0.866 = cosine(30 degrees)
        output = function(input)
```
You can pass both a function
and the list as parameters to
a transformation system.

You can use lists of items
in the input and also
return lists of items.
```
output-list = function(input-list)
output-list = transform(function, input-list)
```

Figure 10.4   Functional programming works similarly to mathematical functions. Instead of methods that modify the state of objects, functional programs transform only input data without side effects.

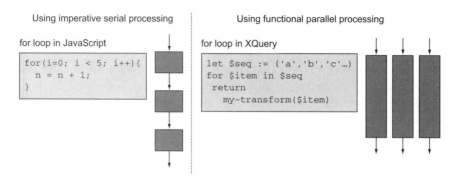

Figure 10.5   Iterations or for loops in imperative languages calculate one iteration of a loop and allow the next iteration to use the results of a prior loop. The left panel shows an example using JavaScript with a mutable variable that's incremented. With some functional programming languages, iteration can be distributed on independent threads of execution. The result of one loop can't be used in other loops. An example of an XQuery for loop is shown in the right panel.

elements serially, with each loop starting only after the prior loop completes, functional programming can process each loop simultaneously and distribute the processing on multiple threads. An example of this is shown in figure 10.5.

As you can see, imperative programming can't process this in parallel because the state of the variables must be fully calculated before the next loop begins. Some functional programming languages such as XQuery keep each loop as a separate and fully independent thread. But in some situations, parallel execution isn't desirable, so there are now proposals to add a sequential option to XQuery functions.

To understand the difference between an imperative and a functional program, it helps to have a good mental model. The model of a pipe without any holes as shown in figure 10.6 is a good representation.

The shift of focus from updating mutable variables to only using immutable variables within independent transforms is the heart of the paradigm shift that underpins many NoSQL systems. This shift is required so that you can achieve reliable and high-performance horizontal scaling in multiprocessor data centers.

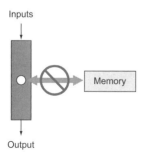

Figure 10.6   The functional programming paradigm relies on creating a distinct output for each data input in an isolated transformation process. You can think of this as a data transformation pipe. When the transformation of input to output is done without modification of external memory, it's called a zero-side-effect pipeline. This means you can rerun the transform many times from any point without worrying about the impact of external systems. Additionally, if you prevent reads from external memory during the transformation, you have the added benefit of knowing the same input must generate the exact same output. Then you can hash the input and check a cache to see if the transform has already been done.

The deep roots of functional programming

A person who's grown up in the imperative world might be thinking, *These people must be crazy! How could people ever write software without changing variables?* The concepts behind functional programming aren't new. They go back to the foundations of computer science in the 1940s. The focus on transformation is a core theme of *lambda calculus*, first introduced by Alonzo Church. It's also the basis of many LISP-based programming languages popular in the 1950s. These languages were used in many artificial intelligence systems because they're ideal for managing symbolic logic.

Despite their popularity in AI research, LISP languages, and their kin (Schema, Clojure, and other languages), functional languages aren't typically found in business applications. Fortran dominated scientific programming because it could be vectorized with specialized compilers. COBOL became popular for accounting systems because it tried to represent business rules in a more natural language structure. In the 1960s, procedural systems such as PASCAL also became popular, followed by object-oriented systems such as C++ and Java in the 1980s and 1990s. As horizontal scalability becomes more relevant, it's important to review the consequences of the programming language choices you've made. Functional programming has many advantages as processor counts increase.

One way to visualize functional programming in a scale-out system is to look at a series of inputs being transformed by independent processors. A consequence of using independent threads of execution is that you can't pass the result of an intermediate calculation from one loop to another. Figure 10.7 illustrates this process.

This constraint is critical when you design transformations. If you need intermediate results from a transformation, you must exit the function and return the output. If the intermediate result needs additional transformation, then a second function should be called.

Another item to consider is that the order of execution and the time that transforms take to complete may vary based on the size of the data elements. For example, if your inputs are documents and you want to count the number of words in each document, the time it takes to count words in a 100-page document will be 10 times longer than the time it takes to count words in a 10-page document (see figure 10.8).

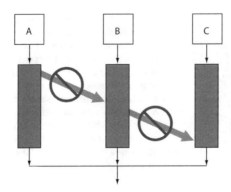

Figure 10.7 Functional programming means that the intermediate results of the transformation of item A can't be used in the transformation of item B, and the intermediate results of B can't be used in calculating C. Only end results of each of these transforms can be used together to create aggregate values.

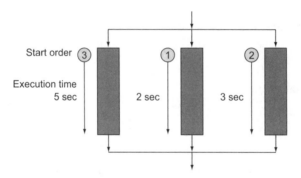

Figure 10.8   Functional programming means that you can't guarantee the order in which items will be transformed or what items will finish first.

This variation in transformation times and the location of the input data adds an additional burden on the scheduling system. In distributed systems, input data is replicated on multiple nodes in the cluster. To be efficient, you want the longest-running jobs to start first. To maximize your resources, the tools that place tasks on different nodes in a cluster must be able to gather processing information from multiple data sources. Schedulers that can determine how long a transform will take to run on different nodes and how busy each node is will be most efficient. This information is generally not provided by imperative systems. Even mature systems like HDFS and MapReduce continue to refine their ability to efficiently transform large datasets.

10.1.3   *Comparing imperative and functional programming at scale*

Now let's compare the capability of imperative and functional systems to support processing large amounts of shared data being accessed by many concurrent CPUs. A comparison of imperative versus functional pipelines is shown in figure 10.9.

You can see that when you prevent writes during a transformation, you get the benefit of no side effects. This means that you can restart a failed transformation and be certain that if it didn't finish, the external state of a system wasn't already updated. With imperative systems, you can't make this guarantee. Any external changes may need to be undone if there's a failure during a transformation. Keeping track of which operations have been done can add complexity that will slow large systems down. The

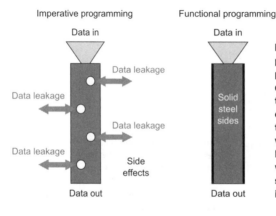

Figure 10.9   Imperative programming (left panel) and functional programming (right panel) use different rules when transforming data. To gain the benefits of referential transparency, output of a transform must be completely determined by the inputs to the transform. No other memory should be read or written during the transformation process. Instead of a pipe with holes on the left, you can visualize your transformation pipes as having solid steel sides that don't transfer any information.

no-side-effect guarantee is critical in your ability to create reproducible transforms that are easy to debug and easy to optimize. Not allowing external side-effect writes during a transform keeps transforms running fast.

The second scalability benefit happens when you prohibit external reads during a transform. This rule allows you to know with certainty that the outputs are completely driven by the inputs of a transformation. If the time to create a hash of the input is small relative to the time it takes to run the transform, you can check a cache to see if the transform has already been run.

One of the central theories of Lambda calculus is that the results of a transform of any data can be used in place of the actual transform of the data. This ability to substitute cached value results, instead of having to rerun a long-running transform, is one way that functional programming systems can be more efficient than imperative systems.

The ability to rerun a transform many times and not alter data is called an *idempotent transform* or an idempotent transaction. Idempotent transforms are transformations that will change the state of the world in consistent ways the first time they're run, but rerunning the transform many times won't corrupt your data. For example, if you have a filter that will insert missing required elements into an XML file, that filter should check to make sure the elements don't already exist before adding them.

Idempotent transforms can also be used in transaction processing. Since idempotent transforms don't change external state, there's no need to create an undo process. Additionally, you can use transaction identifiers to guarantee idempotent transforms. If you're running a transaction on an item of data that increments a bank account, you might record a transaction ID in the bank account transaction history. You can then create a rule that only runs the update if that transaction ID hasn't been run already. This guarantees that a transaction won't be run more than once.

Idempotent transactions allow you to use *referential transparency*. An expression is said to be referentially transparent if it can be replaced with its value without changing the behavior of the program. Any functional programming statement can have this property if the output of the transform can be replaced with the functional call to the transform itself. Referential transparency allows both the programmer and the compiler system to look for ways to optimize repeated calls to the same set of functions on the same set of data. But this optimization technique is only possible when you move to a functional programming paradigm.

In the next section, we'll take a detailed look at how referential transparency allows you to cache results from functional programs.

10.1.4 *Using referential transparency to avoid recalculating transforms*

Now that you know how functional programs promote idempotent transactions, let's look at how these results can be used to speed up your system. You can use these techniques in many systems, from web applications to NoSQL databases to the results of MapReduce transforms.

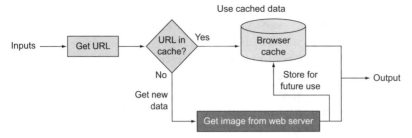

Figure 10.10   Your local browser will check to see if the URL of an image is in a local cache before it goes out to the web to get the image. Once the image is fetched from a remote host (usually a slow process), it can be cached for future use. Getting an image from a local cache is much more efficient.

Referential transparency allows functional programming and distributed systems to be more efficient because they can be clever about avoiding the recalculation of results of transforms. Referential transparency allows you to use a cached version of an item that stands in for something that takes a long time to calculate or a long time to read data from a disk filesystem.

Let's take a simple example, as shown in figure 10.10, to see how an image is displayed within a web browser.

By default, browsers think that all images referenced by the same URL are the same "static" images, since the content of the images doesn't change even if you call them repeatedly. If the same image is rendered on multiple web pages, the image will be retrieved only once from the web server. But to do this, all pages must reference the exact same URL. Subsequent references will use a copy of the image stored in a local client cache. If the image changes, the only way to get the updated image is to remove the original item from your local cache and refresh your screen or to reference a new URL.

By default your browser considers many items static, such as CSS files, JavaScript programs, and some data files if they're marked accordingly by properties in the HTML headers. If your data files do change, you can instruct your server to add information to a file to indicate that the cached copy is no longer valid and to get a new copy from the server.

This same concept of caching documents also applies to queries and transforms used to generate reports or web pages. If you have a large document that depends on many transforms of smaller documents, then you can reassemble the large document from the cached copies of smaller documents that don't change and only re-execute the transforms of smaller documents that do change. The process of using the transform of documents from a cache is shown in figure 10.11.

This transform optimization technique fits perfectly into functional programming systems and serves as the basis for innovative, high-performance website tools. As we move into our case study, you'll see how NetKernel, a performance optimization tool, is used to optimize web page assembly.

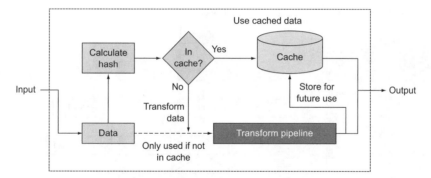

Figure 10.11 You can use referential transparency to increase the performance of any transform by checking to see if the output of a transform is already in a cache. If it's in the cache, you can use the cached value instead of rerunning an expensive transformation process. If the item isn't in the cache, you can store it in a RAM cache such as memcache to reuse the output.

10.2 Case study: using NetKernel to optimize web page content assembly

This case study looks at how functional programming and REST services can be combined to optimize the creation of dynamic nested structures. We'll use as an example the creation of a home page for a news-oriented website. We'll look at how an approach called *resource-oriented computing (ROC)* is implemented by a commercial framework called NetKernel.

10.2.1 Assembling nested content and tracking component dependencies

Let's assume you're running a website that displays news stories in the center of a web page. The web page is dynamically assembled using page headers, footers, navigation menus, and advertising banners around the news content. A sample layout is shown in the left panel of figure 10.12. You use a dependency tree, as shown in the right panel of figure 10.12, to determine when each web page component should be regenerated.

Though we think of public URLs as identifying web pages and images, you can use this same philosophy with each subcomponent in the dependency tree by treating each component as a separate resource and assigning it an internal identifier called a *uniform resource identifier (URI)*. In the web page model, each region of the web page is a resource that can be assembled by combining other static and dynamic resources. Each distinct resource has its own URI.

In the previous section, you saw how functional programming uses referential transparency to allow cached results to be used in place of the output of a function. We'll apply this same concept to web page construction. You can use URIs to check whether a function call has already been executed on the same input data, and you can track dependencies to see when functions call other functions. If you do this, you

Sample HTML news page

Dependency tree of page components

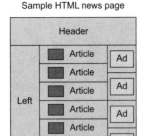

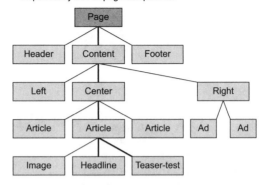

Figure 10.12   Web pages for a typical news site are generated using a tree structure. All components of the web page can be represented in a dependency tree. As low-level content such as news or ads change, only the dependent parts of the web page need to be regenerated. If a low-level component changes (heavy-line links), then all ancestor nodes must be regenerated. For example, if some text in a news article changes, that change will cause the center section, the central content region, and the entire page to be regenerated. Other components such as the page borders can be reused from a cache layer without regeneration.

can avoid calling the same functions on the same input data and reuse information fragments that are expensive to generate.

NetKernel knows what functions are called with what input data, and uses a URI to identify if the function has already generated results for the same input data. NetKernel also tracks URI dependencies, only re-executing functions when input data changes. This process is known as the *golden thread* pattern. To illustrate, think of hanging your clean clothes out on a clothes line. If the clothes line breaks, the clothes fall to the ground and must be washed again. Similarly, if an input item changes at a low level of a dependency tree, all the items that depend on its content must be regenerated.

NetKernel automatically regenerates content for internal resources in its cache and can poll external resource timestamps to see if they've changed. To determine if any resources have changed, NetKernel uses an XRL file (an XML file used to track resource dependencies) and a combination of polling and expiration timestamps.

10.2.2 *Using NetKernel to optimize component regeneration*

The NetKernel system takes a systematic approach to tracking what's in your cache and what should be regenerated. Instead of using hashed values for keys, NetKernel constructs URIs that are associated with a dependency tree and uses models that calculate the effort to regenerate content. NetKernel performs smart cache-content optimization and creates cache-eviction strategies by looking at the total amount of work it takes to generate a resource. NetKernel uses an ROC approach to determine the total effort required to generate a resource. Though ROC is a term specific to NetKernel, it signifies a different class of computing concepts that challenge you to reflect on how computation is done.

ROC combines the UNIX concept of using small modular transforms on data moving through pipes, with the distributed computing concepts of REST, URIs, and caching. These ideas are all based on referential transparency and dependency tracking to keep the right data in your cache. ROC requires you to associate a URI with every component that generates data: queries, functions, services, and codes. By combining these URIs, you can create unique signatures that can be used to determine whether a resource is already present in your cache. A sample of the NetKernel stack is shown in figure 10.13.

As you can see from figure 10.13, the NetKernel software is layered between two layers of resources and services. Resources can be thought of as static documents, and services as dynamic queries. This means that moving toward a service-oriented intermediate layer between your database and your application is critical to the optimization process. You can still use NetKernel and traditional, consistent hashing without a service layer, but you won't get the same level of clever caching that the ROC approach gives you.

By using ROC, NetKernel takes REST concepts to a level beyond caching images or documents on your web server. Your cache is no longer subject to a simple time-stamped eviction policy, and the most valuable items remain in cache. NetKernel can be configured to use complex algorithms to calculate the total effort it takes to put an item in cache, and only evicts items that have a low amount of effort to regenerate or are unlikely to be needed. To get the most benefits, a service-oriented REST approach should be used, and those services need to be powered by functions that return data with referential transparency. You can only begin this journey if your system is truly free from side effects, and this implies you may need to take a close look at the languages your systems use.

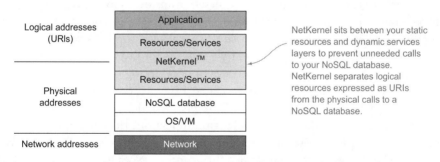

Figure 10.13   NetKernel works similarly to a memcache system that separates the application from the database. Unlike memcache, it's tightly coupled with the layer that's built around logical URIs and tracks dependencies of expensive calculations of objects that can be cached.

In summary, if you associate URIs with the output of referentially transparent functions and services, frameworks such as NetKernel can bring the following benefits:

- Faster web page response time for users
- Reduced wasteful re-execution of the same functions on the same data
- More efficient use of front-end cache RAM
- Decreased demand on your database, network, and disk resources
- Consistent development architecture

Note that the concepts used in this front-end case study can also be applied to other topics in back-end analytics. Any time you see functions being re-executed on the same datasets, there are opportunities for optimization using these techniques.

In our next section, we'll look at functional programming languages and see how their properties allow you to address specific types of performance and scalability issues.

10.3 *Examples of functional programming languages*

Now that you have a feeling for how functional programs work and how they're different from imperative programs, let's look at some real-world examples of functional programming languages. The LISP programming language is considered the pioneer of functional programming. LISP was designed around the concept of no-side-effect functions that work on lists. The concept of recursion over lists was frequently used. The *Clojure* language is a modern LISP dialect that has many benefits of functional programming with a focus on the development of multithreaded systems.

Developers who work with content management and single-source publishing systems may use transformation languages such as *XSLT* and XQuery (introduced in chapter 5). It's no surprise that document stores also benefit from functional languages that leverage recursive processing. Document hierarchies that contain other hierarchies are ideal candidates for recursive transformation. Document structures can be easily traversed and transformed using recursive functions. The XQuery language is a perfect fit with document stores because it supports recursion and functional programming, and yet uses database indexes for fast retrieval of elements.

There has been strong interest by developers working on high-availability systems in a functional programming language called Erlang. Erlang has become one of the most popular functional languages for writing NoSQL databases. Erlang was originally developed by Ericsson, the Swedish telecommunications firm, to support distributed, highly available phone switches. Erlang supports features that allow the runtime libraries to be upgraded without service interruption. NoSQL databases that focus on high availability such as CouchDB, Couchbase, Riak, and Amazon's SimpleDB services are all written in Erlang.

The *Mathematica* language and the *R* language for doing statistical analysis also use functional programming constructs. These ideas allow them to be extended to run on a large numbers of processors. Even SQL, which doesn't allow for mutable values, has some properties of functional languages. Both the SQL-like HIVE language and the PIG system that are used with Hadoop include functional concepts.

Several multiparadigm languages have also been created to help bridge the gap between the imperative and functional systems. The programming language *Scala* was created to add functional programming features to the Java language. For software developers using Microsoft tools, Microsoft created the *F#* (F sharp) language to meet the needs of functional programmers. These languages are designed to allow developers to use multiple paradigms, imperative and functional, within the same project. They have an advantage in that they can use libraries written in both imperative and functional languages.

The number of languages that integrate functional programming constructs in distributed systems is large and growing. Perhaps this is driven by the need to write MapReduce jobs in languages in which people feel comfortable. MapReduce jobs are being written in more than a dozen languages today and that list continues to grow. Almost any language can be used to write MapReduce jobs as long as those programs don't have side effects. This requires more discipline and training when using imperative languages that allow side effects, but it's possible.

This shows that functional programming isn't a single attribute of a particular language. Functional programming is a collection of properties that make it easier to solve specific types of performance, scalability, and reliability problems within a programming language. This means that you can add features to an old procedural or object-oriented language to make it behave more like a pure functional language.

10.4　*Making the transition from imperative to functional programming*

We've spent a lot of time defining functional programming and describing how it's different from imperative programming. Now that you have a clear definition of functional programming, let's look at some of the things that will change for you and your development team.

10.4.1　*Using functions as a parameter of a function*

Many of us are comfortable passing parameters to functions that have different data types. A function might have input parameters that are strings, integers, floats, Booleans, or a sequence of items. Functional programming adds another type of parameter: the function. In functional programming, you can pass a function as a parameter to another function, which turns out to be incredibly useful. For example, if you have a compressed zip file, you might want to uncompress it and pass a filter function to only extract specific data files. Instead of extracting everything and then writing a second pass on the output, the filter intercepts files before they're uncompressed and stored.

10.4.2   *Using recursion to process unstructured document data*

If you're familiar with LISP, you know that *recursion* is a popular construct in functional programming. Recursion is the process of creating functions that call themselves. In our experience, people either love or hate recursion—there's seldom a middle ground. If you're not comfortable with recursion, it can be difficult to create new recursive programs. Yet once you create them, they seem to almost acquire a magical property. They can be the smallest programs that produce the biggest results.

Functional programs don't manage state, but they do use a *call stack* to remember where they are when moving through lists. Functional programs typically analyze the first element of a list, check whether there are additional items, and if there are, then call themselves using the remaining items.

This process can be used with lists as well as tree structures like XML and JSON files. If you have unstructured documents that consist of elements and you can't predict the order of items, then recursive processing may be a good way to digest the content. For example, when you write a paragraph, you can't predict the order in which bold or italic text will appear in the paragraph. Languages such as XQuery and JASONiq support recursion for this reason.

10.4.3   *Moving from mutable to immutable variables*

As we've mentioned, functional programming variables are set once but not changed within a specific context. This means that you don't need to store a variable's state, because you can rerun the transform without the side effects of the variable being incremented again. The downside is that it may take some time for your staff to rid themselves of old habits, and you may need to rewrite your current code to work in a functional environment. Every time you see variables on both the left and right side of an assignment operator, you'll have to modify your code.

When you port your imperative code, you'll need to refactor algorithms and remove all mutable variables used within for loops. This means that instead of using counters that increment or decrement variables in for loops, you must use a "for each item" type function.

Another way to convert your code is to introduce new variable names when you're referencing a variable multiple times in the same block of code. By doing this, you can build up calculations that nest references on the right side of assignment statements.

10.4.4   *Removing loops and conditionals*

One of the first things imperative programmers do when they enter the world of functional programs is try to bring their programming constructs with them. This includes the use of loops, conditionals, and calls to object methods.

These techniques don't transfer to the functional programming world. If you're new to functional programming and in your functions you see complex loops with layers of nested if/then/else statements, this tells you it's time to refactor your code.

The focus of a functional programmer is to rethink the loops and conditionals in terms of small, isolated transforms of data. The results are services that know what functions to call based on what data is presented to the inputs.

10.4.5 *The new cognitive style: from capturing state to isolated transforms*

Imperative programming has a consistent problem-solving (or cognitive) style that requires a developer to look at the world around them and capture the state of the world. Once the initial state of the world has been precisely captured in memory or object state, developers write carefully orchestrated methods to update the state of interacting objects.

The cognitive styles used in functional programming are radically different. Instead of capturing state, the functional programmer views the world as a series of transformations of data from the initial raw form to other forms that do useful work. Transforms might convert raw data to forms used in indexes, convert raw data to HTML formats for display in a web page, or generate aggregate values (counts, sums, averages, and others) used in a data warehouse.

Both object-oriented and functional programming do share one similar goal—how to structure libraries that reuse code to make the software easier to use and maintain. With object orientation, the primary way you reuse code is to use an inheritance hierarchy. You move common data and methods up to superclasses, where they can be reused by other object classes. With functional programming, the goal is to create reusable transformation functions that build hierarchies where each component in the hierarchy is regenerated when the dependent element's data changes.

The key consequence of what style you choose is scalability. When you choose the functional programming approach, your transforms will scale to run on large clusters with hundreds or thousands of nodes. If you choose the imperative programming route, you must carefully maintain the state of a complex network of objects when there are many threads accessing these objects at the same time. Inevitably you'll run into the same scalability problems you saw with graph stores in chapter 6 on big data. Large object networks might not fit within RAM, locking systems will consume more and more CPU cycles, and caching won't be used effectively. You'll be spending most of your CPU cycles moving data around and managing locks.

10.4.6 *Quality, validation, and consistent unit testing*

Regardless of whether imperative or functional programming is used, there's one observation that won't change. The most reliable programs are those that have been adequately tested. Too often, we see good test-driven imperative programmers leap into the world of functional programming and become so disoriented that they forget everything that they learned about good test-driven development.

Functional programs seem to be inherently more reliable. They don't have to deal with which objects need to deallocate memory and when the memory can be released.

Their focus is on messaging rather than memory locks. Once a transform is complete, the only artifact is the output document. All intermediate values are easily removed and the lack of side effects makes testing functions an atomic process.

Functional programming languages also may have type checking for input and output parameters, and validation functions that execute on incoming items. This makes it easier to do compile-time checking and produces accurate runtime checks that can quickly help developers to isolate problems.

Yet all these safeguards won't replace a robust and consistent unit-testing process. To avoid sending corrupt, inconsistent, and missing data to your functions, a comprehensive and complete testing plan should be part of all projects.

10.4.7 Concurrency in functional programming

Functional programming systems are popular when multiple processes need to reliably share information either locally or over networks. In the imperative world, sharing information between processes involves multiple processes reading and writing shared memory and setting other memory locations called *locks* to determine who has exclusive rights to modify memory. The complexities about who can read and write shared memory values are referred to as *concurrency problems*. Let's take a look at some of the problems that can occur when you try to share memory:

- Programs may fail to lock a resource properly before they use it.
- Programs may lock a resource and neglect to unlock it, preventing other threads from using a resource.
- Programs may lock a resource for a long time and prevent others from using it for extended periods.
- Deadlocks occur where two or more threads are blocked forever, waiting for each other to be unlocked.

These problems aren't new, nor are they exclusive to traditional systems. Traditional as well as NoSQL systems have challenges locking resources on distributed systems that run over unreliable networks. Our next case study looks at an alternative approach to managing concurrency in distributed systems.

10.5 Case study: building NoSQL systems with Erlang

Erlang is a functional programming language optimized for highly available distributed systems. As we mentioned before, Erlang has been used to build several popular NoSQL systems including CouchDB, Couchbase, Riak, and Amazon's SimpleDB. But Erlang is used for writing more than distributed databases that need high availability. The popular distributed messaging system RabbitMQ is also written in Erlang. It's no coincidence that these systems have excellent reputations for high availability and scalability. In this case study, we'll look at why Erlang has been so popular and how these NoSQL systems have benefited from Erlang's focus on concurrency and message-passing architecture.

We've already discussed how difficult it is to maintain consistent memory state on multithreaded and parallel systems. Whenever you have multiple threads executing on systems, you need to consider the consequences of what happens when two threads are both trying to update shared resources. There are several ways that computer systems share memory-resident variables. The most common way is to create stringent rules requiring all shared memory to be controlled by locking and unlocking functions. Any thread that wants to access global values must set a lock, make a change, and then unset the lock. Locks are difficult to reset if there are errors. Locking in distributed systems has been called one of the most difficult problems in all of computer science. Erlang solves this problem by avoiding locking altogether.

Erlang uses a different pattern called *actor*, illustrated in figure 10.14.

The actor model is similar to the way that people work together to solve problems. When people work together on tasks, our brains don't need to share neurons or access shared memory. We work together by talking, chatting, or sending email—all forms of *message passing*. Erlang actors work in the same way. When you program in Erlang, you don't worry about setting locks on shared memory. You write actors that communicate with the rest of the world through message passing. Each actor has a queue of messages that it reads to perform work. When it needs to communicate with other actors, it sends them messages. Actors can also create new actors.

By using this actor model, Erlang programs work well on a single processor, and they also have the ability to scale their tasks over many processing nodes by sending messages to processors on remote nodes. This single messaging model provides many benefits for including high availability and the ability to recover gracefully from both network and hardware errors.

Erlang also provides a large library of modules called *OTP* that make distributed computing problems much easier.

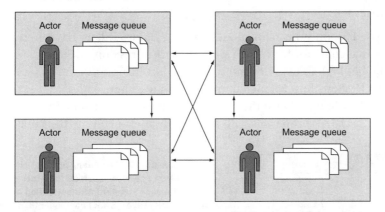

Figure 10.14 Erlang uses an actor model, where each process has agents that can only read messages, write messages, and create new processes. When you use the Erlang actor model, your software can run on a single processor or thousands of servers without any change to your code.

What is OTP?

OTP is a large collection of open source function modules used by Erlang applications. OTP originally stood for Open Telecom Platform, which tells you that Erlang was designed for running high-availability telephone switches that needed to run without interruption. Today OTP is used for many applications outside the telephone industry, so the letters OTP are used without reference to the telecommunications industry.

Together, Erlang and the OTP modules provide the following features to application developers:

- *Isolation*—An error in one part of the system will have minimum impact on other parts of the system. You won't have errors like Java NullPointerExceptions (NPEs) that crash your JVM.
- *Redundancy and automatic failover (supervision)*—If one component fails, another component can step in to replace its role in the system.
- *Failure detection*—The system can quickly detect failures and take action when errors are detected. This includes advanced alerting and notification tools.
- *Fault identification*—Erlang has tools to identify where faults occur and integrated tools to look for root causes of the fault.
- *Live software updates*—Erlang has methods for software updates without shutting down a system. This is like a version of the Java OSGi framework to enable remote installation, startup, stopping, updating, and uninstalling of new modules and functions without a reboot. This is a key feature missing from many NoSQL systems that need to run nonstop.
- *Redundant storage*—Although not part of the standard OTP modules, Erlang can be configured to use additional modules to store data on multiple locations if hard drives fail.

Because it's based around the actor model and messaging, Erlang has inherent scale-out properties that come for free. As a result, these features don't need to be added to your code. You get high availability and scalability just by using the Erlang infrastructure. Figure 10.15 shows how Erlang components fit together.

Erlang puts the agent model at the core of its own virtual machine. In order to have consistent and scalable properties, all Erlang libraries need to be built on this

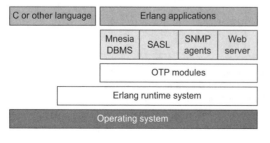

Figure 10.15   The Erlang application runs on a series of services such as the Mnesia database, Standard Authentication and Security Layer (SASL) components, monitoring agents, and web servers. These services make calls to standardized OTP libraries that call the Erlang runtime system. Programs written in other languages don't have the same support that Erlang applications have.

infrastructure. The downside is that because Erlang depends on the actor model, it becomes difficult to integrate imperative systems like Java libraries and still benefit from its high availability and integrated scale-out features. Imperative functions that perform consistent transforms can be used, but object frameworks that need to manage external state will need careful wrapping. Because Erlang is based on *Prolog*, its syntax may seem unusual for people familiar with C and Java, so it takes some getting used to.

Erlang is a proven way to get high availability and scale out of your distributed applications. If your team can overcome the steep learning curve, there can be great benefits down the road.

10.6 Apply your knowledge

Sally is working on a business analytics dashboard project that assembles web pages that are composed of many small subviews. Most subviews have tables and charts that are generated from the previous week's sales data. Each Sunday morning, the data is refreshed in the data warehouse. Ninety-five percent of the users will see the same tables and charts for the previous week's sales, but some receive a customized view for their projects.

The database that's currently being used is an RDBMS server that's overloaded and slow during peak daytime hours. During this time, reports can take more than 10 minutes to generate. Susan, who is Sally's boss, is concerned about performance issues. Susan tells Sally that one of the key goals of the project is to help people make better decisions through interactive monitoring and discovery. Susan lets Sally know in no uncertain terms that she feels users won't take the time to run reports that take more than 5 minutes to produce a result.

Sally gets two different proposals from different contractors. The architectures of both systems are shown in figure 10.16.

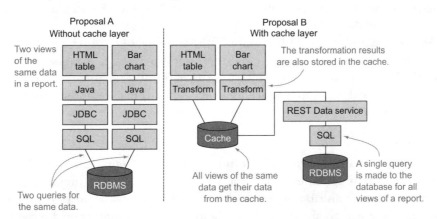

Figure 10.16   Two business intelligence dashboard architectures. The left panel shows that each table and chart will need to generate multiple SQL statements, slowing the database down. The right panel shows that all views that use the same data can simply create new transforms directly from the cache, which lowers load on the database and increases performance.

Proposal A uses Java programs that call a SQL database and generate the appropriate HTML and bitmapped images for the tables and charts of each dashboard every time a widget is viewed. In this scenario, two views of the same data, a bar chart in one view and an HTML table in another view, will rerun the exact same SQL code on the data warehouse. There's no caching layer.

Proposal B has a functional programming REST layer system that first generates an XML response from the SQL SELECT for each user interface widget and then caches this data. It then transforms the data in the cache into multiple views such as tables and charts. The system looks at the last-modified dates in the database to know if any of the data in the cache should be regenerated.

Proposal B also has tools that prepopulate the cache with frequent reports after the data in the warehouse changes. The system is 25% more expensive, but the vendor claims that their solution will be less expensive to operate due to lower demand on the database server. The vendor behind proposal B claims the average dashboard widget generates a view in under 50 milliseconds if the data is in cache. The vendor also claims that if Sally uses SVG vector charts, not the larger bitmapped images, then the cached SVG charts will only occupy less than 30 KB in cache, and less than 3 KB if they're compressed.

Sally looks at both proposals and selects proposal B, despite its higher initial cost. She also makes sure the application servers are upgraded from 16 GB to 32 GB of RAM to provide more memory for the caches. According to her calculations, this should be enough to store around 10 million compressed SVG charts in the RAM cache. Sally also runs a script on Sunday night that prepopulates the cache with the most common reports, so that when users come in on Monday morning, the most frequent reports are already available from the cache. There's almost no load on the database server after the reports are in the cache. When the project rolls out, the average page load times, even with 10 charts per page, are well under 3 seconds. Susan is happy and gives Sally a bonus at the end of the year.

You should notice that in this example, the additional REST caching layer in a software application isn't dependent on your using a NoSQL database. Since most NoSQL databases provide REST interfaces that provide cache-friendly results, they provide additional ways your applications can use a cache to lower the number of calls to your database.

10.7 *Summary*

In this chapter, you've learned about functional programming and how it's different from imperative programming. You learned how functional programming is the preferred method for distributing isolated transformations of data over distributed systems, and how systems are more scalable and reliable when functional programming is used.

Understanding the power of functional programming will help you in several ways. It'll help you understand that state management systems are difficult to scale and that to really benefit from horizontal scale-out, your team is going to have to make some paradigm shifts. Second, you should start to see that systems that are designed with both concurrency and high availability in mind tend to be easier to scale.

This doesn't mean you need to write all your business applications in Erlang functions. Some companies are doing this, but they tend to be people writing the NoSQL databases and high-availability messaging systems, not true business applications. Algorithms such as MapReduce and languages such as HIVE and PIG share some of the same low-level concepts that you see in functional languages. You should be able to use these languages and still get many of the benefits of horizontal scalability and high availability that functional languages offer.

In our next chapter, we'll leave the abstract world of cognitive styles and the theories of computational energy minimization and move on to a concrete subject: security. You'll see how NoSQL systems can keep your data from being viewed or modified by unauthorized users.

10.8 *Further reading*

- "Deadlock." Wikipedia. http://mng.bz/64J7.
- "Declarative programming." Wikipedia. http://mng.bz/kCe3.
- "Functional programming." Wikipedia. http://mng.bz/T586.
- "Idempotence." Wikipedia. http://mng.bz/eN5G.
- "Lambda calculus and programming languages." Wikipedia. http://mng.bz/15BH.
- MSDN. "Functional Programming vs. Imperative Programming." http://mng.bz/8VtY.
- "Multi-paradigm programming language." Wikipedia. http://mng.bz/3HH2.
- Piccolboni, Antonio. "Looking for a map reduce language." Piccolblog. April 2011. http://mng.bz/q7wD.
- "Referential transparency (computer science)." Wikipedia. http://mng.bz/85rr.
- "Semaphore (programming)." Wikipedia. http://mng.bz/5IEx.
- W3C. Example of forced sequential execution of a function. http://mng.bz/aPsR.
- W3C. "XQuery Scripting Extension 1.0." http://mng.bz/27rU.

Security: protecting data in your NoSQL systems

This chapter covers

- NoSQL database security model
- Security architecture
- Dimensions of security
- Application versus database-layer security trade-off analysis

> *Security is always excessive until it's not enough.*
> —Robbie Sinclair

If you're using a NoSQL database to power a single application, strong security at the database level probably isn't necessary. But as the NoSQL database becomes popular and is used by multiple projects, you'll cross departmental trust boundaries and should consider adding database-level security.

Organizations must comply with governmental regulations that dictate systems, and applications need detailed audit records anytime someone reads or changes data. For example, US health care records, governed by the *Health Information Privacy Accountability Act (HIPAA)* and *Health Information Technology for Economic and*

Clinical Health Act (HITECH Act) regulations, require audits of anyone who has accessed personally identifiable patient data.

Many organizations need fine-grained controls over what fields can be viewed by different classes of users. You might store employee salary information in your database, but want to restrict access to that information to the individual employee and a specific role in HR. Relational database vendors have spent decades building security rules into their databases to grant individuals and groups of users access to their tabular data at the column and row level. As we go through this chapter, you'll see how NoSQL systems can provide enterprise-class security at scale.

NoSQL systems are, by and large, a new generation of databases that focus on scale-out issues first and use the application layer to implement security features. In this chapter, we'll talk about the dimensions of database security you need in a project. We'll also look at tools to help you determine whether security features should be included in the database.

Generally, RDBMSs don't provide REST services as they are part of a multitier architecture with multiple security gates. NoSQL databases do provide REST interfaces, and don't have the same level of protection, so it's important to carefully consider security features for these databases.

11.1 A security model for NoSQL databases

When you begin a database selection process, you start by sitting down with your business users to define the overall security requirements for the system. Using a concentric ring model, as shown in figure 11.1, we'll start with some terminology to help you understand how to build a basic security model to protect your data.

This model is ideal for getting started with a single application and a single data collection. It's a simplified model that categorizes users based on their access type and role within an organization. Your job as a database architect is to select a NoSQL system that supports the security requirements of the organization. As you'll see, the number of applications that you run within your database, your data classification, reporting tools, and the number of roles within your organization will dictate what security features your NoSQL database should have.

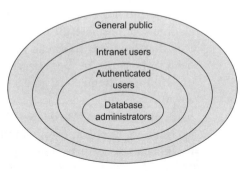

Figure 11.1 One of the best ways to visualize a database security system is to think of a series of concentric rings that act as walls around your data. The outermost ring consists of users who access your public website. Your company's internal employees might consist of everyone on your company intranet who has already been validated by your company local area network. Within that group, there might be a subset of users to whom you've granted special access; for example, a login and password to a database account. Within your database you might have structures that grant specific users special privileges. A special class of users, database administrators, is granted all rights within the system.

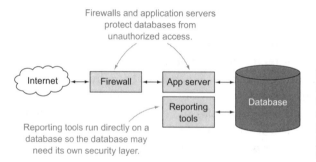

Firewalls and application servers protect databases from unauthorized access.

Reporting tools run directly on a database so the database may need its own security layer.

Figure 11.2   If your database sits behind an application server, the application server can protect the database from unauthorized access. If you have many applications, including reporting tools, you should consider some database-level security controls.

If your concentric ring model stays simple, most NoSQL databases will meet your needs, and security can be handled at the application level. But large organizations with complex security requirements that have hundreds of overlapping circles for dozens of roles and multiple versions of these maps will find that only a few NoSQL systems satisfy these requirements. As we discussed in chapter 3, most RDBMSs have mature security systems with fine-grained permission control at the column and row level associated with the database. In addition, data warehouse OLAP tools allow you to add rules that protect individual cell-based reports. Figure 11.2 shows how reporting tools typically need direct access to the entire database.

There are ways you can protect subsections of your data, and most reporting tools can be customized to access specific parts of your NoSQL database. Unfortunately, not all organizations have the ability to customize reporting tools or to limit the subsets of data that reporting tools can access. To function well, tools such as MapReduce also need to be aware of your security policy. As the use of the database grows within an organization, the need to access data crosses organizational trust boundaries. Eventually, the need for in-database security will transition from "Not required" to "Nice to have" and finally to "Must have." Figure 11.3 is an illustration of this process.

Next, we'll look at two methods that organizations can used to mitigate the need for in-database security models.

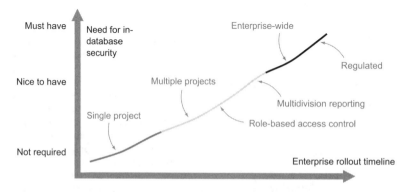

Figure 11.3   As the number of projects that use a database grows, the need for in-database security increases. The tipping point occurs when an organization needs integrated real-time reports for operational data in multiple collections.

11.1.1 Using services to mitigate the need for in-database security

One of the most time-consuming and expensive transitions organizations make is converting standalone applications running on siloed databases with their own security model to run in a centralized enterprise-wide database with a different security model. But if an organization splits its application into a series of reusable data services, they could avoid or delay this costly endeavor. By separating the data that each service provides from other database components, the service can continue to run on a standalone database.

Recall that in section 2.2 we talked about the concept of application layers. We compared the way functionality is distributed in an RDBMS to how a NoSQL system could address those same concerns by adding a layer of services. You can use this same approach to create service-based applications that run on separate lightweight NoSQL databases with independent in-database security models.

To continue this service-driven strategy, you might need to provide more than simple request-response services that take inputs and return outputs. This service-driven strategy works well for search or lookup services, but what if you have data that must be merged or joined with other large datasets? To meet these requirements, you must provide dumps of data as well as incremental updates to users for new and changing data. In some cases, these services can be used directly within ad hoc reporting tools.

How long will the service-oriented strategy work? It starts to fail when the data volume and synchronization complexity becomes too costly.

11.1.2 Using data warehouses and OLAP to mitigate the need for in-database security

The need for security reporting tools is one of the primary reasons enterprises require security within the database, rather than at the application level. Let's look at why this is sometimes not a relevant requirement.

Let's say the data in your standalone NoSQL database is needed to generate ad hoc reports using a centralized data warehouse. The key to keeping NoSQL systems independent is to have a process that replicates the NoSQL database information into your data warehouse. As you may recall from chapter 3, we reviewed the process of how data can be extracted from operational systems and stored in fact and dimension tables within a data warehouse.

This moves the burden of providing security away from standalone performance-driven NoSQL services to the OLAP tools. OLAP tools have many options for protecting data, even at the cell level. Policies can be set up so that reports will only be generated if there's a minimum number of responses so that an individual can't be identified or their private data viewed. For example, a report that shows the average math test score for third graders by race will only display if there are more than 10 students in a particular category.

The process of moving data from NoSQL systems into an OLAP cube is similar to the process of moving from a RDBMS; the difference comes in the tools used. Instead of running overnight ETL jobs, your NoSQL database might use MapReduce processes to extract nightly data feeds on new and updated data. Document stores can run reports using XQuery or another query language. Graph stores can use SPARQL or graph query reporting tools that extract new operational data and load it into a central staging area that's then loaded into OLAP cube structures. Though these architectural changes might not be available to all organizations, they show that the needs of specialized data stores for specific performance and scale-out can still be integrated into an overall enterprise architecture that satisfies both security and ad hoc reporting requirements.

Now that we've looked at ways to keep security at the application level, we'll summarize the benefits of each approach.

11.1.3 *Summary of application versus database-layer security benefits*

Each organization that builds a database can choose to put security at either the application or the database level. But like everything else, there are benefits and trade-offs that should be considered. As you review your organization's requirements, you'll be able to determine which method and benefits are the best fit.

Benefits of application-level security:

- *Faster database performance*—Your database doesn't have to slow down to check whether a user has permission on a data collection or an item.
- *Lower disk usage*—Your database doesn't have to store access-control lists or visibility rules within the database. In most cases, the disk space used by access control lists is negligible. There are some databases that store access within each key, and for these systems, the space used for storing security information must be taken into account.
- *Additional control using restricted APIs*—Your database might not be configured to support multiple types of ad hoc reports that consume your CPU resources. Although NoSQL systems leverage many CPUs, you still might want to limit reports that users can execute. By restricting access to reporting tools for some roles, these users can only run reports that you provide within an application.

Benefits of database-level security:

- *Consistency of security policy*—You don't have to put individualized security policies within each application and limit the ability of ad hoc reporting tools.
- *Ability to perform ad hoc reporting*—Often users don't know exactly what types of information they need. They create initial reports that show them only enough information to know they need to dig deeper. Putting security within the database allows users to perform their own ad hoc reporting and doesn't require your application to limit the number of reports that users can run.
- *Centralized audit*—Organizations that run in heavily regulated industries such as health care need centralized audit. For these organizations, database-level security might be the only option.

Now that you know how a NoSQL system can fit into your enterprise, let's look at how you can qualify a NoSQL database by looking at its ability to handle authentication, authorization, audit, and encryption requirements. Taking a structured approach to comparing NoSQL databases against these components will increase your organization's confidence that a NoSQL database can satisfy security concerns.

11.2 Gathering your security requirements

Selecting the right NoSQL system will depend on how complex your security requirements are and how mature the security model is within your NoSQL database. Before embarking on a NoSQL pilot project, it's a good idea to spend some time understanding your organization's security requirements. We encourage our customers to group security requirements into four areas, as outlined in figure 11.4.

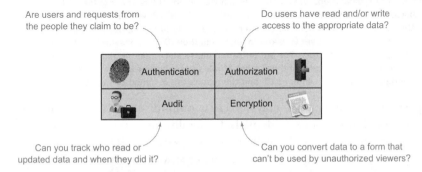

Figure 11.4   The four questions of a secure database. You want to make sure that only the right people have access to the appropriate data in your database. You also want to track their access and transmit data securely in and out of the database.

The remainder of this chapter will focus on a review of authentication, authorization, audit, and encryption processes followed by three case studies that apply a security policy to a NoSQL database. Let's begin by looking at the authentication process to see how it can be structured within your security requirements.

11.2.1 Authentication

Authenticating users is the first step in protecting your data. Authentication is the process of validating the identity of a specific individual or a service request. Figure 11.5 shows a typical authentication process.

As you'll see, there are many ways to verify the identity of users, which is why many organizations opt to use an external service for the verification process. The good news is that many modern databases are used for web-only access, which allows them to use web standards and protocols outside of the database to verify a user. With this model, only validated users will ever connect with the database and the user's ID can then be placed directly in an HTTP header. From there the database can look up the groups and roles for each user from an internal or external source.

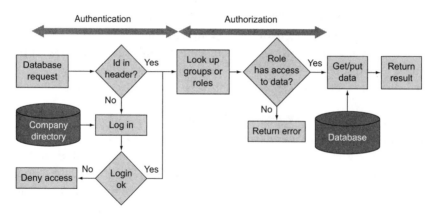

Figure 11.5   The typical steps to validate a web-based query before it executes within your database. The initial step checks for an identifier in the HTTP header. If the header is present, the authentication is done as shown on the left side of the figure. If the user ID isn't in the HTTP header, the user is asked to log in and their ID and password are verified against a company-wide directory. The authorization phase shown on the right side of the figure will look up roles for a user and get a list of roles associated with that user. If any role has the rights, the query will execute and the results are returned to the user.

In large companies, a database may need to communicate with a centralized company service that validates a user's credentials. Generally, this service is designed to be used by all company databases and is called a *single sign-on*, or SSO, system. If the company doesn't provide an SSO interface, your database will have to validate users using a directory access API. The most common version is called the *Lightweight Directory Access Protocol (LDAP)*.

There are six types of authentication: basic access, digest access, public key, multifactor, Kerberos, and Simple Authentication and Security Layer (SASL), as we'll see next.

BASIC ACCESS AUTHENTICATION

This is the simplest level of authenticating a database user. The login and password are put into the HTTP header in a clear plain-text format. This type of authentication should always be used with *Secure Sockets Layer (SSL)* or *Transport Layer Security (TLS)* over a public network; it can also be adequate for an internal test system. It doesn't require web browser cookies or additional handshakes.

DIGEST ACCESS AUTHENTICATION

Digest access authentication is more complicated and requires a few additional handshakes between the client and the database. It can be used over an unencrypted non-SSL/TLS connection in low-stakes situations. Because digest authentication uses a standard MD5 hash function, it's not considered a highly secure authentication method unless other steps have been implemented. Using digest access authentication over SSL/TLS is a good way to increase password security.

PUBLIC KEY AUTHENTICATION

Public key authentication uses what's known as *asymmetric cryptography*, where a user has a pair of two mutually dependent keys. What's encrypted with one of these keys can only be decrypted with the other. Typically, a user makes one of these keys public, but keeps the other key completely private (never giving it out to anyone). For authentication, the user encrypts a small piece of data with their private key and the receiver verifies it using the user's public key. This is the same type of authentication used with the secure shell (SSH) command. The drawback of this method is that if a hacker breaks into your local computer and takes your private key, they could gain access to the database. Your database is only as secure as the private keys.

MULTIFACTOR AUTHENTICATION

Multifactor authentication relies on two or more forms of authentication. For example, one factor might be something you have, such as a smart card, as well as something you know, like a PIN number. To gain access you must have both forms. One of the most common methods is a secure hardware token that displays a new six-digit number every 30 seconds. The sequences of passwords are synced to the database using accurate clocks that are resynchronized each time they're used. The user types in their password and the PIN from the token to gain access to the database. If either the password or the PIN is incorrect, access is denied.

As an additional security measure, you can restrict database access to a range of IP addresses. The problem with this method is that the IP address assignments can change frequently for remote users, and IP addresses can be "faked" using sophisticated software. These types of filters are usually placed within firewalls that are in front of your database. Most cloud hosting services allow these rules to be updated via a web page.

KERBEROS PROTOCOL AUTHENTICATION

If you need to communicate in a secure way with other computers over an insecure network, the Kerberos system should be considered. Kerberos uses cryptography and trusted third-party services to authenticate a user's request. Once a trust network has been set up, your database must forward the information to a server to validate the user's credentials. This allows a central authority to control the access policy for each session.

SIMPLE AUTHENTICATION AND SECURITY LAYER

Simple Authentication and Security Layer (SASL) is a standardized framework for authentication in communication protocols. SASL defines a series of challenges and responses that can be used by any NoSQL database to authenticate incoming network requests. SASL decouples the intent of validating a network request from the underlying mechanism for validating the request. Many NoSQL systems simply define a SASL layer to indicate that at this layer a valid request has entered the database.

11.2.2 *Authorization*

Once you've verified the identity of your users (or their agents), you're ready to grant them access to some or all of the database. The authorization process is shown in figure 11.5. Unlike authentication, which occurs once per session or query request, authorization is a more complex process since it involves applying a complex, enterprise-wide, access-control policy to many data items. If not implemented carefully, authorization can negatively impact the performance of large queries. A second requirement to consider is the issue of security granularity and its impact on performance, as illustrated in figure 11.6.

As you leave the authentication step and move toward the authorization phase of a query, you'll usually have an identifier that indicates which user is making the request. You can use this identifier to look up information about each user; for example, what department, groups, and projects they're associated with and which roles they've been assigned. Inside NoSQL databases, you think of this information as an individual's smart-card badge and your database as a series of rooms in a building with security checkpoints at each door. But most user interfaces use folder icons that contain other folders. Here, each folder corresponds to a directory (or collection) and document within the database. In other systems, this same folder concept uses *buckets* to describe a collection of documents. Figure 11.7 is an example of this folder/collection concept.

You use the information about a user and their groups to determine whether they have access to a folder and what actions they can perform. This implies that if you want to read a file, you'll need read access to the directories that contain the file as well as all the ancestor folders up to the root folder of the database. As you can see, the deeper you go into a directory, the more checks you need to perform. So the checks need to be fast if you have many folders within folders.

In most large database systems, the authorization process will first look up additional information about each user. The most typical information might be what organization you work for in the company, what projects or groups you're associated with, and what roles you've been assigned. You can use the user identifier directly against

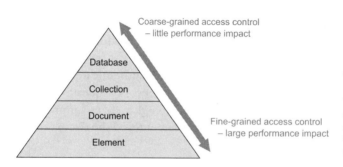

Figure 11.6 Before you create a NoSQL application, you must consider the granularity of security your applications needs. A course grain allows access control at the entire database or collection level. Finer-grained controls allow you to control access to a collection, an individual document, or an element within a document. But fine-grain may have performance impacts on your system.

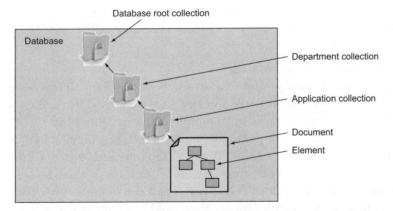

Figure 11.7   A document store is like a collection of folders, each with its own lock. To get to a specific element within a document, you need to access all the containers that hold the element, including the document and the ancestor folders.

your database, but keeping track of each user and their permission gets complicated quickly, even for a small number of users and records using a UNIX permission model.

THE UNIX PERMISSION MODEL

First let's look at a simple model for protecting resources, the one used in UNIX, POSIX, Hadoop, and the eXist native XML database. We use the term *resource* in this context as either a directory or a file.

In the UNIX model, when you create any resource, you associate a user and group as the *owner* of that resource. You then associate three bits with the owner, three bits with the user, and three bits for everyone that's outside the group. This model is shown in figure 11.8.

One positive aspect of a UNIX filesystem permission model is that they're efficient, since you only need to calculate the impact of nine bits on your operations. But the problem with this model is that it doesn't scale, because each resource (a folder or file) is typically owned by one group, and granting folder rights to multiple groups isn't permitted. This prevents organizations from applying detailed access-control

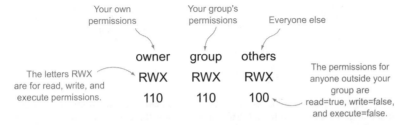

Figure 11.8   UNIX, POSIX, Hadoop, and eXist-db all share a simple approach to security that uses only nine bits per resource. Checks are simple and fast, and won't degrade performance even when large queries are done on many collections of many documents.

policies at the database level. Next, we'll look at an alternative model, role-based access control, which is scalable for large organizations with many departments, groups, projects, and roles.

USING ROLES TO CALCULATE ACCESS CONTROL

An alternative authorization model that associates permissions with roles that has turned out to be scalable and the predominant choice for large organizations is called *role-based access control (RBAC)*, shown in a simplified form in figure 11.9.

Using a role-based, access-control model requires each organization to define a set of roles associated with each set of data. Typically, applications are used to control collections of data, so each application may have a set of roles that can be configured. Once roles have been identified, each user is assigned one or more roles. The application will then look up all the roles for each user and apply them against a set of permissions at the application level to determine whether a user has access.

It's clear that most large organizations can't manage a detailed access-control policy using a simple nine-bit structure like UNIX. One of the most difficult questions for an application architect is whether access can be controlled at the application level, instead of the database level.

Note that some applications need to support more than simple read and write access control. For example, content management systems can restrict who can update, delete, search, copy, or include various document components when new documents are generated. These fine-grained actions on data collections are generally controlled within the application level.

11.2.3 Audit and logging

Knowing who accessed or updated what records and when they took these actions is the job of the auditing component of your database. Good auditing systems allow for a detailed reconstruction and examination of a sequence of events if there are security breaches or system failures. A key component of auditing is to make sure that the

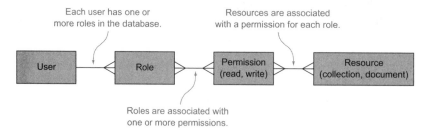

Figure 11.9   This figure shows a simplified role-based access control (RBAC) model that associates one or more roles with each user. The roles are then bound to each resource through a permission code such as read, write, update, delete, and so on. The RBAC model allows a security policy to be more maintainable when users aren't tied to particular resources.

right level of detail is logged before you need it. It's always a problem to say "Yes, we should've been logging these events" after the events have occurred.

Auditing can be thought of as event logging and analysis. Most programming languages have functions that add events to a log file, so almost all custom applications can be configured to add data to event logs at the application layer. There are some exceptions to this rule, for example, when you're using third-party applications where source code can't be modified. In these situations database triggers can be used to add logging information.

Most mature databases come with an extensive set of auditing reports that show detailed activity of security-related transactions, such as

- *Web page requests*—What web pages were requested, by what users (or IP addresses), and when they were accessed. Additional data, such as the response time, can also be added to the log files. This function is typically done by different web servers and merged into central access logs.
- *Last logins*—The last user to log in to the database sorted with the most recent logins at the top of the report.
- *Last updates*—The last user to make updates to the database. These reports can have options for sorting by date or collections modified.
- *Failed login attempts*—The prior login attempts to the database that failed.
- *Password reset requests*—A list of the most recent password reset requests.
- *Import/upload activity*—A list of the most recent database imports or bulk loads.
- *Delete activity*—A list of the most recent records removed from the database.
- *Search*—A list of the most recent searches performed on the database. These reports can also include the most frequent queries over given periods of time.
- *Backup activity*—When data was backed up or restored from backup.

In addition to these standard audit reports, there may be specialized reports that are dependent on the security model you implement. For example, if you're using role-based access control, you might want a detailed accounting of which user was assigned a role and when.

Applications might also require special audit information be added to log files, such as actions that have high impact on the organization. This information can be added at the application level, and if you have control of all applications, this method is appropriate. There's some additional logging that should be done at the database layer. In RDBMSs, triggers can be written to log data when an insert, update, or delete operation occurs. In NoSQL databases that use collections, triggers can be added to collections as well. Trigger-based logging is ideal when there are many applications that can change your data.

11.2.4 *Encryption and digital signatures*

The final concern of NoSQL security is how a database encrypts and digitally signs documents to verify they haven't been modified. These processes can be done at the application level as well as the database level; NoSQL databases aren't required to have built-in libraries to perform these functions. Yet for some applications, knowing the database hasn't been modified by unauthorized users can be critical for regulatory compliance.

Encryption processes use tools similar to the hash functions we described in chapter 2. The difference is that private and public keys are used in combination with certificates to encrypt and decrypt documents. Your job as architects is to determine whether encryption should be done at the application or database layer.

By adding these functions in the database layer, you have centralized control over the methods that store and access the data. Adding the functions at the application layer requires each application to control the quality of the cryptographic library. The key issue with any encryption tool isn't the algorithm itself, but the process of ensuring the cryptographic algorithm hasn't been tampered with by an unauthorized party.

Some NoSQL databases, especially those used in high-stakes security projects, are required to have their cryptographic algorithms certified by an independent auditor. The US National Institute of Standards and Technology (NIST) has published *Federal Information Processing Standard (FIPS)* Publication 140-2 that specifies multiple levels of certification for cryptographic libraries. If your database holds data that must be securely encrypted before it's transmitted, then these standards might be required in your database.

XML SIGNATURES

The World Wide Web consortium has defined a standard method of digitally signing any part of an XML file using an XML Signature. XML Signatures allow you to verify the authenticity of any XML document, any part of an XML document, or any resource represented in a URI with a cryptographic hash function. An XML Signature allows you to specify exactly what part of a large XML document should be signed and how that digital signature is included in the XML document.

One of the most challenging problems in digitally signing an entire XML document is that there are multiple ways a document might be represented in a single string. In order for digital signatures to be verified, both the sender and receiver must agree on a consistent way to represent XML. For example, you might agree that elements shouldn't be on separate lines or have indented spaces, attributes should be in alphabetical order, and characters should be represented using UTF-8 encoding. Digital signatures can avoid these problems by only signing the data within XML elements, not the element and attribute names that contain the values.

As an example, US federal law requires that all transmissions of a doctor's prescriptions of controlled substances be digitally signed before they're transmitted between computer systems. But the entire prescription doesn't need to be verified. Only the critical elements such as the doctor prescribing the drug, the drug name, and the drug quantity need to be digitally signed and verified. An example of this is shown in listing 11.1, which shows how the rules of extracting part of the text within a document are specified before they're signed. In the example, the prescriber (Drug

Enforcement Agency ID Number), drug description, quantity, and date are digitally signed, but other parts of the document aren't included in the final string to be signed.

Listing 11.1   Adding a digital signature to a document

```
<ds:Signature>
  <ds:SignedInfo>                                              Use SHA-256
    <ds:CanonicalizationMethod Algorithm="xml-exc-cl4n#"/>     hash
      <ds:SignatureMethod Algorithm="xmldsig#rsa-sha256"/>  ◁─ algorithm
        <ds:Reference>
          <ds:Transforms>
            <ds:Transform
              Algorithm="http://www.w3.org/TR/1999/REC-xpath-19991116">
                <ds:XPath> concat ( Message/Body/*/Prescriber/Identification/
                  DEANumber/text(),
                  Message/Body/*/MedicationPrescribed/DrugDescription/text(),
                  Message/Body/*/MedicationPrescribed/Quantity/Value/text(),
                  Message/Body/*/MedicationPrescribed/WrittenDate/text() )
                </ds:XPath>
              </ds:Transform>
          </ds:Transforms>
          <ds:DigestMethod Algorithm="http://www.w3.org/2000/09/
            xmldsig#sha256"/>
          <ds:DigestValue>UjBsR09EbGhjZ0dTQUxNQUFBUUNBRU1tQ1p0dU1GGUXhEUzhi
          </ds:DigestValue>
        </ds:Reference>
  </ds:SignedInfo>
  <ds:SignatureValue>XjQsL09EbGhjZ0dTQUxNQUFBUUNBRU1tQ1p0dU1FGUXhEUzhi
  </ds:SignatureValue>
  <ds:KeyInfo> ...
  </ds:KeyInfo>
</ds:Signature>
```

Rules to get text within the document you sign ▷ (points to the `<ds:Transforms>` block)

One useful rule in digital signatures is to "only sign what the users see." To get consistent digital signatures of XML prescriptions and avoid the problems with changing element names and canonicalization, XPath expressions can be used to extract only the values from XML elements and exclude all the element names and paths from the string that's signed. As long as both the transmitter and receiver use the same XPath expressions, the digital signature will match. The DigSig standard allows you to specify precisely the path expressions that you used to sign the documents.

11.2.5 *Protecting pubic websites from denial of service and injection attacks*

Databases with public interfaces are vulnerable to two special types of threats: *denial of service (DOS)* and *injection attacks.*

A DOS attack occurs when a malicious party attempts to shut down your servers by repeatedly sending queries to your website with the intention of overwhelming it and preventing access by valid users. The best way to prevent DOS attacks is by looking for repeated rapid requests from the same IP address.

An injection attack occurs when a malicious user adds code to an input field in a web form to directly control your database. For example, a SQL injection attack might run a SQL query within a search field string to get a listing of all users of the system. Protecting NoSQL systems is no different; all input fields that have public access, such as search forms, should be filtered to remove invalid query strings before processing. Each public interface must have filters that remove any invalid queries to your system.

Preventing these types of attacks isn't usually the job of your database. This kind of task is the responsibility of your front-end application or firewall. But the libraries and code samples for each database should have examples to show you how to prevent these types of attacks.

This concludes our discussion on security requirements. Now we'll look at three case studies: security in practice for one key-value store, one column family store, and one document store.

11.3 Case Study: access controls on key-value store— Amazon S3

Amazon Simple Storage Service (S3) is a web-based service that lets you store your data in the cloud. From time to time our customers ask, "Aren't you worried about security in the cloud? How can you make sure your data is secure?"

Authentication mechanisms are important to make sure your data is secure from unwanted access. Industries such as health insurance, government agencies, or regulations (like HIPAA) require you to keep your customer's data private and secure, or face repercussions.

In S3, data such as images, files, or documents (known as objects) is securely stored in buckets, and only bucket/object owners are allowed access. In order to access an object, you must use the Amazon API with the appropriate call and credentials to retrieve an object.

To access an object, you must first build a signature string with the date, GET request, bucket name, and object name (see the following listing).

Listing 11.2 XQuery code for creating a string to sign using your AWS credentials

```
let $nl := "&#10;"  (: the newline character :)
let $date := aws-utils:http-date()
let $string-to-sign := concat('GET', $nl, $nl, $nl, $nl,
    'x-amz-date:', $date, $nl, '/', $bucket, '/', $object)
```

Once the signature string is built, the signature and your S3 secret key are encrypted, as shown in the following listing.

Listing 11.3 XQuery for signing a string with AWS secret key and `hmac()`

```
let $signature := crypto:hmac($string-to-sign, $s3-secret-key,
  "SHA-1", "base64")
```

Finally, the headers are constructed and the call to retrieve the object is made. As you can see in listing 11.4, the encrypted signature is combined in the header with your S3 access key and the call is made.

Listing 11.4   XQuery for REST HTTP GET with the AWS security credentials

```
let $headers :=
<headers>
  <header name="Authorization" value="AWS {$s3-access-key}:{$signature}"/>
  <header name="x-amz-date" value="{$date}"/>
</headers>
let $url := concat($amazon-s3:endpoint, $bucket, '/', $object)
let $results := httpclient:get($url, false(), $headers)
```

In addition to the security for retrieving objects, S3 provides additional access-control mechanisms (ACMs) that allow others to view, download, and update your buckets and objects. For example:

- Identity and Access Management (IAM)
- Access-control lists (ACLs)
- Bucket policies

11.3.1   *Identity and Access Management (IAM)*

IAM systems allow you to have multiple users within an AWS account, assign credentials to each user, and manage their permissions. Generally, IAM systems are found in organizations where there's a desire to grant multiple employees access to a single AWS account. To do this, permissions are managed using a set of IAM policies that are attached to specific users.

For example, you can allow a user dan to have permission to add and delete images from your web-site-images bucket.

11.3.2   *Access-control lists (ACL)*

Access-control lists can be used to grant access to either buckets or individual objects. Like IAM systems, they only grant permissions and are unable to deny or restrict at an account level. In other words, you can only grant other AWS accounts access to your Amazon S3 resources.

Each access-control list can have up to 100 grants, which can be either individual account holders or one of Amazon's predefined groups:

- *Authenticated Users group*—Consists of all AWS accounts
- *All Users group*—Consists of anyone, and the request can be signed or unsigned

When using ACLs, a grantee can be an AWS account or one of the predefined Amazon S3 groups. But the grantee can't be an IAM User.

11.3.3 *Bucket policies*

Bucket policies are the most flexible method of security control, because they can grant as well as deny access to some or all objects within a specified bucket at both account and user levels.

Though you can use bucket policies in conjunction with IAM policies, bucket policies can be used on their own and achieve the same result. For example, figure 11.10 demonstrates how two users (Ann and Dan) have been granted authority to put objects into a bucket called bucket_kma.

Perhaps you're wondering when to use a bucket policy versus an ACL. The answer is that it depends on what you're trying to accomplish. Access-control lists provide a coarse-grained approach to granting access to your buckets/objects. Bucket policies have a finer-grained approach. There are times when using both bucket policies and ACLs make sense, such as

- You want to grant a wide variety of permissions to objects but you only have a bucket policy.
- Your bucket policy is greater than 20 KB in size. The maximum size for a bucket policy is 20 KB. If you have a large number of objects and users, you can grant additional permissions using an ACL.

There are a few things to keep in mind when combining bucket policies and ACLs:

- If you use ACLs with bucket policies, S3 will use both to determine whether the account has permissions to access an object.
- If an account has access to an object through an ACL, it'll be able to access the requested bucket/object.

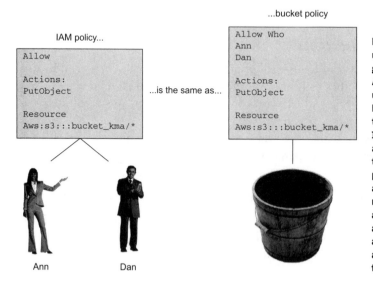

Figure 11.10 You can use a bucket policy to grant users access to your AWS S3 objects without using IAM policies. On the left, the IAM policy allows the PutObject action for bucket_kma in an AWS account, and then gives the users Ann and Dan permission to access that account/action. On the right, the bucket policy is attached to bucket_kma and like the IAM gives Ann and Dan permission to access PutObject on the bucket.

- When using a bucket policy, a deny statement overrides a grant statement and will restrict an account's ability to access a bucket/object, essentially making the bucket policy a superset of the permissions you grant an ACL.

As you can see, S3 offers multiple mechanisms for keeping your data safe in the cloud. With that in mind, is it possible to grant fine-grained security on your tabular data without impacting performance? Let's look at how Apache Accumulo uses roles to control user access to the confidential information stored in your database.

11.4 *Case study: using key visibility with Apache Accumulo*

The Apache Accumulo project is similar to other column family architectures, but with a twist. Accumulo has an innovative way of granting fine-grained security to tabular data that's flexible and doesn't have a negative performance impact for large datasets.

Accumulo's method of protecting fine-grained data in the database layer is to place role, permissions, or access list information directly in the key of a key-value store. Since organizations can have many different models of access control, this could make the size of keys unwieldy and take considerable disk space. Instead of putting multiple security models into multiple fields of a key, Accumulo adds a single general field, called *Visibility*, that's evaluated for each query and returns true or false each time the key is accessed. This is illustrated in figure 11.11.

The format of the Visibility field isn't restricted to a single user, group, or role. Because you can place any Boolean expression in this field, you can use a variety of different access-control mechanisms.

Every time you access Accumulo, your query context has a set of Boolean authorization tokens that are associated with your session. For example, your username, role, and project might be set as authorization tokens. The visibility of each key-value is calculated by evaluating the Boolean AND (&) and OR (|) combinations of authorization strings that must return true for a user to view the value of a key-value pair.

For example, if you add the expression (admin|system)&audit, you'd need either admin OR system authorization AND the audit to be able to read this record.

Although putting the actual logic of evaluation within the key itself is unusual, it allows many different security models to be implemented within the same database.

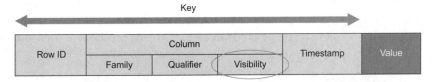

Figure 11.11 Apache Accumulo adds a Visibility field to the column portion of each key. The Visibility field contains a Boolean expression composed of authorization tokens that each return true or false. When a user tries to access a key, the Visibility expression is evaluated, and if it returns true, the value is returned. By restricting the Visibility expression to be only Boolean values, there's a minimal performance penalty even for large datasets.

As long as the logic is restricted to evaluating simple Boolean expressions, there's a minimal impact on performance.

In our last case study, we'll look at how to use MarkLogic's role-based, access-control security model for secure publishing.

11.5 Case study: using MarkLogic's RBAC model in secure publishing

In this case study, we'll look at how role-based access control (RBAC) can protect highly sensitive documents within a large organization and still allow for fine-grained status reporting. Our example will allow a distributed team of authors, editors, and reviewers to create and manage confidential documents and yet prevent unauthorized users from accessing the text of the confidential documents.

Let's assume you're a book publisher and you have a contract to create a new book on a hot, new NoSQL database that's being launched in a few months. The problem is that the company developing the database wants assurances that only a small list of people will be able to access the book's content during its development. Your contract specifically states that no employees other than the few listed in the contract can have access to the text of the documents. Your payments are contingent on the contents of the book staying private. The contract only allows high-level reports of book metrics to be viewed outside the small authoring team.

Your publishing system has four roles defined: Author, Editor, Publisher, and Reviewer. Authors and Editors can change content, but only users with the Publisher role can make a document available to reviewers. Reviewers have collections configured so that they can add comments in a comment log, but they can't change the main document content.

11.5.1 Using the MarkLogic RBAC security model to protect documents

MarkLogic has built-in, database-layer support for role-based access control, as described in "Using roles to calculate access control" in section 11.2.2. The MarkLogic security model uses many of these same RBAC concepts as well as implements some enhanced functionality.

MarkLogic applies its security policy at the collection and the document levels and allows users to create functions that have elevated permissions. This feature enables element-level control of selected documents without compromising performance.

This case study will first review the MarkLogic security model and then show how it can be applied in a secure publishing example. Finally, we'll review the business benefits of this model.

A logical diagram of how MarkLogic security models work is shown in figure 11.12. Here are some of the interesting points of the MarkLogic RBAC security model:

- *Role hierarchy*—Roles are configured in a hierarchy, so a lower-level role will automatically inherit the permissions of any parent roles.

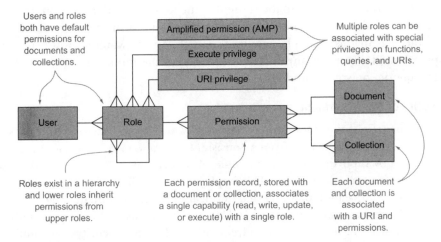

Figure 11.12   The MarkLogic security model is based on the role-based access control (RBAC) model with extensions to allow elevated permissions for executing specific functions and queries. Documents and collections each have a set of permissions that consist of role-capability pairs.

- *Default permissions*—Users and roles can each be configured to provide default permissions for both documents and collections.
- *Elevated security functions*—Functions can run at an elevated security level. The elevated security only applies within the context of a function. When the function finishes, the security level is lowered again.
- *Compartments*—An additional layer of security beyond RBAC is available with an optional license. Compartmentalized security allows complex Boolean AND/OR business rules to be associated with a security policy.

11.5.2 *Using MarkLogic in secure publishing*

To enforce the contract rules, create a new role for the project called `secret-nosql-book` using the web-based role administration tools and associate the new role with the collection that contains all of the book's documents including text, images, and reviewer feedback. Then configure that collection to include the role of `secret-nosql-book` to have read and update access to that collection. Also remove all read access for people not within this group from the collection permissions. Make sure that all new documents and subcollections created within this collection use the correct default permission setting. Finally, add the role of `secret-nosql-book` to only the users assigned to the project.

The project also needs to provide a book progress report that an external project manager can run on demand. This report counts the total number of chapters, sections, words, and figures in the book to estimate chapter-by-chapter percentage completion status. To implement this, give the report elevated rights to access the content using functions that use amplified permission (AMP) settings. External project managers don't need access to the content of the book, since the functions that use the amplified permissions will only gather metrics and not return any text within the book.

Note that in this example, application-level security wouldn't work. If you used application-level security, anyone who has access to the reporting tools would be able to run queries on your confidential documents.

11.5.3 Benefits of the MarkLogic security model

The key benefit of the RBAC model combined with elevated security functions is that access control can be driven from a consistent central control point and can't be circumvented by reporting tools. Element-level reports can still be executed on secure collections for specialized tasks. This implementation allows flexibility with minimal performance impact—something that's critical for large document collections.

MarkLogic has many customers in US federal systems and enterprise publishing. These industries have stringent requirements for database security and auditing. As a result, MarkLogic has one of the most robust, yet flexible, security models of any NoSQL database.

The MarkLogic security model may seem complex at first. But once you understand how roles drive security policy, you'll find you can keep documents secure and still allow reporting tools full access to the database layer.

Experienced MarkLogic developers feel that the security model should be designed at an early stage of a project to ensure that the correct access controls are granted to the right users. Careful definition of roles within each project is required to ensure that security policies are correctly enforced. Once the semantics of roles has been clearly defined, implementing the policy is a straightforward process.

In addition to the RBAC security model supported by MarkLogic, there are also specialized versions of MarkLogic that allow the creation of collections of highly sensitive containers. These containers have additional security features that allow for the storage and auditing of classified documents.

MarkLogic also integrates auditing reports with their security model. Auditors can view reports every time elevated security functions are executed by a user or roles are changed. A detailed history of every role change can be generated for each project. These reports show how security policy has been enforced and which users had access to collection content and when.

The RBAC security model isn't the only feature that MarkLogic has implemented to meet the security demands of its customers. Other security-related features include tamper-resistance of cryptography and network libraries, extensive auditing tools and reports, and third-party auditing of security libraries. Each of these features becomes more important as your NoSQL database is used by a larger community of security conscious users.

11.6 Summary

In this chapter, you've learned that, for simple applications, NoSQL databases have minimal security requirements. As the complexity of your applications increases, your security requirements grow until you reach the need for enterprise-grade security within your NoSQL database.

You've also learned that by using a service-oriented architecture, you can minimize the need for in-database security. Service-driven NoSQL databases have lower in-database security requirements and provide specialized data services that can be reused at the application level.

Early implementations of NoSQL databases focused on new architectures that had strong scale-out performance. Security wasn't a primary concern. In the case studies, we've shown that there are now several NoSQL databases that have flexible security models for key-value stores, column family stores, and document stores. We're confident that other NoSQL databases will include additional security features as they mature.

So far, we've covered many concepts. We've given you visuals, examples, and case studies to enhance learning. In our last chapter, we'll pull it all together to see how these concepts can be applied in a database selection process.

11.7 *Further reading*

- Apache Accumulo. http://accumulo.apache.org/.
- ———"Apache Accumulo User Manual: Security." http://mng.bz/o4s7.
- ———"Apache Accumulo Visibility, Authorizations, and Permissions Example." http://mng.bz/vP4N.
- AWS. "Amazon Simple Storage Service (S3) Documentation." http://aws.amazon.com/documentation/s3/.
- "Discretionary access control." Wikipedia. http://mng.bz/YB0o.
- GitHub. ml-rbac-example. https://github.com/ableasdale/ml-rbac-example.
- "Health Information Technology for Economic and Clinical Health Act." Wikipedia. http://mng.bz/R8f6.
- "Lightweight Directory Access Protocol." Wikipedia. http://mng.bz/3I24.
- MarkLogic. "Common Criteria Evaluation and Validation Scheme Validation Report." July 2010. http://mng.bz/Y73g.
- ———"Security Entities." Administrator's Guide. http://docs.marklogic.com/guide/admin/security.
- ———"MarkLogic Server Earns Common Criteria Security Certification." August 2010. http://mng.bz/ngJI.
- National Council for Prescription Drug Programs Forum. http://www.ncpdp.org/standards.aspx.
- "Network File System." NFSv4. Wikipedia. http://mng.bz/11p9.
- NIAP CCEVS—http://www.niap-ccevs.org/st/vid10306/.
- "Role-based access control." Wikipedia. http://mng.bz/idZ7.
- "The Health Insurance Portability and Accountability Act." US Department of Health & Human Services. http://www.hhs.gov/ocr/privacy/.
- W3C. "XML Signature Syntax and Processing." June 2008. http://www.w3.org/TR/xmldsig-core.

12

Selecting the right NoSQL solution

Marry your architecture in haste, and you can repent in leisure.

—Barry Boehm
(from *Evaluating Software Architectures:
Methods and Case Studies*, by Clements et al.)

If you've ever shopped for a car, you know it's a struggle to decide which car is right for you. You want a car that's not too expensive, has great acceleration, can seat four people (plus camping gear), and gets great gas mileage. You realize that no one car has it all and each car has things you like and don't like. It's your job to figure out which features you really want and how to weigh each feature to help you make the final decision. To find the best car for you, it's important to first understand which features are the most important to you. Once you know that, you can prioritize your requirements, check the car's specifications, and objectively balance trade-offs.

Selecting the right database architecture for your business problem is similar to purchasing a car. You must first understand the requirements and then rank how important each requirement is to the project. Next, you'll look at the available database options and objectively measure how each of your requirements will perform in each database option. Once you've scored how each database performs, you can tally the results and weigh the most important criteria accordingly. Seems simple, right?

Unfortunately, things aren't as straightforward as they seem; there are usually complications. First, all team stakeholders might not agree on project priorities or their relative importance. Next, the team assigned to scoring each NoSQL database might not have hands-on experience with a particular database; they might only be familiar with RDBMSs. To complicate matters, there are often multiple ways to recombine components to build a solution. The ability to move functions between the application layer and the database layer make comparing alternatives even more challenging.

Despite the challenges, the fate of many projects and companies can depend on the right architectural decision. If you pick a solution that's a good fit for the problem, your project can be easier to implement and your company can gain a competitive advantage in the market. You need an objective process to make the right decision.

In this chapter, we'll use a structured process called *architecture trade-off analysis* to find the right database architecture for your project. We'll walk through the process of collecting the right information and creating an objective architecture-ranking system. After reading this chapter, you'll understand the basic steps used to objectively analyze the benefits of various database architectures and how to build quality trees and present your results to project stakeholders.

12.1 What is architecture trade-off analysis?

Architecture trade-off analysis is the process of objectively selecting a database architecture that's the best fit for a business problem. A high-level description of this process is shown in figure 12.1.

The qualities of software applications are driven by many factors. Clear requirements, trained developers, good user interfaces, and detailed testing (both functional and stress testing) will continue to be critical to successful software projects. Unfortunately, none of that will matter if your underlying database architecture is the wrong architecture. You can add more staff to the testing and development teams, but changing an architecture once the project is underway can be costly and result in significant delays.

For many organizations, selecting the right database architecture can result in millions of dollars in cost savings. For other organizations, selecting the wrong database

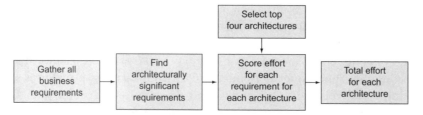

Figure 12.1 The database architecture selection process. This diagram shows the process flow of selecting the right database for your business problem. Start by gathering business requirements and isolating the architecturally significant items. Then test the amount of effort required for each of the top alternative architectures. From this you can derive an objective ranking for the total effort of each architecture.

architecture could mean they'll no longer be in business in a few years. Today, business stakes are high, and as the number of new data sources increases, the stakes will increase proportionately.

Some people think of architecture trade-off analysis as an insurance package. If they have strong exposure to many NoSQL databases, senior architects on a selection team may have an intuitive sense of what the right database architecture might be for a new application. But doing your analysis homework will not only create assurance that the team is right, it'll help everyone understand why the fit is good.

An architecture trade-off analysis process can be completed in a few weeks and should be done at the beginning of your project. The artifacts created by the process will be reused in later phases of the project. The overall costs are low and the benefits of a good architectural match are high.

Selecting the right architecture should be done before you start looking at various products, vendors, and hosting models. Each product, be it open source or commercial license, will add an additional layer of complexity as it introduces the variables of price, long-term viability of the vendor, and hosting costs. The top database architectures will be around for a long time, and this work won't need to be redone in the short term. We think that selecting an architecture before introducing products and vendors is the best approach.

There are many benefits to doing a formal architecture trade-off analysis. Some of the most commonly cited benefits are

- Better understanding of requirements and priorities
- Better documentation on requirements and use cases
- Better understanding of project goals, trade-offs, and risks
- Better communication among project stakeholders and shared understanding of concerns of other stakeholders
- Higher credibility of team decisions

These benefits go beyond the decision of what product and what hosting model an organization will use. The documentation produced during this process can be used throughout the project lifecycle. Not only will your team have a detailed list of critical success factors, but these items will be logically categorized and prioritized.

Many government agencies are required by law to get multiple bids on software systems that exceed a specific cost amount. The processes outlined in this chapter can be used to create a formal *request for proposal (RFP)* which can be sent to potential vendors and integrators. Vendors that respond to RFPs in writing are legally obligated to state whether they satisfy requirements. This gives the buyer control of many aspects of a purchase that they wouldn't normally have.

Let's now review the composition and structure of a NoSQL database architecture selection team.

12.2 *Team dynamics of database architecture selection*

Your goal in an architecture selection project is to select the database architecture that best fits your business problem. To do this, you should use a process that's objective, fair, and has a high degree of credibility. It would also be ideal if, in the process, you can build consensus with all stakeholders so that when the project is complete, everyone will support the decision and work hard to make the project successful. To achieve this, it's important to take multiple perspectives into account and weigh the requirements appropriately; see figure 12.2.

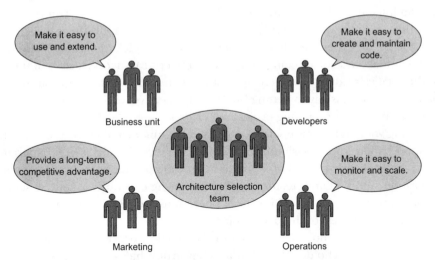

Figure 12.2   The architecture selection team should take into account many different perspectives. The business unit wants a system that's easy to use and to extend. Developers want a system that's easy to build and maintain. Operations wants a database that can be easily monitored and scaled by adding new nodes to a cluster. Marketing staff want to have a system that gives them a long-term competitive advantage over other companies.

12.2.1 *Selecting the right team*

One of the most important things to consider before you begin your analysis is who will be involved in making the decision. It's important to have the right people and keep the size of the team to a minimum. A team of more than five people is unwieldy, and scheduling a meeting with too many calendars is a nightmare. The key is that the team should fairly represent the concerns of each stakeholder and weigh those concerns appropriately. If you have a formal voting process to rank feature priorities, it's good to have an odd number of people on the team or have one person designated as the tie-breaker vote.

Here's a short list of the key questions to ask about the team makeup:

- Will the team fairly represent all the diverse groups of stakeholders?
- Are the team members familiar with the architecture trade-off process?
- Does each member have adequate background, time, and interest to do a good job?
- Are team members committed to an objective analysis process? Will they put the goals of the project ahead of their own personal goals?
- Do the team members have the skills to communicate the results to each of the stakeholders?

If the architecture selection process is new to some team members, you'll want to take some time initially to get everyone up to speed. If done well, this can be a positive shared learning experience for new members of the selection team. These steps are also the initial phase of agreeing, not only on the critical success factors of the project, but the relative priority of each feature of the system. Building consensus in the early phases of a project is key to getting buy-in from the diverse community of people that will fund and support ongoing project operations.

Getting your architecture selection team in alignment and even creating enthusiastic support about your decision involve more than technical decisions. Experience has shown that the early success of a project is part organizational psychology, part communication, and part architectural analysis. Securing executive support, a senior project manager, and open-minded head of operations are all factors that will contribute to the ultimate success of the pilot project.

One of the worst possible outcomes in a selection process is selecting a database that one set of stakeholders likes but another group hates. A well-run selection process and good communication can help everyone realize there's no single solution that meets everyone's needs. Compromises must be made, risks identified, and plans put in place to mitigate risk. Project managers need to determine whether team members are truly committed or using passive-aggressive behavior to undermine the project. Adopting new technologies is difficult even when all team members are committed to the decision. If there's division, the process will only be more difficult.

Keeping your database selection *objective* is one of the most difficult parts of any database selection process. As you'll see, there are some things, such as experience bias and using outside consultants, that impact the process. But if you keep these in mind, you can make adjustments and still make the selection process neutral.

12.2.2 Accounting for experience bias

When you perform an architecture trade-off analysis, you must bear in mind that each person involved has their own set of interests and biases. If members of your project team have experience with a particular technology, they'll naturally attempt to map the current problem to a solution they're familiar with. New problems will be applied to the existing pattern-matching circuits in their brains without conscious thought. This doesn't mean the individual is putting self-interest above the goals of the project; it's human nature.

If you have people who are good at what they do and have been doing it for a long time, they'll attempt to use the skills and experience they've used in previous projects. People with these attributes may be most comfortable with existing technologies and have a difficult time objectively matching the current business problems to an unfamiliar technology. To have a credible recommendation, all team members must commit to putting their personal skills and perspectives in the context of the needs of the organization.

This doesn't imply that existing staff or current technologies shouldn't be considered. People on your architecture trade-off team must create evaluations that will be weighted in ways that put the needs of the organization before their personal skills and experience.

12.2.3 Using outside consultants

Something each architecture selection team should consider is whether the team should include external consultants. If so, what role should they play? Consultants who specialize in database architecture selection may be familiar with the strengths and weaknesses of multiple database architectures. But there's a good chance they won't be familiar with your industry, your organization, or your internal systems. The cost-effectiveness of these consultants is driven by how quickly they can understand requirements.

External consultants can come up to speed quickly if you have well-written detailed requirements. Having well-written system requirements and a good glossary of business terms that explain internal terminology, usage, and acronyms can lower database selection costs and increase the objectivity of database selection. This brings an additional level of assurance for your stakeholders.

High-quality written requirements not only allow new team members to come up to speed, they can also be used downstream when building the application. In the end, you need someone on the team who knows how each of these architectures works. If your internal staff lacks this experience, then an outside consultant should be considered. With your team in place, you're ready to start looking at the trade-off analysis process.

12.3 Steps in architectural trade-off analysis

Now that you've assembled an architectural selection team who'll be objective and represent the perspectives of various stakeholders, you're ready to begin the formal architectural trade-off process. Here are the typical steps used in this process:

1 *Introduce the process*—To begin, it's important to provide each team member with a clear explanation of the architecture trade-off analysis process and why the group is using it. From there the team should agree on the makeup of the team, the decision-making process, and the outcomes. The team should know that the method has been around for a long time and has a proven track record of positive results if done correctly.

2 *Gather requirements*—Next, gather as many requirements as is practical and put them in a central structure that can be searched and reported on. Requirements are a classic example of semistructured data, since they contain both structured fields and narrative text. Organizations that don't use a requirements database usually put their requirements into MS Word or Excel spreadsheets, which makes them difficult to manage.

3 *Select architecturally significant requirements*—After requirements are gathered, you should review them and choose a subset of the requirements that will drive the architecture. The process of filtering out the essential requirements that drive an architecture is somewhat complex and should be done by team members who have experience with the process. Sometimes a small requirement can require a big change in architecture. The exact number of architecturally significant requirements used depends on the project, but a good guideline is at least 10 and not more than 20.

4 *Select NoSQL architectures*—Select the NoSQL architectures you want to consider. The most likely candidates would include a standard RDBMS, an OLAP system, a key-value store, a column family store, a graph database, and a document database. At this point, it's important not to dive into specific products or implementations, but rather to understand the architectural fit with the current problem. In many cases, you'll find that some obvious architectures aren't appropriate and can be eliminated. For example, you can eliminate an OLAP implementation if you need to perform transaction updates. You can also eliminate a key-value store if you need to perform queries on the values of a key-value pair. This doesn't mean you can't include these architectures in hybrid systems; it means that they can't solve the problem on their own.

5 *Create use cases for key requirements*—Use cases are narrative documents that describe how people or agents will interact with your system. They're written by *subject matter experts* or *business analysts* who understand the business context. Use cases should provide enough detail so that an effort analysis can be determined. They can be simple statements or multipage documents, depending on the size of the project and detail necessary. Many use cases are structured

around the lifecycle of your data. You might have one use case for adding new records, one for listing records, one for searching, and one for exporting data, for example.

6 *Estimate effort level for each use case for each architecture*—For each use case, you'll determine a rough estimate of the level of effort that's required and apply a scoring system, such as 1 for difficult and 5 for easy. As you determine your effort, you'll place the appropriate number for each use case into a spreadsheet, as shown in figure 12.3.

7 *Use weighted scores to rank each architecture*—In this stage, you'll combine the effort level with some type of weight to create a single score for each architecture. Items that are critical to the success of the project and that are easy to implement will get the highest scores. Items that are lower in priority and not easy to implement will get lower scores. By adding up the weighted scores, as shown in figure 12.4, you'll generate a composite score that can be used to compare each architecture.

In the first pass at weighting, effort and estimation may be rough. You can start with a simple scale of High, Medium, and Low. As you become more comfortable with the results, you can add a finer scale of 1–5, using a higher number for lower effort.

How each use case is weighted against the others should also help your group build consensus on the relative importance of each feature. Use cases can also be used to understand risk factors of the project. Features marked as critical will need special attention by project managers doing project risk assessment.

8 *Document results*—Each step in the architecture trade-off process creates a set of documents that can be combined into a report and distributed to your stakeholders. The report will contain starting points for the information you need to communicate to your stakeholders. These documents can be shared in many forms, such as a report-driven website, MS Word documents, spreadsheets and

Architectural Trade-off Analyis for Project ABC

Category	Use Case	Database Architecture					
		RDBMS	OLAP Cube	Key-Value Store	Col-Family	Graph	Document
Injest	Load data						
	Load code tables						
	Add record						
Validate	Structure						
	Required fields						
	Optional fields						
Update	Batch						
	Record-by-record						
Search	Fulltext						
	Change sort order						
Export	Reports in HTML						
	Export as XML						
	Export as JSON						
	Totals						

Figure 12.3 A sample architecture trade-off score card for a specific project with categorized use cases. For simplicity, all of the use cases have the same weighted value.

slide presentations, colorful wall-sized posters, and quality trees, which we'll review later in this chapter.

9 *Communicate results*—Once you have your documentation in order, it's time to present the results. This needs to be done in a way that will focus on building credibility for your process team. Sending a 100-page report as an email attachment isn't going to generate excitement. But if you present your case in an interactive method, you can create a sense of urgency using vocabulary the audience understands.

The communication job isn't done until you've ensured that the stakeholders understand the key points you want to communicate. Creating an online quiz will usually turn people off. You want to create two-way dialogs that verify the information has been transmitted and understood so the stakeholders can move on to the next stage of the project.

An example of a weighted scorecard is shown in figure 12.4.

We want to make it clear that we think that selecting an architecture before selecting a specific NoSQL product is the preferred method. We've been involved in situations where a team is trying to decide between two products that use different architectures. The team must then combine both architectural decisions and vendor-specific issues in one session. This prevents the team from understanding the real underlying architectural fit issues.

It might be interesting to compare the steps in the trade-off analysis process with a similar process developed by the Software Engineering Institute (SEI) at Carnegie

	RDBMS	Native XML	Document Management	Hybrid
Critical				
Import XML Data	0	4	4	4
Index Imported Documents	0	4	4	4
Indexes	4	4	0	4
Use XML	2	4	3	4
Web Access	2	4	3	3
weighted subtotal - 100% weight	8	20	14	19
Very High				
Display as HTML	2	4	2	3
Easy to Modify Business Rules	2	3	1	2
Leverage OpenSource Software	3	4	4	3
Search Score	0	4	4	3
Standards	3	4	2	3
weighted subtotal - 75% weight	7.5	14.25	9.75	10.5
High				
Use Standards to Express Business Rules	3	3	0	3
Customizable by Non Programmers	3	3	0	1
Transform	1	4	0	1
weighted subtotal - 50% weight	3.5	5	0	2.5
Medium				
Source Customizable Search Rank	0	3	4	4
weighted subtotal - 25% weight	0	0.75	1	1
Total Score	19	40	24.75	33

Figure 12.4 **A weighted scorecard for a software selection process for a statute management system. The grid shows the ease of performing a task for four alternative architectures. A score of 0–4 is used, with a 4 indicating the lowest effort. The most critical features have the highest weight in the total score.**

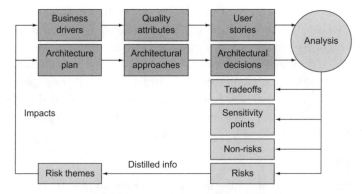

Figure 12.5　High-level information flow for the SEI ATAM process.
Although this process isn't specifically targeted at NoSQL database
selection, it shares many of the same processes that we recommend in
this chapter. Business requirements (driven by marketing) and
architectural alternatives (driven by your knowledge of the NoSQL
options available) have separate paths into the analysis process. The
outcome of this analysis is a set of documents that shows the strengths
and weakness of one architecture.

Mellon. A high-level description of the Architecture Trade-off Analysis Method
(ATAM) process developed by Carnegie Mellon is shown in figure 12.5.

Originally, the ATAM process was designed to analyze the strengths and weaknesses
of a single architecture and highlight project risk. It does this by identifying the high-
level requirements of a system and determining how easily the critical requirements fit
into a given architecture. We'll slightly modify the ATAM process to compare different
NoSQL architectures.

12.4　*Analysis through decomposition: quality trees*

The heart of an objective evaluation is to break a large application into smaller discrete
processes and determine the level of effort each architecture demands to meet the system requirements. This is a standard divide-and-conquer decomposition analysis process. To use decomposition, you continue to break large pieces of functionality into
smaller components until you understand and can communicate the relative strengths
and weaknesses of each architecture for the critical areas of your application.

Although there are several ways you can use decomposition, the best practice is to
break up the overall functionality of an application into small stories that describe
how a user will interact with the system. We call these the system's *scenarios* or *use cases.*
Each process is documented in a story that describes how actors will interact with a system. This can be as simple as "loading data" or as complex as "upgrading software with
new releases." For each process, you'll compare how easy or difficult it is to perform
this task on each of the systems under consideration. Using a simple category (easy,
medium, hard) or 1–5 ranking is a good way to get started.

One of the keys to objective comparison is to group requirements into logical hierarchies. Each upper node within a hierarchy will have a label. Your goal is to create a hierarchy that has no more than 10 top-tier branches with meaningful labels.

Once you've selected an architecture, you're ready to build a *quality tree*. Quality trees are hierarchies of quality attributes that determine how well your specific situation fits with the system you're selecting. These are sometimes called the *-ilities* as a shorthand for properties such as scalability, searchability, availability, agility, maintainability, portability, and supportability that we've discussed.

12.4.1 *Sample quality attributes*

Now that you have an idea of what quality trees are and how they're used to classify system requirements, let's take a look at some sample qualities that you might consider in your NoSQL database selection.

- *Scalability*—Will you get incremental performance gain when you add additional nodes to a cluster? Some people call this *linear* or *horizontal scalability*. How difficult is it to add or remove nodes? What's the operational overhead when you add or remove nodes from a cluster? Note that read and write scalability can have different answers to this question.

  We try to avoid using the word *performance* in our architectural quality trees, as it means different things to different people. Performance can mean a number of transactions per second in an RDBMS, the number of reads or writes per second in a key-value store, or the time to display a total count in an OLAP system. Performance is usually tied to a specific test with a specific benchmark. You're free to use it as a top-level category as long as you're absolutely clear that everyone on the team will use the same definition. When in doubt, use the most specific word you can find.

  One good example of how difficult it is to measure performance is the degree that data will be kept in a caching layer of a NoSQL database. A benchmark that selects distinct data may run slowly on one system, but it may not represent the real-world query distribution of your application.

  We covered many issues related to horizontal scale-out in chapter 6 on big data and the issues of referential transparency and caching in chapter 10.

- *Availability*—Will the system keep running if one or more components fail? Some groups call this attribute *reliability*, but we prefer availability. We covered high availability in chapter 8, including the subtleties of measuring performance and the pros and cons of different distribution models.

  In chapter 2 and in other case studies, we also discussed that when network errors occur, many NoSQL systems allow you to make intelligent choices about how services should deal with partition tolerance.

- *Supportability*—Can your data center staff monitor the performance of the system and proactively fix problems before they impact a customer? Are there high-quality monitoring tools that show the status of resources like RAM cache, input and output queries, and faults on each of the nodes in a cluster? Are there data feeds that provide information that conforms to monitoring standards such as SNMP?

Note that supportability is related to both scalability and availability. A system that automatically rebalances data in a cluster when a node fails will get a higher score for both scalability and availability as well as supportability.

- *Portability*—Can you write code for one platform and port it to another platform without significant change? This is one area where many NoSQL systems don't perform well. Many NoSQL databases have interfaces and query languages that are unique to their product, and porting applications can be difficult. This is one area where SQL databases have an advantage over NoSQL systems that require database developers to use proprietary interfaces.

  One method you can use to gain portability is to build database-independent wrapper libraries around your database-access functions. Porting to a new database could be done by implementing a new version of your wrapper library for each database. As we discussed in chapter 4, building wrappers can be easy when the APIs are simple, such as GET, PUT, and DELETE. Adding a wrapper layer for increased portability becomes more expensive when there are many complex API calls to the database.

- *Sustainability*—Will the developers and vendors continue to support this product or this version of the product in the future? Is the data model shared by other NoSQL systems? How viable are the organizations supporting the software? If the software is open source, can you hire developers to fix bugs or create extensions?

  The way that document fragments are addressed using path expression is a universal data-access pattern common in all document stores. Path expressions will be around for a long time. In contrast, there are many new key-value stores that store structures within values and have their own way of accessing this data that's unique to that system. It's difficult to predict whether these will become future standards, so there's higher risk in these areas.

  Note that the issues of portability and sustainability are tied together. If your application uses a standard query language, it'll be more portable, so the concerns of sustainability are lower. If your NoSQL solution locks you into a query language that's unique to that solution, you'll be locked in to a single solution.

- *Security*—Can you provide the appropriate access controls so that only authorized users can view the appropriate elements? What level of granularity does the database support?

  The key element we considered is whether security should be placed within the database layer itself or whether there are methods of keeping security at the application layer.

- *Searchability*—Can you quickly find the items you're looking for in your database? If you have large amounts of full text, can you search by using a keyword or phrase? Can you rank search results according to how closely a record matches your keyword search? This topic was covered in chapter 7.

- *Agility*—How quickly can the software be modified to meet changing business requirements? We prefer the term agility over *modifiability*, since agility is associated more closely with a business objective, but we've seen both terms in use. This topic was covered in chapter 9.

Beware of vendor-funded performance benchmarks and claims of high availability

Several years ago, one of us was working on a database selection project when a team member produced a report which claimed that vendor A had a tenfold performance advantage over the other vendors. It took our team several days of research to find that the benchmark was created by an "independent" company that was paid by vendor A. This so-called independent company selected samples and tuned the configuration of the funding vendor to be optimized. No other databases were tuned for the benchmark. Most external database performance benchmarks are targeting generic read, write, or search metrics. They won't be tuned to the needs of a specific project and as such aren't useful for making valid comparisons.

We avoid using external benchmarks in comparing performance. If you're going to do performance bake-offs, you must make sure that each database is configured appropriately and that experts from each vendor are given ample time to tune both the hardware and software to your workload. Make sure the performance benchmark will precisely match the data types you'll use and use your predicted peak loads for reads, writes, updates, and deletes. Also make sure that your benchmark includes repeated read queries so that the impact of caching can be accounted for.

Vendor claims of high availability should also be backed up by visits to other customers' sites that can document service levels. If something sounds too good to be true, it probably is. Any vendor with astounding claims should back up the claims with astounding evidence.

12.4.2 Evaluating hybrid and cloud architectures

It's usually the case that no single database product will meet all the needs of your application. Even full NoSQL solutions that leverage other tools such as search and indexing libraries may have gaps in functionality. For items like image management and read-mostly BLOB storage, you might want to blend a key-value store with another database. This frequently requires the architectural assessment team to carefully partition the business problem into areas of concern that need to be grouped together.

One of the major themes of this book has been the role of simple, modular, database components that can snap together like Lego blocks. This modular architecture makes it easier to customize service levels for specific parts of your application. But it also makes it difficult to do an apples-to-apples comparison. Running a single database cluster might be operationally more efficient than running one cluster for data, one cluster for search, and one cluster for key-value stores.

This is why in many of our evaluations we include a separate column for a hybrid solution that uses different components for different aspects of an application. Supporting multiple clusters can allow the team to use specialized databases that will be tuned for different tasks. Tuning each cluster needs its own operational budget extending out over multiple years.

A best practice is to use cloud-based services whenever possible. These services can reduce your overhead operational costs and, in some cases, make them more predictable. Predicting the costs of cloud-based NoSQL services can be complicated, since the services chart is based on many factors, such as disk spaced used, the number of bytes of input and output, and the number of transactions.

There are times when cloud computing shouldn't be used—say, if your business problem requires data to be constantly moved between a private data center and the cloud. Storing all static resources on a public cloud works well when your users are based on the internet. This means that the I/O of users hitting your local site will be much lower. Since I/O is sometimes a key limitation for a website, removing static data from the site can be a great way to lower overall cost.

As you complete your analysis, you begin thinking about the best way to communicate your findings and recommendations to your team and stakeholders and move forward with the project.

12.5 Communicating the results to stakeholders

To move your NoSQL pilot project forward, you need to present a compelling argument to your stakeholders. Frequently, those who make this important decision are also the least technical people in the organization. To receive serious consideration, you must communicate your results and findings clearly, concisely, and in a way everyone understands. Drawing detailed architecture diagrams will only be valuable if your intended audience understands the meaning of all the boxes and lines in the diagram.

Many projects do select the best match of a business problem to the right NoSQL architecture, yet they fail to communicate the details of why a decision was made to the right people and so the endeavor fails. The architecture trade-off analysis process should be integrated with the project communication plan. To create a successful outcome, you need to trade your analyst hat for a marketing hat.

12.5.1 Using quality trees as navigational maps

A goal of this book is to create a vocabulary and a set of tools for helping everyone, including nontechnical staff, to understand the key issues of database selection.

One of the most difficult parts of presenting results to your stakeholders is creating a shared navigational map that helps everyone orient themselves to the results of the evaluation. Navigational maps help stakeholders determine whether their concerns have been addressed and how well the solution meets their concerns.

For example, if a group of stakeholders has expressed concerns about using roles to grant users access to data, they should be able to guess that roles are listed in your map in the area labeled Security. From within that part of the map, they will see how role-based access is listed under the authorization area. Although there are multiple ways to display these topic maps, one of the most popular is a tree-like diagram that places the highest category of concern (the -ilities) on the left side of a tree, and then presents increasing levels of detail as you move to the right. We call these structures *quality trees.* An example of a quality tree is shown in figure 12.6.

This example uses a three-level structure to break down the concerns of the project. Each of the seven qualities can be further broken down into subfeatures. A typical single-page quality tree will usually stop at the third level of detail because of the limitations of reading small fonts on a single page. Software tools can allow interactive sites to drill further down to a requirements database and view use cases for each requirement.

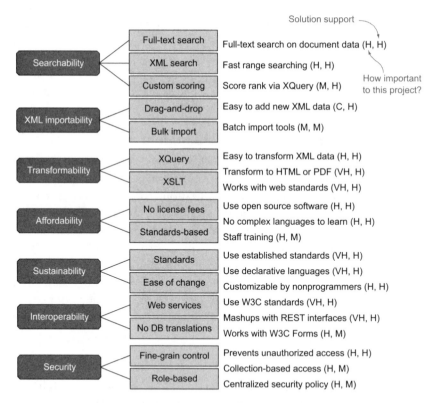

Figure 12.6 Sample quality tree—how various qualities (-ilities) are grouped together and then scored. High-level categories on the left are broken down into lower-level categories. A short text describing the quality is followed by letter codes to show how important a feature is (C=Critical, VH=Very High, H=High, M=Medium, L=Low) and how well the proposed solution meets the requirement.

Quality trees are one method of using graphical presentations to quickly explain the process and findings of your project to stakeholders. Sometimes the right image or metaphor will make all the difference. Let's see how finding the right metaphor can make all the difference in the adoption of new technologies.

12.5.2 *Apply your knowledge*

Sally is working on a team that has looked at two options to scale out their database. The company provides data services for approximately 100 large corporate customers who run reports on only their own data. Only a small number of internal reports span multiple customers' files. The team is charged with coming up with an architecture that can scale out and allow the customer base to continue to grow without impacting database performance.

The team agrees on two options for distributing the customer data over a cluster of servers. Option A puts all customer data on a single server. This architecture allows for scale-out and new database servers can be added as the customer base grows. When new servers are added, they'll use the first letter of the customer's name to divide the data between the servers. Option B distributes customer records evenly across multiple servers using hashing. Any single customer will have their data on every node in the cluster and replicated three times for high availability.

Sally's team is concerned that some stakeholders might not understand the trade-offs and believe that storing all customer data on a single node with replication might be a better option. But if they implement option A, half of the nodes in the cluster will be idle and only in use when a failure occurs.

The team wants to show everyone how evenly distributing the queries over the cluster will return faster results even if queries are running on each node in the cluster. Yet, after a long discussion, the team can't convince their stakeholders of the advantages of their plan. One of the team members has to leave early. He has to catch a plane and is worried about the long lines at the airport. Suddenly, Sally has an idea.

At their next meeting Sally presents the drawings in figure 12.7.

The next time the group meets, Sally uses her airport metaphor to describe how most of the nodes in the cluster would remain idle, even when a customer is waiting many hours for long reports to run. By evenly distributing the data over the cluster, the load will be evenly distributed and reports will run on every node until the report finishes. No long lines!

Sally's metaphor works and everyone on the project understands the consequences of uneven distribution of data in a cluster and how costs can be lower and performance improved if the right architecture is used. Though you can create a detailed report of why one scale-out architecture works better than another using bulleted lists, graphics, models, or charts, using a metaphor everyone understands gets to the heart of matter quickly and drives the decision-making process.

Like buying a car, there will seldom be a perfect match for all your needs. Every year the number of specialized databases seems to grow. Not many free and standards-compliant open source software systems scale well and store all data types

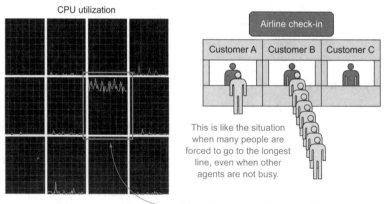

CPU utilization

Airline check-in

Customer A   Customer B   Customer C

This is like the situation when many people are forced to go to the longest line, even when other agents are not busy.

This customer is running a report that takes a long time to run on a single system. With a NoSQL solution, the report would be evenly distributed on all servers and run in half the time.

Figure 12.7   Rather than only creating a report that describes how one option provides better distribution of load over a cluster, use graphs and metaphors to describe the key differences. While many people have seen CPU utilization charts, waiting in line at the airport is a metaphor they've most likely experienced.

automatically without the need for programmers and operations staff. If they did, we would already be using them. In the real world, we need to make hard choices.

12.5.3 *Using quality trees to communicate project risks*

As we mentioned, the architectural trade-off process creates documentation that can be used in subsequent phases of the project. A good example of this is how you can use a quality tree to identify and communicate potential project risks. Let's see how you might use this to communicate risk in your project.

A quality tree contains a hierarchy of your requirements grouped into logical branches. Each branch has a high-level label that allows you to drill down into more detailed requirements. Each leaf of the tree has a written requirement and two scores. The first score is how important the feature is to the overall project. The second is how well the architecture or product will implement this feature.

Risk analysis is the process of identifying and analyzing the gaps between how important a feature is and how well an architecture implements the feature. The greater the gap, the greater the project risk. If a database doesn't implement a feature that's a low priority to your project, it may not be a risk. But if a feature is critical to project success and the architecture doesn't support it, then you have a gap in your architecture. Gaps equal project risk, and communicating potential risks and their impact to stakeholders is necessary and important, as shown in figure 12.8.

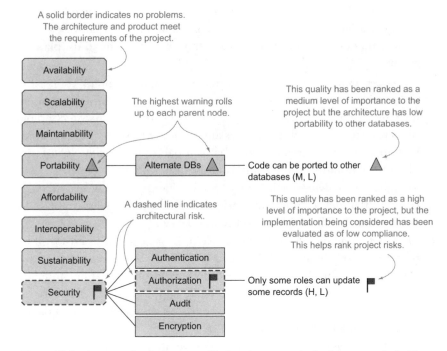

Figure 12.8 An example of using a quality tree to communicate risk-gap analysis. You can use color, patterns, and symbols to show how gaps in lower-level features will contribute to overall project risk. The way we do this is by having each branch in our tree inherit the highest level of risks from a subelement.

12.6 Finding the right proof-of-architecture pilot project

After you've finished your architecture trade-off analysis and have chosen an architecture, you're ready for the next stage: a *proof-of-architecture (POA)* pilot project sometimes called a proof-of-concept project. Selecting the right POA project isn't always easy, and selecting the wrong project can prevent new technologies from gaining acceptance in an organization.

The most critical factor in selecting a NoSQL pilot project is to identify a project with the right properties. In the same way Goldilocks waited to find the item that was "just right," you want to select a pilot project that's a good fit for the NoSQL technology you're recommending.

A good POA project looks at

1 *Project duration*—Pilot projects should be of a medium duration. If the project can be completed in less than a week, it might be discarded as trivial. If the project duration is many months, it becomes a target for those opposed to change and new technology. To be effective, the project should be visible long enough to achieve strategic victories without being vulnerable to constantly changing budgets and shifts in strategic direction.

Though this may sound like an overly cautious tone, introducing new technology into an organization can be a battle between old and new ideas. If you assume that enemies of change are everywhere, you can adjust plans to ensure victory.

2 *Technology transfer*—Using an external consultant to build your pilot project without interaction with your staff prevents internal staff from understanding how the systems work and getting some exposure to the new technology. It prevents your team from finding allies and building bridges of understanding. The best approach is to create teams that will pair experienced NoSQL developers with internal staff who will support and extend the databases.

3 *The right types of data*—Each NoSQL project has different types of data. It may be binaries, flat files, or document-oriented. You must make sure the pilot project data fits the NoSQL solution you're evaluating.

4 *Meaningful and quality data*—Some NoSQL projects are used in pilot projects because there's high-variability data. This is the right reason to move from a SQL database. But the data still needs to have strong semantics and data quality. NoSQL isn't a magic bullet that will make bad data good. There are many ways that schema-less systems can ingest and run statistical analysis on data and integrate machine learning to analyze data.

5 *Clear requirements and success criteria*—We've already covered the importance of understandable, written requirements in NoSQL projects. A NoSQL pilot project should also have clearly defined written success criteria associated with measurable outcomes that the team agrees to.

Finding the right pilot project to introduce a new NoSQL database is critical for a project's successful adoption. A NoSQL pilot project that fails, even if the reason for failure isn't associated with architectural fit, will dampen an organization's willingness to adopt new database technologies in the future. Projects that lack strong executive support and leadership can be difficult, if not impossible, to move forward when problems arise that aren't related to the new architecture.

Our experience is that getting high-quality data into a new system is sometimes the biggest problem in getting users to adopt new systems. This is often not the fault of the architecture, but rather a symptom of the organization's ability to validate, clean, and manage metadata.

Before you proceed from the architecture selection phase to the pilot phase, you want to stop and think carefully. Sometimes a team is highly motivated to get off of older architectures and will take on impossible tasks to prove that new architectures are better. Sometimes the urge to start coding immediately overrides common sense. Our advice is to not accept the first project that's suggested, but to find the right fit before you proceed. Sometimes waiting is the fastest way to success.

12.7 Summary

In this chapter, we've looked at how a formal architecture trade-off process can be used to select the right database architecture for a specific business project. When architectures were few in number, the process was simple and could be done informally by a group of in-house experts. There was no need for a detailed explanation of their decisions. But as the number of NoSQL database options increases, the selection process becomes more complex. You need an objective ranking system that helps you narrow down the options and then compares the trade-offs.

After reading the cases studies, we believe with certainty that the NoSQL movement has and will continue to trigger dramatic cost reductions in building applications. But the number of new options makes the process of objectively selecting the right database architecture more difficult. We hope that this book helps guide teams through this important but sometimes complex process and helps save both time and money, increasing your ability to adapt to changing business conditions.

When Charles Darwin visited the Galapagos Islands, he collected different types of birds from many of the islands. After returning to England, he discovered that a single finch had evolved into roughly 15 different species. He noted that the size and shape of the birds' beaks had changed to allow the birds to feed on seeds, cacti, or insects. Each island had different conditions, and in time the birds evolved to fit the requirements.

> Seeing this gradation and diversity of structure in one small, intimately related group of birds, one might really fancy that from an original paucity of birds in this archipelago, one species had been taken and modified for different ends. (Charles Darwin, *Voyage of the Beagle*)

NoSQL databases are like Darwin's finches. New species of NoSQL databases that match the conditions of different types of data continue to evolve. Companies that try to use a single database to process different types of data will in time go the way of the dinosaur. Your task is to match the right types of data to the right NoSQL solutions. If you do this well, you can build organizations that are healthy, insightful, and agile, and that can take advantage of a changing business climate.

For all the goodness that diversity brings, standards are still a must. Standards allow you to reuse tools and training and to leverage prebuilt and preexisting solutions. Metcalf's Law, where the value of a standard grows exponentially as the number of users increases, applies to NoSQL as well as to network protocols. The diversity-standardization dilemma won't go away; it'll continue to play a role in databases for decades to come.

When we write reports for organizations considering NoSQL pilot projects, we imagine Charles Darwin sitting on one side and Robert Metcalf sitting on the other—two insightful individuals using the underlying patterns in our world to help organizations make the right decision. These decisions are critical; the future of many jobs depends on making the right decisions.

We hope this book will guide you to an enlightening and profitable future.

For up-to-date analysis of the current portfolio of SQL and NoSQL architectures, please refer to http://manning.com/mccreary/, or go to http://danmccreary.com/nosql.

Good luck!

12.8 Further reading

- Clements, Paul, et al. *Evaluating Software Architectures: Methods and Case Studies.* 2001, Addison-Wesley.
- "Darwin's finches." Wikipedia. http://mng.bz/2Zpa.
- SEI. "Software Architecture: Architecture Tradeoff Analysis Method." http://mng.bz/54je.

index